Ray Cantagyene
Feb 08

ALL (

New Library of Pastoral Care

ALL GOD'S CHILDREN

An Introduction to
Pastoral Work with Children

Marian Carter

First published in Great Britain in 2007

Society for Promoting Christian Knowledge
36 Causton Street
London SW1P 4ST

British Library Cataloguing-in-Publication Data
A catalogue record for this book is available from the British Library

ISBN 978–0–281–05888–4

1 3 5 7 9 10 8 6 4 2

Typeset by Kenneth Burnley
Printed in Great Britain by Ashford Colour Press

Contents

And if you would know God,
be not therefore a solver of riddles,
rather look around you and you shall see him
playing with your children.

Khalil Gibran

Preface

This book arises from a commitment to children. It is a tribute to the children with whom I have had the privilege to work and grow in the Christian faith: to those who have surprised, challenged, taught, annoyed, exasperated and kept me on my toes by their insights, questions and actions. Throughout this book the children and their experiences are reflected in my thinking.

The book is written for all those working with children in the Church. It is interactive; its purpose is to share understanding and knowledge. Every reader will have an experience of being with and learning from children. Bring this to bear on what I have said: enter a dialogue. In each chapter there are boxes containing questions designed to aid thinking. It may be possible for you to work with the material as a group; if not you could share thinking with a friend.

I first examine the historical development of the concept of childhood, the aspects of the cultures in which our children are born and socialized, followed by an exploration of the images we as adults have of them. I then look at the resources, both from the human sciences and biblical, which help us to understand what it is to be a child. Next, I move to the practical issues and ask what pastoral care is and who offers it to children. This brings me to the roles of parents, minister, children's workers, the child's peer group and the community of faith, and how we support one another. I move to explore how pastoral care functions for and with children in times of need and times of joy, through relationships, nurture, teaching and worship, looking at particular examples. I finally offer a challenge to us all to be alongside, nurture and encourage the children of today, for in them we meet the one who himself shared our human life and childhood – even Jesus.

marian.carter@care4free.net

CHAPTER ONE

Our Children: Context and Perceptions

A conversation arose in our local post office. Diane was posting a birthday present for her seven-year-old granddaughter. The girl had told her mother she was joining an after-school club, called a 'mental club'. Her mother was mystified. Asking about the club, she discovered that it involved activities such as watching insects, planting seeds, observing and identifying birds. She suggested hesitantly (and correctly) that it might be an 'environmental club'. On hearing the story, Diane decided to buy a junior membership of the Royal Society for the Protection of Birds (RSPB) for her granddaughter, together with a fun piece of clothing for a girl already into fashion. In the superstore she was horrified to discover knickers for girls emblazoned with the slogan 'I'm sexy'. Diane sent a letter to the chief executive of the superstore. There was no response. 'Children grow up too fast. I want her to have a proper childhood, like mine. I want her to be natural, enjoy her club, and love the world, not get prematurely into sex and boys,' stated Diane. The mother of the girl could not see what all the fuss was about.

'When I was a child . . .' How often does one hear that?

Is there an idealized past? Was it really that different from the present?

How does your childhood affect your attitudes to children today?

Diane, as a grandmother, had a very different childhood from her granddaughter's. Her memory of childhood is associated with innocence, asexuality, being in tune with nature and gradual development. As adults our memories of our own childhood colour how we understand the children of today. In this chapter I shall examine the development of the concept of childhood: aspects of the cultures in which our children are born and socialized, followed by an exploration of the way we see children.

We all know about children. Every adult has experience of the child, through memories of our own childhood and from observing children at home and in the supermarket, whether we are parents, godparents, relatives or members of the public. Our memories of childhood may be idealized, romanticized, falsified or distorted by the passage of time, but because of our experiences we view our notion of the child and childhood as normal and universal. Yet knowing what a child 'is' and how childhood is constructed is a complex and difficult task. Our own memories of childhood are not easily accessed, covered over as they are by years of subsequent experiences. However, we *can* observe and listen to how children define themselves. They do not adopt the perception of adults that they are 'incomplete', yet they know that they are growing and changing. Children simply see themselves as children: they just 'are'. The child is born into a world defined by adults and influenced by societal concepts.

Very young children have little control of their environment. Their world is unpredictable and they have neither the language nor reason to explain it. For example, young children do not understand a sudden thunderstorm and explain it in animistic ways such as 'God moving the furniture about'. Chronological age gives only guidelines to development, for each child is an individual. Commonly children walk at one year and talk at two years. However, some children crawl and move in many different ways before they walk. Children change rapidly and stages of development are transitory. They become aware of their growth and herald new skills with glee. They use fantasy and imagination, have languages of their own and a freedom from responsibilities. This may evoke in a parent a sense of envy of a child's relative freedom and greater opportunities, or a sense of relief that the dependency of childhood is far behind. This generational imbalance may lead to the abuse, oppression or marginalization of the child.

In the twentieth and early twenty-first centuries the child and childhood have become an increasingly significant area of study. Prior to this, 'children' were either included in research on the family and marriage or simply thought unworthy of serious research. The explanations for the neglect of research on children are various:

- ideological: men dominate the writing of history;
- political: children exist in the home, the domestic rather than the public sphere;
- social and cultural: children are subsumed under women, who are themselves considered marginal by society, and therefore children are too ordinary to be mentioned;
- economic: children are economically unproductive;
- biological: childhood is a transition stage to adulthood, lacking any continuing significance;
- theological: Christianity is about maturity, therefore it deals with adults.

THE 'EMERGENCE' OF CHILDHOOD

The work of the French researcher Philippe Ariès (1914–84) was groundbreaking.[1] He focused on historical changes in ideas about childhood: concepts such as stages of development, the portrayal of childhood in pictures, children's dress, the history of games, and the notion that children were naturally innocent and in need of protection. His work was exploratory and tentative in its conclusions. However, the greater part of his thesis centred on the development of universal education, which he believed had 'created' childhood.

Ariès suggests that 'in medieval society the idea of childhood did not exist . . . Children were present in paintings of the period, they were not neglected, forsaken or despised.' There was affection for children, but what was missing was the 'idea of childhood', that is, 'the awareness of the particular nature of childhood which distinguished the child from the adult'. Ariès proposed that the differentiation of child from adult began to emerge in the late seventeenth century. Prior to this infants who survived were incorporated into adult life, and into domestic and economic work; everyone in the family had a part to play; children were not distinctive. Children were seen simply as immature adults, important not for their present but their future value.

In Ariès's thesis the seventeenth century marked a transformation of ideas about childhood. Two concepts developed. First, parents moved from their pleasure in watching children's antics and 'coddling' them as 'playthings' to considering childhood as a 'distinct way of being in the world'. The Enlightenment's positioning of rationality as the chief characteristic of humanity created a new category of being – 'children', who were irrational, frail and in need of correction and training. Second, Ariès noted a 'moralization of society' promulgated by the reformers of the sixteenth and seventeenth centuries. The child was no longer regarded as amusing or agreeable. Children must be understood so that they could be corrected and educated appropriately. Education gradually became universal for both genders and all classes. Linked with education was the idea of children's subservience and dependence on adults. Some scholars have challenged Ariès's thesis.[2] However, his significance lies in the fact that he recognized childhood as a *construct* which has changed over time and across cultures.

More recently, Hugh Cunningham has researched childhood in the UK, noting the changes in patterns of work from predominantly agricultural communities based around the home in the sixteenth and seventeenth centuries to the industrial cities of the eighteenth and nineteenth centuries.[3] Many children worked long hours in domestic service, climbing chimneys, in mines, factories and mills, selling articles on the streets and in prostitution. Children were abandoned by their parents and roamed the streets; they appeared as 'wizened adults', precocious beyond their years. Gradually, during the early nineteenth century the physical and moral damage of this work was recognized and questioned. Children came to be regarded as victims, slaves who needed saving from exploitation by industrialists, negligent parents and the vices of urban life.

A new concept of childhood arose. Children were seen as having a separate and distinct set of characteristics, and as requiring protection, though many people still accepted child labour as a positive good, which encouraged the habit of work and moral principles.[4] Nevertheless the Factory Acts of 1802, 1833 and 1847 began to regulate child labour. Philanthropic individuals established Sunday schools and charitable day schools to provide a rudimentary education for street children. The idea of a 'natural childhood' took root, embedded in a middle-class 'family ideal' that was characterized by order, respect for one's elders, love and duty to parents. Children came to be seen not simply as a workforce but as 'children of God' who needed to be safeguarded and reformed.

The Education Act of 1870 was a pivotal moment, when the state adopted greater responsibility for children while separating them from the adult world. However, compulsory education had repercussions, particularly for working-class children, whose self-esteem gained through wage-earning employment was devalued, while they were often thought to be 'duffers' at learning the three Rs. The new *concept* of childhood required dependence and deference to authority and assumed that children were characteristically ignorant (therefore needing teaching) and innocent of adult life (although children lost their innocence in the workplace). There was a legal right to punish children physically, reinforcing the idea of the child as being in 'need' of discipline. Wage-earning became an adult responsibility. In summary, the setting up of free schooling institutionalized children, separating them from adults and confirming a separate 'child' identity, and a 'national childhood' which ignored divisions of sex and class.

Ariès's work became the benchmark for further research which indicated that over time there had been major changes in attitudes to, and treatment of, childhood.[5] Analyses of childhood in the late twentieth century have raised issues of the influence of technology and suggested the demise of childhood as a construct as it is once again absorbed into adulthood.[6]

Today childhood is recognized as a variable 'social construct', although it has physical connotations as a stage in human development towards maturity. Social constructs are culturally determined and reflect the social, economic, political and religious conditions of particular historical periods. Those in power, adults, create these constructs which have formative effects on children's lives but must not be confused with the actual lives of children.[7] However, not all constructs support the thriving of children.

BEING A CHILD TODAY

In the last two decades the societal context of children has dramatically changed. The immediate context of children's lives, the family, is under threat as an institution, though considerable government legislation has sought to make the two-parent family a priority. Changes in education are headline news, and the rights of children have received much attention. Working practices, internet communication, the world as a global village, markets and advertising have all impinged directly and indirectly on children. The review that follows is selective and personal;

readers might like to consider for themselves the implications of changes in society for children today.

The family

The family now provides the primary socialization of a child. Having, and raising, children has become a lengthy commitment, which may be extended if a recent suggestion to raise the school-leaving age from 16 to 18 years is implemented. Research shows the importance that children attach to family life. From birth, children are sociable and need relationships and a safe and secure environment in which to grow. The memories from our childhood may be 'gift' or 'baggage', but they have a profound effect on the development of our personalities. However, in the twenty-first century there is no benchmark model of 'the family'.

Families come in various shapes and sizes. As adults, we experiment with relationships, procreation and nurture. Self-value and self-worth are put above the worth of others, which generates a sense of an absolute right to personal fulfilment and may be at the cost of responsibility for others. This 'pleasure-seeking' is evident in increased cohabitation (no commitment to permanence), marriage breakdown (there must be more to life than this relationship), divorce, separation and re-partnering, which all create complex varieties of family structure and disruption for children. Families may include stepchildren, children living with each birth parent at different times, or a child or children in a one-parent family. Some children live in extended families, with several generations sharing a home. It is possible for same-sex couples to adopt, or for one of a lesbian couple to have children through artificial insemination.

Family structure has been changed by cultural shifts. The women's movement challenged male dominance and raised the expectations for women of mutual enjoyment of sexuality and equality in career prospects. Marriage is undermined by a modern emphasis on adult fulfilment, which may be achieved at the expense of children. Sex is considered by many as a 'leisure' activity and separated from procreation. Life expectancy has increased, while women's reproductive lives have reduced from 20 years a generation ago to between 5 and 10 years today. Families are smaller, since contraceptives allow choice. Increasing numbers of women are in paid employment, balancing work and family commitments. This is made possible for mothers with babies by increased nursery provision, but the financial and emotional cost is high and some mothers are now questioning the long-term effects of maternal separation for very young infants.

The birth of children can be delayed and controlled through advances in medical technology, reflecting a society in which adult choice is paramount. Other medical advances help childless couples to conceive, but the emotional support for them is not as advanced. Donor sperm can be bought over the internet, enabling single women and lesbian couples to procreate. Ethical issues face would-be parents, yet rarely are the consequences for the unborn child mentioned. It seems that the needs of adults determine the existence, or not, of children, as if they were commodities.

Societal attitudes often blame parents for much of the antisocial behaviour of children and young people. The UK government has responded by creating Parenting Orders (requiring the parents of offending children to attend classes) and Asbos (antisocial behaviour orders, such as curfews on children). These orders are interpreted by some parents as interference by the 'nanny state'. The situation is complex. It includes adults inexperienced in parenting (infants do not come with a manual); parents who feel inadequate after watching TV parenting programmes; fears for the safety of children playing out of doors; lack of safe play facilities. On 21 November 2006 the UK government announced the allocation of £4 million to pay for support and advice workers in 77 areas of England to work on a one-to-one basis with parents who were experiencing difficulties with their children. It is anticipated that 20,000 parents a year will be helped; already 50 'parenting' schemes exist.

Families need fathers

The experience of fatherhood has changed dramatically in recent years. Research from the Equal Opportunities Commission shows that currently fathers of under-fives do one-third of the parental childcare. Males and females tend to play with their children in different ways: mothers are verbal and sensory, implicitly developing emotional skills; fathers' play is physical – 'rough and tumble', helping children gain control of their bodies. Psychologists have suggested that children need fathers both as role models and to help them develop autonomy and self-identity as they move away from the mother. These examples prompt a rethink on the significance of fathers in children's lives.

Fathers Direct is the UK national information centre on father-hood, providing news, information on training, policy updates, research summaries and guides to support fathers and families. It is a charitable organization, launched in 1999 with a grant from the Department of Health. A 'Dad Pack', funded by the then Department for Education and Skills, was launched in June 2006. The pack fulfils government guidelines that require children's centres, maternity units and nurseries to provide fathers with the support given traditionally only to mothers. Children need fathers to spend time with them, but following divorce children are more likely to be given into the custody of mothers and many lose touch with their fathers.

> Jot down a list of all the words you associate with the word 'family'.
>
> What are your concerns about the future of the family?
>
> What insights might Christians bring to the family?
>
> What do children gain from fathers?

Families and parental work

Work has changed dramatically over the last half-century from an industrial to a post-industrial service society. For some parents this provides flexible working hours, giving more time for children. For others home-based work is possible. Increasingly mothers work, many outside the home, necessitating flexible childcare. Large internationally owned companies often require work abroad and absence from home; sometimes moving the whole family abroad to another culture becomes necessary. The arrangements of parental work create challenges for children. The increasing cost of housing means that two incomes are needed to afford housing, so that many never get on the housing ladder. Some families, through circumstances such as ill health, disability, unemployment, or as one-parent families, have little option but to manage on benefits. The conditions of employment, unemployment and poverty of parents affect their children.

Families and legislation

Legislation to support children and families has become a political priority in recent years, suggesting either a growing concern for children or conversely a government reaction to counteract fears of a destabilizing society. State finance to support families is being reviewed constantly. Paid maternity and paternity leave, Child Benefit and Family Credit, free dental care and free prescriptions for those under 16 have all benefited parents and children. There are government information services including registers of child-minders and nurseries.

The number of high-profile cases of (alleged) child abuse and death has increased in the last decade. The Cleveland Inquiry of 1987 into alleged abuse stated 'the child is a person and not an object of concern'. The well-being of children was at the centre of the inquiry. The Sexual Offences Act (2003) reframed legislation to include a new offence of 'grooming' children on the internet; the word 'incest' was replaced by 'family sex abuse'. Protection from abuse is a difficult issue, particularly as children reach puberty at a younger age and imitate adult obsessions with sexuality.

The Children Act 1989 for the first time emphasized the responsibility of parents. It stated: the welfare of children is paramount; birth families give the best provision; court procedures involving children and families in divorce cases should be improved; there should be a partnership of children, parents and local authorities (LAs); parents should have rights of appeal against court decisions; parents' rights must be protected when children are cared for by the LA, with a high standard of care expected in LA homes and the right of a child to be consulted if there was a possibility of him or her being taken into care. Other acts attempted to legislate divorce humanely. The Child Support Act (1991) created the Child Support Agency (CSA), which required fathers to provide financial support when paternity was established. The administration of the CSA has been problematic and it is to be disbanded; nevertheless the principle of paternal financial responsibility has been established, reflected in the government Green Paper *Parental Separation: Children's Needs and Parents' Responsibilities* (2004). The Family Law Act (1996) states that courts are to require information on the financial provision and future care of children after a divorce. Divorce is considered a private matter but it has public financial implications in the provision of state childcare and education. The Act has the welfare of children at its heart.

The Special Educational Needs and Disability Act (2001) was the government commitment to a 'significant extension of the rights of children'. It aimed to 'strengthen the right' of disabled children to be educated in mainstream schools where appropriate, though recognizing the 'vital' role of special schools. LAs were to provide information and advice for parents when there were disputes regarding schooling. All these childcare acts have been significant in providing guidance on children's welfare.

Lord Laming's report in January 2003 on the tragic death of eight-year-old Victoria Climbié was influential in raising questions about the weak accountability and poor integration of local authority and voluntary services which were designed to protect children. The government subsequently published *Every Child Matters: the Next Steps* and the Children Act 2004 forwarded Lord Laming's work, incorporating the results of consultation with children's services, parents and children, and making the welfare and protection of the child a legal requirement. Work on a database of 12 million children in England (from birth to 18 years) is under way, called the Integrated Children's System. It is intended to combine data from education, youth justice, health and social services, together with a personal profiling tool known as the Common Assessment Framework. Concern has been expressed that this scheme could categorize a child from birth, jeopardizing children's own self-determination. There are also worries about the misuse of data and fears that the cost of the scheme might take money needed for day-to-day support services.[8] Theoretically, *Every Child Matters* places better outcomes for children (from birth to age 19) firmly at the centre of all policies and initiatives involving children's services. The intended outcomes are that every child should

- be healthy;
- stay safe;
- enjoy and achieve through learning;
- make a positive contribution to society;
- achieve economic well-being.

In 2003 the government programme Sure Start introduced centres to promote the welfare of children under five years old. These are 'one-stop shops' where parents will have access to integrated health, education and social services, and to work opportunities and training, so that families can receive 'seamless, holistic, integrated services'. Despite all this legislation, the Child Poverty Action Group stated in March 2006 that a quarter of our children (three million) still live in poverty although the UK is one of the richest countries in the world.

Children's rights

Children's rights were highlighted in the 1989 United Nations (UN) Convention on the Rights of the Child (CRC). What were previously seen as *protection* rights (adults deciding for the child how it should be protected) became *choice* rights (children as agents being involved in deciding issues that concern them). Recognizing the vulnerability of children through physical and mental immaturity, the CRC focused on nutrition, housing, recreation, medical services, education and protection from neglect and exploitation. Article 12 of the Convention stated a set of principles: that children have the right to be consulted and taken account of, to have access to information, to freedom of speech and opinion, and to challenge decisions made on their behalf.

The countries which have agreed to the Convention experience regular checks and reports from the UN. Internationally, energy has been expended on research and monitoring. Governments are required to present a report to the monitoring body two years after ratification, and then every five years, to provide 'general information about their country and its children and indicating measures and progress, as well as difficulty in implementing the treaty'. The life chances of the child are being gradually recognized, though for many adults children are not a priority.

The UK was not a signatory to the CRC but enacted a Children Act in 1989, discussed earlier. In 1991 the UK government agreed to the Convention with certain provisos; in 1992 it created a Children's Rights Development Unit. A cabinet appointment as Minister for Children was announced on 14 June 2003. In March 2005 the government appointed Professor Al Aynsley-Green as England's first Children's Commissioner. He aims to give a voice to all children, especially the disadvantaged and the vulnerable. Independent of government, the Commissioner's remit is to

> promote awareness of [the] views and interests of children. He is expected to raise the profile of the issues that affect and concern children in England, and promote awareness and

understanding of their views and interests among all sectors of society, both public and private.[9]

The language of rights has been positive for children, challenging social constructions that see them as powerless dependants, separated from adult society and effectively excluded from participation. Rights have empowered children to participate, for example, in the process of defining their needs and treatment in health services. A further example was the first Special Session of the United Nations General Assembly devoted exclusively to children (8–10 May 2002), which also included children as delegates. Many children have responsibilities such as caring for younger siblings, a sick or handicapped sibling or a parent; all should become aware of their need to respect other children and adults. However, children may abuse their rights by accusing adults of inappropriate behaviour: a child may do this to be mischievous or vengeful.

Education

The provision of nurseries supports mothers who desire to return to work when their child is very young. Because significant relationships and bonding with one adult carer are central to young children's development, legislation requires a generous ratio of carers to child; the younger the infant, the greater this should be. This allows mothers to return to work immediately after maternity leave. However, carers may work varying shifts, so that the child lacks the consistent bonding with one adult. Long hours spent in a nursery by infants only a few weeks old are considered by some to jeopardize a child's development.

The government has extended financial provision to ensure a free place in nursery education for all three-year-olds. Nursery education has brought increased opportunities to children of every ability and social class and is a great boon to both children and parents. For some children nursery education is invigorating, an 'escape' from a dysfunctional family, which enables them to play with other children and toys in a rich educational environment. However, the National Curriculum has introduced guidelines for nurseries that state the purpose of every activity. Some child researchers believe that concentration on these guidelines restricts teachers and infants rather than allowing the development of imagination through free play.

The introduction of a National Curriculum in 1988 was followed by Ofsted inspections to maintain standards. A positive result of this has been raised standards, with additional attention and funding for poorer-achieving schools. The educational process of recognizing and planning suitable education for individual children, 'differentiation', has affirmed the individual nature of each child. Underachievement among boys in the junior school has been recognized and research instigated. Children with learning and behavioural difficulties may be 'statemented', which entitles the teacher to additional classroom assistance. However, the National Curriculum has been criticized for being too prescriptive and mechanistic. Inspections and Standard Attainment Targets (SATs) have resulted in strain for some children and teachers, though the system of assessment is continually being refined, and has been reduced for younger children. Because league tables of school SAT results are published, it has been suggested that schools work towards the SAT tests rather than giving teachers the freedom to work with the interests and experiences of the children and educate creatively. SATs have highlighted cognitive development, ignoring social, emotional and spiritual growth and the freedom to question and explore. Sadly, children are marginalized and thought of as failures if they do not reach 'cognitive' targets in literacy and numeracy, although they may be talented in other ways. Music, drama and art are being squeezed within the curriculum; playtimes have been cut. Lack of time and space to play may be one cause of the increasing levels of stress reported in young children.

The Education Act (2002) contributed to the outcomes of *Every Child Matters*: school governing bodies were permitted to provide facilities and services in the community, the concept of 'extended schools'. These schools work with local providers to give access to extended childcare services from 8 a.m. to 6 p.m., all year round, not necessarily on the school site. These may include:

- parenting and family support;
- a varied range of after-school activities and study support, including sport and music clubs;
- swift and easy referral to specialist services such as speech therapy and health drop-ins;
- community use of facilities, including adult and family learning and ICT.

Ofsted reports that extended schools and children's centres have helped to enhance children's self-confidence, improve their relationships, raise their aspirations and lead to better attitudes to learning.[10] Unfortunately the implementation of extended schools and children's centres has been limited by lack of will and finance.

Is there an emphasis in education on creating future workers rather than feeding the open minds of children and enthusing them with a love of learning? Is education a function of the economic system, with children cogs in the system, being prepared for their future productive role? The purpose of education appears to be to move children as quickly as possible from childhood to adulthood. The moral values underlying the educational system and into which our children are socialized are rarely questioned. Questions need to be raised concerning an education system in which, despite all its benefits, many children are failing to thrive.

SOCIETAL INFLUENCES ON CHILDREN

Consumerism

Britain is a capitalist society. Capitalism has fuelled 'shop till you drop' consumerism and the violence of a 'have and have not' society that is increasingly reliant on credit card borrowing. There is pressure for children to become adult consumers, with advertisers targeting them, creating and satisfying needs for special foods, clothes, toys and video games, and for merchandise linked to leisure activities such as watching films and wearing football strips.

Ownership has become a status symbol in the adult world and children are caught up in the same culture. We acquire possessions, not because we necessarily need them, but for what they say about us. Advertisers promise children that buying will make them happier or more successful, or will bring them friends. Educational toys promise 'development' out of the stage of dependency. The assumption made by consumer culture is that happiness is found in possessions. Children are exposed to the relentless saturation of consumerism, while their powerlessness leaves them vulnerable to exploitation. Within the logic of capitalism children are not beings of intrinsic worth but primarily consumers, spending pocket money provided by their parents and being economic burdens, doubly unproductive since they do not earn and have to be maintained. This materialist outlook on life dampens and threatens to destroy children's spirituality, openness and naturalness.

> **Think of examples of how advertising influences children.**
>
> **What, if anything, should parents do about this?**

Sexualization

Freud helped us realize that children have sexual feelings from an early age. Gender is natural and something to celebrate. Childhood is a time of curiosity, a time for the discovery of bodies and difference, for experimenting and learning who we are. It is not a time of sexual innocence or naivety, but rather a period of latency that children need in order to develop an identity and become secure adults. As adults we seem to have forgotten this period. Our highly sexualized adult culture fails to respect children and creates a precociousness among them. The emphasis on child sexuality is seen in overtly sexy underwear marketed for young girls, in pre-teen magazines with articles on girls' sexual experience, and sexual imagery on television. In some respects it is adults who are guilty of sexualizing children's behaviour before children are sexually mature. However, it is likely that children's relationships with parents shape how they react to the 'sexuality' in advertisements, not the advertisements themselves, which possess little, if any, intrinsic power. This places a responsibility on parents. Parents who are willing to answer their children's questions reduce what may become an unhealthy obsession. Good communication with children reduces their fascination with premature sexuality.

Communications

The explosion in the communications industry has created a 'global village'. Through television our children have become aware of the needs and conditions of life of other children in the developing world. Many children have been moved to act, for example, raising funds for the victims of the 2004 Asian tsunami. But terrorist violence is seen almost instantaneously on the screens in our living rooms. Many young children have TVs and internet access in their bedrooms, and most have mobile phones. The easy availability of chatlines and pornography creates a risk when a child's viewing is not supervised. Children are curious and are sometimes encouraged by friends to look at unsuitable material. Growing numbers of children are abusing other children because they have seen pornography and are encouraged to experiment. Parents need to think about their responsibility.

Violence

The United Nations document *Study on Violence against Children* (2006)[11] records widespread violence against children which society continues to accept. At least 106 countries allow corporal punishment in schools, 147 in care homes. Only 16 outlawed corporal punishment at home. Worldwide, 53,000 children died in homicides in 2002, and between 80 and 98 per cent of all children were physically punished at home, one-third of them beaten with a stick. The World Health Organization (WHO) estimates that 150 million girls and 73 million boys experienced forced sexual intercourse or other sexual violence in 2002. A further 100 to 140 million girls and women were subjected to female genital mutilation (3 million in sub-Saharan Africa, Egypt and Sudan). The International Labour Organization estimates that 218 million children are involved in child labour, more than half in hazardous work. Violence perpetrated against children is hidden. Children and families are afraid to report it, because the perpetrator might be a member of the family or powerful in the community; those who report violence fear being ostracized, raped or killed. In the developed world children fear being taken away from home and placed in care if they speak of family abuse.

CHILDREN IN THE DEVELOPING WORLD

UNICEF produces an annual report entitled *The State of the World's Children*. In the developing world children lose their childhood and many their lives through poverty, disease and malnutrition – known as the 'Silent Emergencies'. A child dies every three seconds from malnutrition. Annually a total of 10.4 million children under five years die from respiratory infections, diarrhoea, measles, whooping cough and malaria. The risk of death from any of these diseases when associated with malnutrition is doubled. Approximately one-third of children are underweight as a result of illness, which depresses the appetite and drains the body of nutrients, combined with poor parental understanding of childcare and feeding practices. Through lack of immunization, children die of measles, poliomyelitis, tuberculosis, diphtheria, whooping cough and tetanus, diseases that have been largely eradicated in the developed world. In 1998, 510,000 children under 15 years became infected with AIDS, mostly in sub-Saharan Africa, and the disease is now becoming endemic in parts of southern India. Girls may be infected because intercourse with young virgins is believed in some groups to be a 'cure' for AIDS. AIDS leads to the disintegration of the 'traditional' family, the ancient kinship pattern of family that, until AIDS, had continued to be influential. Children become orphans, losing one or both parents. Many orphans become street scavengers, fending for themselves, some turn to crime, others are 'adopted' by pimps and led into prostitution in order to buy food to survive. Without the influence of nurturing adults, children are thrust into adult responsibilities and lifestyles, thus losing their childhood. Child prostitution is increasing in Thailand, sustained by Western sex tourism, where, because of the risk of AIDS, clients are using increasingly younger girls, forced into prostitution through economic circumstances.

Children are the most vulnerable in the 'Loud Emergencies' of war and civil unrest. Fathers may be forced to join armies, and are frequently brutalized by their experiences. Families are reduced to mothers and children; losing homes and livelihoods, they become dependent on handouts from governments or aid agencies. The cultivation of food becomes impossible without labour for planting or harvesting crops. Young children are recruited or abducted into the army, becoming victims of war. Many are maimed by landmines. In Sierra Leone and Sudan, a report from a UN officer responsible for child rehabilitation stated that children as young as four years old were deposited in 'camp' conditions, deprived of love and emotional attachments, in order to train them as single-minded fighters. These children are used to carry messages, since they are not suspected of involvement. The United Nations estimates there are 250,000 child soldiers in the world. Yet war is the result of adult activity and beyond the control of children.

Children also lose their childhood through premature entry into the labour market. Yet the issue of child labour is complex. Children want to imitate their parents and may be driven by family poverty into child labour. Work *per se* is not wrong. The child's financial contribution may be essential for family survival, give the child a sense of self-worth, and provide an education in useful skills. However, children are expected to carry adult responsibility prematurely and to risk their present and future health through long hours in cramped, unsafe and unhealthy conditions. Western media have highlighted scandals of child exploitation, making carpets in India and Kashmir and fireworks and matches in the factories of China. Child consumers in the West are the beneficiaries of labouring children in, for example, Indonesia, China and Pakistan through the products of multi-nationals such as Nike, Disney and Mattel. The first world is complicit in perpetuating this 'trade' in child labour in the interests of buying cheap goods.

There are gender issues in education and differences between the possibilities open to boys and girls. The spread of the internet and television has made the world into a 'global village'; access to pictures of lifestyles in the developed world leads to the desire for betterment. This is not wrong in itself, though it has resulted in the developing world inheriting the emphasis on materialism and has brought about an individualism which lessens and destroys the influence of kinship groups. Within these countries a division between rich and poor is developing.

It is a challenging world in which to raise children. Having indicated the changing societies in which children grow up, I now turn to examine critically some of the different ways in which adults perceive children today. Adults hold varied and contradictory 'images' or 'concepts' of children, which have their roots in the past. It is useful to understand something of how these concepts emerged and their implications, in order that we may challenge and expose 'images' of children that are false and demeaning to them, yet not fall into the trap of idolizing or romanticizing them.

HOW CHILDREN ARE PERCEIVED

Children as sinners

The concept of the child as sinner has influenced Western society's definition and treatment of children for many centuries. It is found in the Hebrew Scriptures: 'I was born guilty, a sinner when my mother conceived me' (Ps. 51.5); and taken up by Paul:

'sin came into the world through one man, and death . . . because all have sinned' (Rom. 5.12–21). An indication of this thinking today is parents' views about the wilfulness of children. Wilfulness is seen in a young child who repeatedly disobeys a parent who has forbidden him to touch the TV plug or in the sibling jealousy of a toddler who is spiteful to a younger baby in the family.

It was Augustine (354–430), interpreting Paul's words, who popularized thinking about the origin of sin.[12] With reference to children, he quoted Psalm 51.5, asking, 'where, I ask you, Lord, where or when was I, your servant, ever innocent?'[13] Augustine's reflections on memories of his own childhood and his observation of other children led him to believe that even the infant grasping for the breast was symbolic of a habit of selfish desire, by which the infant became dominated. He interpreted as nothing other than jealousy the rage of a fed baby who screamed at another infant feeding. He concluded, however, that children were neither innately innocent nor utterly depraved, suggesting a third possibility that the child had harmful desires but not the physical strength to express them. We now see a baby's instinct for survival as accounting for the 'self-centredness' which Augustine interprets as sin. Augustine remembered how as a child he stole, lied, cheated and committed perjury, while in adolescence there were deliberate acts of sin. He recounted stealing pears with a gang of friends, not because they were hungry, but for the sheer delight of wrongdoing. He noted, 'By myself I would not have committed that robbery. It was not the takings that attracted me but the raid itself, and yet to do it by myself would have been no fun and I should not have done it. This was friendship of a most unfriendly sort, bewitching my mind in an inexplicable way' (*Confessions*, Book 2, sect. 9). He confessed to God, 'no one is pure of sin before you, not even a small child who is no older than a day' (Book 1, sect. 7).

Augustine's thinking led him to believe in 'original sin' and guilt. Sin meant 'desire', inherent in the sexual act, through which it passed to children. In *infancy*, from birth to the acquisition of language, a baby could not be punished because it could not understand. However, as language and reasoning developed, a child had a growing moral responsibility and accountability. Augustine's powerful theology influenced much subsequent thinking on childhood. If children inherited sin, they needed to be kept safe for 'their own good', taught or trained how to behave morally. Augustine had the insight that as children develop language and reason they have an increasing level of moral accountability, while he recognized that there is a predisposition to destructive tendencies which is greater in adults.

Augustine's theology continues to flourish. During the Reformation the 'wilful indulgence of children' was identified as a common error of parents, one requiring increased parental authority. The Puritans compared children to 'an unbroken horse [which] turns out stubborn' (Sir. 30.8). Children bore the marks of original sin, evident in pride, self-centredness and above all will. Parents were to suppress and control what was understood as natural depravity through weekly catechism, daily prayer and Scripture reading, warnings and, if necessary, physical punishment. For John Wesley, in the movement known as the Evangelical Revival, all, including children, were 'fallen', in need of conversion and a life of holiness. Wesley advised parents 'to break the will of your child, to bring his will into subjection to yours that it may be afterward subject to the will of God'. Child-rearing was punitive, yet Wesley's words arose from an active concern for the 'soul' of the child and his moral and spiritual development. Indulgent parenting would result in a headstrong child, with dire results (Prov. 13.24; 22.15).

The image of the child as sinner continues today in some conservative Christian traditions. It is found in manuals of guidance for child-rearing.[14] Such manuals state that it is the responsibility of parents to break, challenge and frustrate the child's natural will, so that he will obey unquestioningly, 'honour parents' and live within the will of God. Physical punishment, from the age of six months, is advocated as the Christian method of discipline, essential to create morality, spirituality and character, and vital to a child's salvation. God holds parents accountable for the discipline of their children: parental failure incurs God's wrath. Abdicating this God-given obligation cheats children of the deep personal satisfaction of knowing that God loves them as their heavenly father. However, research shows that physical discipline demeans and degrades a child: it may be an exercise of the parents' power rather than related to the needs of the child.

Little theological thought has been given to the relationship between sin and children. Theologians have seemed to equate children's early stages of development, such as instinct, with sin. But it is repugnant to modern minds to attribute sin and guilt to babies before they are capable of understanding right from wrong or have developed moral responsibility. Children are born into 'a state of sin', that is, a world that is not what it ought to be. They experience 'good enough' but not perfect parents and broken relationships, and live in an unjust society. It is easy for children in a consumerist society to become self-centred. Gradually, children become aware of brokenness within themselves. They become moral agents, acquiring responsibility for their actions. Children do commit wrong against others; children who commit crimes have sometimes lacked good parenting and guidance in moral values. They may be forced or drawn by adults into actions that they do not realize are sinful: premature sexual acts or killings by child soldiers. These children are more sinned against than sinning.

> **What in your experience of children agrees with the idea of the child as sinner?**
>
> **What is useful/not useful about Augustine's thinking today?**

Children as innocent

Children are often thought of today as 'innocent'. Innocence is related to naivety, simplicity, vulnerability and lack of adult knowledge of sexuality and suffering. The innate goodness and innocence of humanity was an idea particularly associated with the Enlightenment of the eighteenth century, which challenged humanity's enslavement to religion, particularly the idea of 'man' as a sinner. Humanity would become enlightened by knowledge, and progress to greater happiness and freedom.

The concept of childhood innocence was popularized by Jean-Jacques Rousseau in *Émile* (1762), a landmark book in the history of childhood.[15] He believed that the child was innocent, having a natural goodness that could be tarnished by the evil influence of society: 'Everything is good as it comes from the hands of the Author of Nature; but everything degenerates in the hands of man' (Preface, p. 1). As the bearers of this goodness, children were to be educated and socialized according to 'natural' principles. Education develops from the child's inborn interests and instincts and must be related to the needs and characteristics of the child at each successive stage of his development. Learning is about the present, not a preparation for the future. Rousseau wrote: 'Nature wants children to be children, before they are men. If we deliberately pervert this order, we shall get premature fruits which are neither ripe nor well-flavoured, and which soon decay' (Book 2, p. 54). Childhood was to be appreciated for itself, not simply as a developmental stage towards adulthood.

No attempt was made to 'form the mind prematurely', particularly in moral and spiritual development. 'Keep the soul fallow as long as you can. If he learns about it too soon, there is a risk of his never really knowing anything about it.'[16] Rousseau believed that moral training in childhood developed from natural consequences. Faults were due to bad training: 'A child is only naughty because he is weak; make him strong and he will be good; if we could do everything we should never do wrong' (*Émile*, Book 1, p. 33). The aim of education was not knowledge but wisdom. 'There will always be time to learn; but there is not a moment to be lost in forming the disposition . . . There is not the least need for a man to be a scholar, but nothing is more needful for him than to be wise and good.'[17]

The appeal of Rousseau was to those who despised the changes of the Industrial Revolution and desired to return to the simplicity of nature. Rousseau was an idealist and anti-establishment. Some may think his ideas were unrealistic; nature is not moral nor good. Yet his emphasis on childhood as a unique and significant stage of life was influential. Rousseau's belief in the innate goodness of children and his advocacy of child-centred education marked the beginning of child developmental studies.

Among those influenced by Rousseau's thinking were the poets William Wordsworth (1770–1850) and William Blake (1757–1827). Wordsworth recalled childhood as a time of innocence and wonder that were lost in adulthood, and he saw this as a loss of paradise. Blake saw childhood as the *source* of 'innocence', not merely a preparation for adulthood. Wordsworth's perception of childhood was of a special (genderless) time of life, filled with childlike spiritual qualities.

> Not in entire forgetfulness,
> And not in utter nakedness,
> But trailing clouds of glory do we come
>   From God, who is our home:
> Heaven lies about us in our infancy!
>   *Ode. Intimations of Immortality*

Nature would implant the foundations for moral virtue and appreciation of beauty and these in turn would shape the adult life. The family was understood as an agent of repression, while schools crippled minds. Urban life, mechanization, and a puritanism gone sour had turned the child's life into a nightmare. Society needed to recapture a childlike vitality. In this way the poets set out an ideal of childhood in which it was transformed from being a preparation phase for adulthood to being the spring which should nourish the whole life.[18] Similar sentiments are found in Cardinal Newman (1830): a child is 'one out of the hands of God, with all lessons and thoughts of Heaven fresh marked upon him'; and in the Revd Stopford Brooke (1872), for whom children 'are fresh from the hand of God, living blessings which have drifted down to us from the imperial palace of the love of God'.[19]

The protest of Wordsworth and Blake was set against the exploitation of children in the Industrial Revolution and the evangelical doctrine of original sin. In Victorian art, Blake Morrison has noted, 'every baby [is] a God, worshipped by kneeling adults'.[20] Illustrative of the late-Victorian understanding of the child was Thomas Gotch's painting *The Child Enthroned* (1894), which can be seen as the 'personification of childhood'. A child dominates the picture, richly dressed in an embroidered gown, seated alone on a throne facing the viewer, a halo around the head. The picture 'invites' the viewer to kneel before the child. At its first exhibition in the Royal Academy this was taken to be the child Jesus. In fact, it was the artist's daughter. The adult idealization of the innocence of the child had passed from sentimentality to idolization.

In the late twentieth century childhood innocence has been challenged by child violence, such as the murder of the toddler James Bulger on 12 February 1993 by two 10-year-old boys. In part the public horror was that the perpetrators were themselves children, who at their trial had to stand on boxes to be seen in the dock. Marina Warner in the 1994 Reith Lectures stated, 'public grief focuses obsessively on the loss of an ideal of childhood, of their playfulness, their innocence, their tenderness, their beauty. The child holds up an image of origin.'[21] The reality is that children can be cruel to those more vulnerable than themselves. They are capable of both good and evil. Warner suggested that 'children are perceived as innocent because they're outside society, pre-historical, pre-social, instinctual, creatures of unreason, primitive, kin to unspirited nature. Whether this is seen as good or evil often reflects the self-image of society.' In 2003, ten years after the murder, adult emotions on the subject were still as raw and mixed.

Adults seem to need the concept of childhood innocence. Examples can be found in literature, such as James Barrie's play *Peter Pan*, and in real life in the attempt by Michael Jackson to 'remain a child'. However, the idea of innocence is challenged by William Golding's book *Lord of the Flies* and by Jackson's trial for child abuse. Childhood innocence is a myth. If we insist on children's innocence, it deprives them of the human ability to be agents of their own actions. As children grow emotionally and psychologically they can recognize their responsibility for their own actions and they begin to realize that adults also do wrong, that the possibility of doing wrong is intrinsic to a shared human condition.

What do you understand by innocence?

In what ways today might children be considered innocent?

Do adults have a need to see children as innocent? If so, why?

Children as emotionally priceless

Historically, the advent of compulsory education in 1870 completed the concept of childhood as a period of dependence. This was a fundamental change, as working-class children now became a drain, even a burden, on the family economy. Zelizer noted a change in the valuation of children, 'from one where they were valued according to their contribution to the family economy to one where they became productively useless but emotionally priceless'.[22] Market forces saw children as worthless: in contrast, parents saw them as priceless. The focus changed from the idea of controlling the child to the need for nurture, and to cater to the special needs of the innocent and underdeveloped child.

The family today continues to fulfil the emotional needs of its members while many of its traditional functions, for example, employment, education and socialization, are met by outside agencies such as the state. The decrease in family size may have increased the emotional 'value' of children (in 1960 there were

2.95 children per UK family; in 2004 the figure was 1.77). A
further example of the emotional pricelessness of children may be
seen in the intense desire for some infertile couples to have
children. Fertility treatment necessitates intrusive and costly
procedures. If a child results, it may become a priceless treasure,
putting great pressure on him or her to succeed and fulfil the
parents' expectations. Another example of 'emotional pricelessness' is seen in custody battles over children by emotionally
needy and divorcing parents.

What is the evidence that children are priceless?

What is the downside of this image of childhood?

Children as possessions

There is a justifiable pride in being the parent of a newborn baby,
yet the child can be thought of as belonging to its parents in a
possessive way. An example is the story of Caroline. She took her
young son Richard to the children's playground in the park. As he
played she noticed another child hurtling down the slide, about to
crash. Her maternal instincts moved her to put a hand out to save
the child. Another mother challenged her immediately, appearing
suddenly and yelling, 'Don't you dare touch my child'.

As parents we may assume we have power over what we
possess, including our children, and consider it our right to bring
up our child as we wish. The family is private – 'an Englishman's
home is his castle'; we think our children belong to us. But we
need to recognize that children are not our possessions. A child is
a gift, since from the moment the umbilical cord is cut he or she is
other. In one sense the child is a stranger. The infant is a person
in his or her own right, although initially highly dependent, a
blood-related human but with an independent will. Infants are
physically and emotionally demanding, needing nurture, love,
food and sleep, without which they will die, but we need to
respond to our infant's needs as a person.

Children can become a 'lifestyle choice', 'a fashion accessory',
expected to fill a niche in our personal expectations. As parents,
consciously or unconsciously, we may want children to meet some
unfulfilled need in our lives and psyches, to achieve unrealized
dreams, to succeed where we have failed, to give and receive

unconditional love in place of, or because of, the inadequacy of a partner, or to meet a media-engendered romantic ideal of family. Many of these are expectations that children cannot meet. All tend to reduce children's role to fulfilling the needs of adults, as 'psychic commodities'. It is as if an inversion of nature takes place so that 'parents need children' rather than children needing parents. In this paradoxical situation the mutual recognition between parent and child, child and parent, is lacking. Parenthood is a trust, however, not a right. Children are a gift to us, not a possession. As we shall see, infant baptism is a reminder and declaration that children are a gift of God entrusted to our care.

Children as dependent

An infant is powerless and dependent. As it develops through the stages of sitting independently, crawling, walking, talking, its needs change but it remains dependent on the parent. Dependency in children challenges adult norms of self-sufficiency and autonomy. The infant is devalued in society since self-sufficiency is an attribute of twenty-first century society. Yet dependency on human relationships changes through the life cycle, and mutual dependency and relationships are the essence of our humanity (Gen. 2.18).

Our society is adult-oriented. Jon Davies describes society as one of 'autonomous self-directing adults'. In contrast, he comments, 'children are dependent, not independent; vulnerable, not autonomous; inchoate, not finalized; ignorant, not wise; wrong, not right'.[23] In a modern society dependent children can be considered a burden, a 'cost' which is physical, emotional and financial. 'It has become clear that adults no longer need children in their lives, at least not in economic terms. The problem is that children, as much as they ever did, still need adults.'[24] Words such as 'commitment' and 'sacrifice' have been re-examined, particularly in situations where women are expected to sacrifice careers for their children. Yet, although it is true that children are dependent on parents for a considerable number of years, participation in the development of another human being is still felt by many parents to far outweigh the sacrifices that are involved.

Children as incomplete

Even today children are considered to be incomplete, immature, a stage of humanity which is left behind when adult maturity is reached. Children are simply 'adults in the making'. There are resonances of this in Paul's comment 'when I became a man I put away childish things' (1 Cor. 13.11, NKJV), as if childhood had no significance in the long term.

This is perhaps the most influential understanding of childhood. It was the accepted view of Aristotle and other Greek philosophers: 'childhood was seen as a weak, insignificant, biographical stage, a preface to adulthood.'[25] Children were 'symbols of human fear as well as physical frailty',[26] unable to participate in warfare, which made them, like women and the elderly, peripheral to the state. The Latin word for a young child, *infans*, translates as 'a non-speaker'. 'The child's inability to communicate made him a symbol of non-participation in the rational world of an adult citizen.'[27] Reason was thought to be the attribute that most likened humans to the gods; the exercise of reason was the route to eventual unity with God. This underlies the thinking of Aquinas, who wrote of the infant, 'so long as he has not the use of reason he is like a non-rational animal'. Aquinas noted the importance of parental and ecclesial care to 'guide children into fuller humanity', through which the child develops free will and 'begins to be his own master and to provide for himself in matters of divine and natural rights'.[28] For Aquinas reason is the marker of true humanity. But why reason alone?

Aquinas is concerned not with children but with the adults they will become. This understanding is challenged by Anderson and Johnson, who state, 'All people are children. We do not lose childhood when we become adults. It endures as a quality of being that must be lived through and accepted as part of our humanity.'[29] The authors use the metaphor 'childness' to identify qualities of childhood – vulnerability, openness, immediacy and neediness – that continue into adult life and distinguish what it is to be human. Accepting the qualities of childhood that we retain in adulthood leads to an empathy and respect for the child as unique.

Children as signs of hope

The birth of a child brings to life infinite possibilities. Who is this child? What will it become? It offers the possibility of openness to the future as the child's individuality becomes daily more evident.

The child became a symbol of Israel's hope for salvation during a period of despair in captivity. Hopes included an idyllic age of

peace: 'Old men and old women shall again sit in the streets of
Jerusalem . . . And the streets of the city shall be full of boys and
girls playing in its streets' (Zech. 8.4–5). A child will come named
'Immanuel' (Isa. 7.14; 9.6–7), in a time characterized by peace for
all creation and a return to Eden (Isa. 11.6). Other cultures had a
similar expectation of a golden age. In 40 BCE, Virgil combined the
ancient myth of a golden age with the birth of a boy, both human
and divine, as saviour.[30]

The Victorian cleric and academic Henry Scott Holland (1847–
1918) understood children as 'signs of hope'. In a sermon wrestling with Matthew 18.1–3, he contrasted the child with the adult.
'Childhood is open to everything; childhood knows no fixity, no
finality, no prison house of routine, no shell of egotistic self-interest . . . It has adventures to face, risks to run, visions to follow,
hopes to fulfil . . . That is the child, the child that we are meant to
be, the child that will be greatest in the kingdom of heaven.'[31]
This model of the child has much to offer in imagery today, but
sadly many children are damaged by dysfunctional families and
become hopeless rather than signs of hope.

The concepts discussed above overlap and interweave. They
exist as a complex and contradictory web of thinking and attitudes to children which continue to influence us. The way we
understand our children in the twenty-first century continues
to be ambivalent. Bonnie Miller-McLemore, an American scholar,
notes 'modernity's fundamentally unsatisfying answer: the re-
definition of children as economically useless, emotionally
priceless, socially invisible, and in the end morally and spiritually innocent'.[32]

SUMMARY POINTS FOR DISCUSSION

- Understanding the distinctive nature of children is a modern
  concept.

- Twenty-first-century society is adult-orientated, emphasizing
  autonomy and independence.

- Children are vulnerable, powerless and dependent.

- Advocacy for children is a political priority.

- Images of children are historically based and continue to
  influence our thinking.

CHAPTER TWO

Insights from Child Development

Stephanie, aged three, regularly visited an elderly neighbour, Doris. She always asked Doris for a sweet. Her mother suggested to Stephanie that this was not polite. 'Be a friend. Ask Doris how she is today. Then she may offer you a sweet.' On the next visit it was evident that the suggestion had been considered. Stephanie asked Doris how she was, waited for a reply, and then said, 'Now may I have my sweet?' Stephanie was learning about relationships, gaining and practising the necessary social skills for living.

Find some photographs of yourself as a child.

What are your earliest memories?

What adults were significant in your life? In what ways?

This chapter explores key aspects of normal patterns of child development, drawing on the disciplines of human biology, psychology, linguistics, sociology and theology. Examining the vulnerabilities and strengths of children at various stages of growth provides insights into the way these shape and influence spiritual and religious development and growth. An understanding of the development of the child is the context of our pastoral care.

The Jesuit educator St Francis Xavier said, 'Give me a child until he is seven and I will give you the man.' The first seven years of life are the most influential and formative for the patterning of the personality. The 'imprint' of parental relationships during these early years continues into adulthood. The growth of bodies and minds is a natural process of biological maturation which arises from our genetic inheritance but is dependent also on the child's environment, particularly people. The relative influence of genes and environment is usually expressed as 'nature versus nurture'.

The changes of childhood include the development of:

- physical abilities (sitting up, crawling, walking, jumping, sexual maturing);
- thought processes (imagining, conceptualizing, symbolizing, hypothesizing);
- communication (using signs, gestures, symbols, body language, words);
- social relations (gender identity and belonging);
- emotions (rage, pleasure); and
- spiritual responses (awe, wonder, worship).

There is a similar sequence of development for all children, though variations in rate may relate to culture.[1] Children change rapidly: their growth is organic and holistic. Growth is based on previous growth, as the child is always becoming something new and yet summates the essence of his or her past. The personality at five years (or 15 or 25) is an outgrowth of what happened in previous years. Children themselves become aware of this growth, as they recognize their increasing mastery of skills. Each child is an individual and develops at his or her own rate. Parents need to be sensitive to their child and encourage what seems to be the next step. There are optimum times for each stage of development to occur. If these times are missed through illness or low self-esteem, the child usually catches up.

BEGINNINGS

Even before birth the foetus makes its presence known. Looking at foetal scans excites a sense of mystery and marvel at this growing new life. As a pregnant woman experiences changes in her body, so her attention is drawn to the new life growing within her. This will gradually alter her relationship with her partner, since he is no longer the sole recipient of her attention. It is important that the woman shares her feelings, positive and negative, with her partner. As birth approaches questions arise about the care of the infant, both immediate and long term, maternity and paternity leave, family finances and the division of domestic labour. There are changes as each partner prepares to take on the new role of parent, often adapting the model received from his or her own parents.

BIRTH

For parents the emotions around birth are varied, including thanksgiving for this miracle of life, relief, delight, fear and uncertainty about the adequacy of their skills to nurture this highly dependent life. A baby is born with parental and family expectations. For example, if a child is born with a disability its parents may need to let go of particular dreams for the child; or a birth may coincide with an event within the wider family such as a death. The new baby may be given a name of the deceased person, with an unspoken expectation that somehow the baby will 'replace' the one who has died. Eric Berne, the 'creator' of Transactional Analysis, believed that children inherit 'scripts', that is, expectations to fulfil. Friends and family may make comments like 'He's got his dad's eyes' or 'Her hair is the colour of her mum's', but the baby, though inheriting attributes from each parent, is a unique person from the beginning of his life. This was highlighted when a maternity unit in Halifax hit the headlines. Notices appeared, 'Don't touch the babies', 'Please respect my baby.' Visitors, strangers to the babies' families, were cooing over them, asking their names, even picking up a baby and cuddling it. Certainly babies respond to touch and attention. But, as a spokesperson said, in a hospital babies need privacy – they are their own people.[2] This resonates with biblical insights into the uniqueness of each child created 'in the image and likeness of God'.

At birth the mother and baby are the centre of attention. The father may be forgotten and feel like an intruder. This can be a difficult time for him. Childbirth changes a couple's relationship; for example, for a period of time there is likely to be a loss of intimacy between them, since the mother is of necessity engrossed in the baby physically, emotionally and psychologically. The father can feel he is doing all the work as breadwinner, while the mother has all day at home; in fact, this is an exhausting time for the mother too. Penelope Leach[3] writes that the father may wonder if either mother or baby needs him. The answer is that they both do – not as a competitor with the woman who is mothering, nor with the baby who is being mothered: they need him in the uniquely male role of father. The availability of paid maternity and paternity leave helps the development of bonding between each parent and the child.

Every parent responds differently to parenthood. There may be feelings of resentment and jealousy that one parent is able to spend time with the child while the other is in paid employment; anger at a disturbed lifestyle and the loss of regularity in meals and sleep; feeling trapped by recognition of the years of responsibility ahead; or conversely pride, delight, pleasure and joy at the new life created. These varied and volatile emotions are a normal part of parenthood. The pastoral care of the parents, and indirectly of the child, may be helping parents to recognize the normality of these conflicting emotions, to acknowledge them, and to talk openly about them to one another in a safe place, in confidence with an experienced person, preferably another but older parent. This may be a service that the community of faith could offer.

A baby influences his or her parents and their fixed patterns of interaction. A baby challenges any inclinations to selfishness and short-term thinking, since raising a child is a long-term process. Leach notes that birth brings a sense of omnipotence and self-completion to parents, but that it may also reopen aspects of their own infancy and infantile relationships.[4] For example, in the daily routine of childcare the mother may lose self-esteem, or feel lonely within the severe limits to her freedom. The support of an experienced mother, who has time to listen, is helpful at this time. The infant may bring its parents into a rewarding world of love, which takes them out of themselves in participating in the growth of a new human being. However, having a child is not an act of self-interest; it is impossible to raise a child without sacrifice. Anderson and Johnson comment that 'it takes faith to have a child'.[5]

What do you understand by Anderson and Johnson's comment 'It takes faith to have a child'?

How does having a baby change a couple's home, work and social life?

What pastoral support might the parents of a newborn need? How can that be given?

DEVELOPMENTAL STAGES

Physical development

A baby at birth is powerless and dependent on its parents for food, warmth, shelter, protection and love. It is therefore important that attachment develops between the infant and the mother (or father, or caregiver).[6] The bonding of mother and child involves adjusting to one another and learning how to read signals. Some mothers can anticipate their infants' needs, while for others the early weeks of life can be frustrating for both as the mother learns new skills of intuition, imagining and interpreting. It is then that the baby teaches the mother. Child-rearing is not predictable; it entails both routine and the sense of 'not knowing' the needs of another. This may tax the mother's endurance and energy. It is important to realize that the parent grows as the child grows. This resonates with biblical insights of learning from children and of learning as a continuous process throughout life.

Babies need physical contact, continuing the intimacy of the womb. The sensation of touch is needed for physical and emotional health. Some young children may know only a negative touch. It may be rough handling, a smack or abuse but even this may be preferable to no touch. The mutual blessing of touch, adult for child and child for adult, is a biblical concept. Jesus healed by touch. He embraced the children brought to him for a blessing, knowing the significance of physical contact to well-being.

All parents make mistakes; they get things wrong. The child psychologist Donald Winnicott talks about 'good enough' parents, since none 'get it right all the time'.[7] It is enough that parents are giving of their best. Many new parents have a fragile sense of their competence; for example, feeling guilty if their child cries. Parents need the support of friends, neighbours, family and child-care specialists.

At 18 months infants are gaining confidence in walking, beginning to develop physical independence. They can climb, kneel, squat and carry things around with them. With a pincer grasp they can pick up small objects, build a tower of several bricks and scribble on paper. By two years the child is very mobile, a confident climber on to furniture, can manage stairs and can kick a ball. If a toddler's efforts in walking or climbing on to a chair are unsuccessful, he or she will give up and be hesitant. However, with encouragement to try again, the child will blossom. This is an age when children receive messages, both verbal and non-verbal, from parents. Sometimes toddlers try to please but are uncertain what the parent wants.

The years between three and five mark a distinct physical change from the toddler stage, which is accompanied by the development of language, social play and emotions. From single words the child begins to use sentences, copy and experiment with sounds. Those who have an older sibling may communicate by means other than speech and develop speech later. This does not mean that they are not 'making sense' of the world. Infants become active interpreters, constantly asking 'Why?', and building pictures of the world they experience in order to make sense of it. Language is now seen not as an egotistical expression but a means of relating. The pre-school child's increasing command of language gives an increased sense of self-determination and ability to exercise will, resulting in conflicts between parents and child.

In the early school years (five to seven) children discover and learn new abilities and skills, physical, academic and social. Physically, the child can play on a slide, swing and climbing frame, skip, hop and play ball games. Co-ordination continues to improve and by seven years the child has the confidence to ride a two-wheeled bicycle. Social skills increase with an increase in language use.

From seven to 11 years there is a level of sophistication in movements, sometimes outgrowing strength. In the last years of the junior school physical development is characterized by the beginning of hormonal changes and onset of puberty.

Psycho-social development

The work of Erik Erikson is a useful aid to understanding a child's psycho-social development. Erikson suggests that the human lifespan is a sequence of eight stages, and that development depends on the positive or negative resolution of particular psycho-social and emotional conflicts.[8] He suggests that positive outcomes strengthen the personality, while negative outcomes leave a scar and frustrate future growth. The stages of childhood development identified by Erikson are summarized in Table 2.1.

Table 2.1 Erikson's stages of childhood development

Stage	Psycho-social conflict	Outcome
Infancy	Basic trust or mistrust Primary social interaction with mother/or substitute; oral concerns; trust in life-sustaining care, feeding, nurturing	Hope or withdrawal
Toddler	Autonomy or shame and doubt Interaction with parents; toilet training; beginning of control; self-identity	Will or compulsion
Pre-school	Initiative or guilt Development of language skills; increasing exercise of will; physical and emotional growth	Purpose or inhibition
School age	Industry or inferiority Awareness of peer group and teachers; awareness of differing abilities	Competence or inertia
Adolescence	Identity or identity crisis Becoming self-conscious; sense of identity	Faith or role repudiation

The conflict for the infant is between basic trust or mistrust. The infant needs to know that it can trust its mother (or substitute) for life-sustaining feeding and nurturing.[9] In the baby's early life the mother is focused on him. A baby gains a sense of omnipotence, a joining of desire and satisfaction, when his mother recognizes his need and feeds him. At first his mother is an extension of him, and his desires and the satisfaction of his needs appear to be one. Gradually the mother's sensitivity to the child's needs is challenged by her own needs and the baby experiences a gap between desire and satisfaction from which a sense of 'not me' arises. From three to eight months the child experiences something new: he and his mother are separate; she is independent of

him. The mother becomes an object to his subject. A baby begins
to form an idea of himself which is the beginning of the distinctively human skill of 'symbolization', that is, of being able to represent one thing or person by another. The first instance of this
stage is a baby's attachment to an object, which may be part of a
blanket, a teddy bear, a doll or an article of clothing. Winnicott
calls this a *transitional object*.[10] The child chooses the object. It
represents the mother when she is absent and is a constant
companion. Winnicott believed that all infants learn early in life
to carry with them ideas and feelings connected to persons, places
and things, represented by the transitional object, and that these
show the beginnings of an intimate space, '*a transitional space*'
between what 'is me' and what 'is not me', marking the start of
the capacity for self-identity. Transitional objects are the beginnings for the infant of the world of thought, symbol and memory.
Ana-Maria Rizzuto (1979) puts a strong emphasis on 'object relations', seeing the infant's mind as constantly responding to and
reflecting interpersonal relationships, and suggests that the 'self'
is formed by the internalizing of his relationships. The relationship between parent and infant parallels a religious experience
in which a parent 'represents' a powerful, yet loving, omnipotent
God. These 'representations' are transferred to the transitional
object. The infant's range of experiences will be vital ingredients
of faith, for example, security, intimacy, dependence, personhood
and trust. Trust leads to an outcome of hope; mistrust leads to
withdrawal.

It is likely that the most fundamental experience for a child is
that of feeling secure. A child who has the security to trust
someone who will not fail him or her, usually the mother, is able
to form a relationship. The quality of this experience of trust is
crucial for the child's later understanding of what is meant by
God's love. Any failure of human relationships during childhood
impairs growth. This inner development of emotion and attitudes
begins to happen before a child acquires language. If a mother is
erratic and cannot be relied upon, or ignores her child's needs,
then the infant will mistrust her. The child will become insecure
in knowing and interpreting the mother and withdraw. Between
parent and child there is inevitably an imbalance of power that
may lead to abuse, oppression, or the marginalizing of the child.
The intuitive 'knowing' of trust and security are foundational to
the development of healthy religious experience.

In their mothers' provision for their needs infants discover they

are accepted and loved for themselves. They then have the security to trust that their mothers will not fail them; this trust
is vital to the development of personality. As important as trust is
the child's acceptance of discipline and guidance. The child learns
the limits of what is possible and what is not, although he or she
cannot yet know reasons.

Winnicott wrote of 'mirroring', a term which he used to describe
the transaction when the baby gazes into his mother's face and
finds himself there. This is necessary if he is to believe in his self-
worth. A baby goes to great lengths to secure recognition. The
opposite of recognition is indifference. We notice the infant who is
ignored and the 'emptiness' in such an infant's face. To develop,
an infant needs to recognize its own lovableness, yet as Christians we may have 'hang-ups' about self-love, despite Psalms 8
and 139.15–16, Jeremiah 1.5, Jesus' embrace of children, and the
command to 'love your neighbour as yourself'. The baby's presence needs to be recognized as that of a unique individual and is
a central factor in the sense of identity.

**What are the most significant needs of an infant (birth to two
years)?**

**Why are the first years of life so influential for the foundation of
faith in a child?**

At the toddler stage, 'I' gradually enters the child's consciousness
and vocabulary. With the development of self-consciousness and
beginnings of identity the will also develops. This is a critical
stage, when the parent needs to create a safe environment,
physical and emotional, to give the toddler freedom to explore.
Toddlers challenge parental authority. This is the stage of temper tantrums. Boundaries need to be set, establishing what is
acceptable and what is not. Needs should be recognized so
toddlers know that they are loved but are not the centre of the
world. Erikson understands the conflict for the two-year-old
between being able to do things (autonomy) and a basic sense
of doubt leading to shame. This stage is about the beginnings of
self-identity.

Children of three to five years develop increasing language
skills. These are accompanied by an increasing exercise of will,

physical and emotional. Erikson's conflict is the development of conscience influencing the showing of initiative, or guilt in holding back. Children learn to negotiate, to give and take; they experiment with feeling powerful, having a sense of control; and they quarrel with other children. Pre-schoolers have vivid imaginations, easily becoming afraid of the dark. Children in a group of three-year-olds are very forgiving and will help another child who is distressed. However, children's behaviour tends to reflect their own experience. If they are laughed at and smacked at home, they are likely to laugh at and hit others, especially children younger than themselves.

During the primary school years the child is affected by interacting with a wider group, including peers and teachers. The child becomes aware of differing abilities and compares himself with others. The conflict is 'Am I basically competent or inferior?' This is a time when children learn to win recognition by producing things in school. It is a time when it is painful to be different. Friendship and peer groups become important. In a school where a group of boys become friends and decide that it is 'uncool' to learn to read, preferring to play football, it is painful for the nonathletic boy or for the one who has books at home and has learnt to read, yet wants to appear 'one of the lads'.

Boys become increasingly boisterous and some start to underachieve academically. Research suggests that this may be due to differing male and female styles of teaching and learning and care must be given to encourage all efforts.

Social development

Researchers have transformed our knowledge about newborns.[11] An infant who is touched near the mouth turns towards the touch to seek both physical nourishment by sucking and a relationship. This parallels biblical insights of a basic human need to establish relationships. Newborns smile and cry, and the caregiver responds by smiling, picking up the infant and talking. The infant thus learns the social consequences of smiling and crying and responds in turn. Within a few weeks of birth the infant is able to distinguish the sound of the mother from that of a stranger. One-month-old babies imitate facial expressions. When an adult 'coos', there is a pause and the baby responds. 'Infant' means 'wordless', yet babies are born with a voice and an urge to communicate emotions and needs which cannot be ignored. The baby creates a relationship without words, inviting adults to participate in non-verbal communication. Mothers are particularly expert at interpretation and the baby experiences pleasure and satisfaction in communicating. By six months babies imitate sounds; towards nine months they begin to understand words, repeat sounds, will point at objects when asked, and use intonation in their voice; by 18 months they will try to sing as well as listen to music, join in action songs and look at books with pictures.

A toddler will happily explore toys if his or her mother is present. However, if social signals for help and attention are ignored, a child will become frustrated and detached, and relate poorly to people. The loss of a carer through hospitalization, death or divorce or a toddler being taken into care for whatever reason creates disbelief, numbness, shock, despair, and a yearning for the lost person. The transitional object may be central at this point.

The years three to five see the early development of a gender role as a child becomes aware of being either like mummy or like daddy. Roles are tried for fit. My niece of three announced to her parents one morning that she was Geoffrey. For several days this was the only name to which she would respond; then she reverted to her own name. New social relationships outside the family are entered with other children in a mothers and toddlers group or in nursery. Pre-schoolers make friends and are interested in having friends. Helping a child who is isolated from others for whatever reason is crucial. A child can be helped to develop a strategy of access. If a child looks at other children and imitates what they are doing, he or she is likely to be accepted and invited to join the activity. Imaginative play is good for joining in, as is friendship based on a shared interest.

Young children can only socialize for part of the day; they need personal space on their own and to feel nurtured and loved for themselves, to be given individual attention without the pressure of being in a group. Children need time to withdraw in daydreams, as a release from the bombardment of stimulus in our culture, or to find space for imaginative play in order to come to terms with all that is happening in their environment.

During the early school years the child is beginning to move away from dependence on parents, yet still needs reassurance that he or she is of worth. The giving of unconditional love is essential for healthy personal growth. At school a child's peer group becomes important, but even more important is the teacher. Young children return home and challenge their parents with, 'My teacher says . . .' The power of the teacher is absolute. The authority of parents begins to be questioned. The child realizes adults are fallible and needs assurance that there is someone or something greater.

At this age, children need to be given more opportunities for their own decision-making: what to wear, hair-style, choosing new clothes, food eaten and birthday treats. The transition of power from parent to child needs to be gradual, appropriate to the age of the child and the situation. This may cause issues with an older generation in the family who still have romantic notions of children's innocence, which lead to the view that children are incapable of thinking and acting for themselves. The general opinion is that children should be obedient to parents and be shaped into socially acceptable human beings. But they should be recognized as their own people, gradually taking and being given responsibility for their own actions or behaviour.

For seven- to nine-year-olds, friendships become important, usually focusing on friends as people who help each other whether asked or spontaneously. Children attempt to find their identity, helped by an intense interest in what makes people tick. There is a tendency to hero-worship, and this is the gang stage. Children search for meaning and significance in themselves and their world, as well as sorting out acceptable behaviour. Trust and compatible traits are features in children's understandings of friendships. Thus we observe the early emergence of friendship groups.

From nine to twelve years self-awareness comes to be as important as friendships. Friends are defined as other individuals with whom the child shares thoughts, feelings and secrets, who help each other physically and may give psychological support. Children negotiate rules, roles and personal relationships. They create their autonomy, and balance this with their dependence. They take responsibility for their own well-being and that of others. Children emerge as workers (in the home – washing up, preparing meals, doing household chores); consumers (of fashionable clothes, using pocket money and gifts from parents); carers (to disabled parents); counsellors (to a divorced parent); clients of services (health and education); representatives within a peer group (elected on to a school council, defining school rules and ways of combating bullying). Children take responsibility, challenging conventional assumptions about the childishness of their everyday activities, and their intellectual and emotional status. The theory of childhood deficiency becomes one of childhood competency.[12]

Emotional development

Emotional development is allied with cognitive development. It is dependent on a child's immediate feelings in reaction to a situation, a sense of his or her own identity and a growing ability to handle concepts. A baby is at the mercy of its emotions, which can be very volatile. Gradually these are modified. The child's emotional experience is intense, because verbal and conceptual skills are still developing, so that he or she can be overwhelmed by feelings. Cognitively the child can focus on only one situation or idea at a time. For example, a three-year-old becomes upset if an adult interrupts him when he is playing, exclaiming 'I hate you'. The adult is upset. But this is the only way for the child to show his displeasure and anger. Within minutes he has forgotten and is ready for fun again. He senses no contradiction and cannot link the action with the emotion.

The four- to six-year-old can reflect more on feelings and emotional responses; for example, she begins to realize she is a girl, from whom certain responses are to be expected. Children watch and observe, imitating the emotional responses of those with whom they identify. They learn that 'girls cry and get kissed better' but 'big boys don't cry'. Children learn to control emotions in socially acceptable ways. They observe others' expressions of anger, fear, disgust, joy, excitement or happiness, and learn how to react in different situations. In play they try out emotions and imitate significant adults. Emotions such as anger, happiness and fear are immediate and straightforward but emotions such as pride and shame are more complex and depend on children's understanding of their own behaviour in the light of the reactions or expectations of others. For example, children feel pride when they have done something which gains the approval of a parent and shame if their behaviour incurs disapproval. A four- to six-year-old lives in the moment.

Friendships for six- to nine-year-olds bring emotional attachment to others. A new area of values becomes clearer: a child will co-operatively perform a less enjoyable task in order to participate in a desired activity later. In mid-childhood there is an increased ability to empathize with others in their particular situation. A child can co-ordinate several social perspectives with increased ability, can reflect on his or her own feelings and emotional responses as well as those of others. A child can now understand mixed feelings, sadness and anger occurring at the same time, and that someone else can feel a different emotion from the one expressed. For example, they can be told the story of how Brian falls over in the playground, badly grazing his knee. He knows that the other children will laugh if he shows how he feels. So he tries to hide his feelings. Six-year-olds are able to say that Brian will try to look happy and they explain that he didn't want other children to know his sadness in falling over. The child begins to make judgements on how others feel.

In later childhood, ten- to twelve-year-olds can begin to construct abstract concepts and to imagine the situation of others with whom they have no contact, such as children in the developing world. The child owns his or her emotions and can begin to appreciate those of others. At times emotions can interfere, dominate and even over-ride the cognitive. Understanding is not that of an adult – but children strive to make sense and create an understanding that will enable them to enter into a new relationship with the world and the self.

Play

Play is a significant memory of our childhood: making dens and tree-houses, secret places, gangs, fights and games, balls that become cannon balls, dressing up and pretending, a sense of fantasy and magic, of timelessness, the world of the imagination. In play children rehearse the future and reflect on the past, organize their own learning and problem-solving, come to explore and control their bodies (co-ordination, motor skills, balance, spatial awareness) and emotions (exploration and control), and develop social skills (co-operating with others). Examples of play are: a baby lying in a pram watching the sunlight as it plays through the trees; an infant crawling; a toddler pushing a doll's pram or building a tower of bricks; pre-schoolers running against the wind, picking up stones and flowers. A young child 'tries on' the role of adult, plays at being Mum who is angry with the child, becomes the evil witch, tries out 'being dead', 'magics' dead an adult who has challenged him; older children build dens, play in boats, have cycling adventures. Play, through laying down neural patterns in the brain, is important for the future learning of imaginative thinking, for personal identity and appreciating the otherness of another person. Play is safe; children are free to make mistakes, since within the world of imagination there are no 'consequences' or 'responsibilities'. Play may be solitary or communal. The essence of play is that it is an activity for its own sake rather than having a purpose or function, yet for the child it is utterly serious. It is the world of the child's imagination away from the watchful eyes and ears of adults. The characteristics of play are reflected in good children's literature.

Observers of children have recognized the unconscious aspect of play, the replay in fantasy of a child's own experiences and the feelings evoked. As such, it is a significant tool of learning. For this reason therapists and counsellors use play in their work with damaged and disturbed children. Winnicott emphasizes the importance of seeing play as a creative experience and that it is only in being creative that we discover ourselves. Play is a basic component of a child's growth process: by playing out feelings, the child faces them, learns to control them or abandons them. Then he 'begins to realize the power within himself to be an individual in his own right, to think for himself, to make his own decisions, to become psychologically more mature, and, by so doing, to realize selfhood'.[13]

Children need the freedom to play with emotions, ideas, words, relationships, to try out and find meaning for themselves which makes sense of their world and of their relationships with others. In our society adults can thwart a child's need for play by filling time with adult-chosen and adult-directed activities such as reading, playing an instrument, playing computer games. Many of these activities are good in themselves but do not have the same function as play. Play comes from within the child. It is a biological drive, but to develop play fully children need other people, peers and adults. Research suggests lack of childhood play may be linked with attention deficit hyperactivity disorder (ADHD). Boys who do not play are more likely to bring personal and social tragedy on themselves; for example, becoming persistent drunk drivers.[14] Some children do not learn to play, owing to sickness, unhappiness, abuse or a culture that does not encourage play.

Play is significant in the spiritual and religious development of children. In play children replay their own experiences and make meaning of it. This is part of the process of becoming a person. If Christian faith is a process of becoming what we truly are, the children of God, then it is a growth towards that maturity. The philosopher Nietzsche's idea of true maturity was to attain the seriousness of a child at play. By that, I understand Nietzsche to mean the total involvement of body, mind, imagination and spirit in play. The image of play is found in the Scriptures and in tradition. Wisdom plays at creation (Prov. 8.22–31, NJB); the ideal future for the people of God is seen as children playing in the streets (Zech. 8.4–5) and as a nursing child playing (Isa. 11.8); and Mechtild of Magdeburg, a Beguine of the thirteenth century, gives insight into the relationship of the believer and God by using the imagery of a child at play: 'I, God, am your playmate! I will lead the child in you.'[15]

What are your childhood memories of play?

Why was play important to you?

What is the significance of play to spiritual growth and faith?

Moral growth

Moral growth is influenced by environment and by an innate sense, conscience. For example, children of one to three years begin to develop a sense of what pleases people. Through play and in conversation in the family they observe and imitate how people behave: how they hurt and help each other. They learn how other people feel, they learn to think beyond themselves. Conversely, if the child lives in a family where there is little concern for others, or where relationships are ignored or even violent, it is likely that the child will grow up with this as the 'norm'.

Children aged three to eight, with support, can develop concepts like being helpful and forgiving, and having a sense of fairness. Issues arise when there is a conflict between the values of home and what is expected at school. Children begin to work out the difference between social rules, which vary with culture (the way to greet someone), display rules, which govern how we show our feelings (hiding disappointment when a present is not the one hoped for) and moral values, which govern our treatment of others (not hitting someone).

From nine years old children understand more abstract concepts: justice, right and wrong, good versus evil, beauty and nature, the arts and scientific achievements. Children of this age have an ability to understand and choose between alternatives. For some children there is a fear of God, conscience or penitence.

Cognitive development

A newborn's learning is immediate, dominated by innate reflexes such as sucking, looking and assimilating what is happening around it. The long biological dependence of the child allows it time to discover and learn, but it needs human stimulation. Thinking develops as a result both of a child's biological maturing and of environmental stimulation. Babies' minds are as rich, abstract, complex and powerful as those of adults, although 'what they think is often radically different from what adults think'.[16] This has implications for the kind of thinking children are capable of and how we relate to them: the adult must make an effort to enter the child's experience and perspective.

PIAGET'S THEORY

Theories of children's thinking have been dominated by the research of Jean Piaget, which began in the 1930s.[17] He argued that children had systematic ideas about people, the world and language that were qualitatively different from those of adults. Piaget's observations led him to propose chronological and hierarchical ordered stages of thinking, from *sensori-motor* and *pre-operational* in infancy, through a *concrete operations* stage to *formal operations*, found in adolescence and adulthood (see Table 2.2). His stages came to be regarded as benchmarks of 'normality' for all children.

Sensori-motor stage

Piaget believed that the infant from birth to two years learns through bodily experiences: exploring through the senses, discovering how things feel, look, sound, taste and smell (banging rattles and bricks, chewing rattles and toys) and extending perception of the world through physical activities (grasping, holding, rolling, watching and listening). Piaget called this the sensori-motor stage. He understood cognitive development as a continuous process of *assimilation* (taking in what is known) and

Table 2.2 Piaget's cognitive development stages

Age	Stage
0–2 years	*Sensori-motor* The child experiences the environment and learns through the senses; schemas or patterns of thought occur and become increasingly co-ordinated; the child is egocentric; has own point of view; by end of first year understands people and objects as permanent even when they cannot be seen.
2–7 years	*Pre-operational* Children think through the senses, feelings and imagination; are able to represent people in drawings and in imaginative play (symbolic thinking); can begin to refer to things and people not present (memory); begin to share what they know with others; assume objects have consciousness (animism); deal with one aspect at a time.
7–11 years	*Concrete operations* Patterns of thinking depend on the presence of objects; with 'hands-on experience' children sort out understanding through basic literal reasoning but still find abstract thinking difficult; can see someone else's point of view and enter their experience; begin to understand about conservation in volume, number and weight; enjoy games and understand about rules.
12–14 years	*Formal operations* Children engage in abstract and hypothetical reasoning; they use abstract concepts of ideas – fairness, justice; principles and analogies become possible.

accommodation (adjusting to what is new). The balance between assimilation and accommodation helps a child to organize past experiences into concepts (ideas). This is an active process: Piaget considered children active learners. Young babies begin to organize their perceptions and link them with earlier experiences of people and events. They use these concepts to work out what will happen next. Piaget called these concepts *schemas*.

Pre-operational stage

Between two and four years new capacities emerge in learning. Most psychologists agree that by the end of the sensori-motor period the child is no longer ruled by reflex actions and motor behaviour but has begun to use internal 'mental' processes to solve problems. This new capacity for *symbolic* thought is the basis for the next stage: the two- to four-year-old infant's thinking is pre-operational. The normal toddler at two is mobile, has the beginnings of language, is showing insight in solving problems and possesses an early form of symbolic thought. Piaget held that thought grows out of action. This is supported by research on the cognitive abilities of deaf children, who reason and solve problems despite language limitations.

The activity of a three-year-old's brain is twice that of an adult. Symbolic thought is expressed in imaginative play, dressing up, imitation and constructive activities with toys such as building bricks and jigsaws. Thinking, however, is limited by *animistic* thoughts, in that feelings and intentions are attributed to objects: 'the moon follows the child', 'teddy has a sore head'. It is also egocentric. Since the infant's view is centred on himself and his own perspective, he finds it hard to take the perspective of another person. This is an example of the thinking of a three-year-old:[18]

Adult: Have you any brothers or sisters?
John: Yes, a brother.
Adult: What is his name?
John: Sammy.
Adult: Does Sammy have a brother?
John: No.

John sees things only from his own point of view. He cannot decentre to realize that from Sammy's perspective he (John) is a brother.

Intuitive stage

From four to seven years there is a shift in thinking: the intuitive period. At about four, the child begins to develop the mental operation of ordering, classifying and quantifying in a more systematic way. Piaget classifies this period as intuitive because the child cannot explain why something happens – mostly things just are. Thinking is unrelated, fragmented and inconsistent. A child may hold two contradictory ideas at once because he or she cannot relate them. Children's thinking and interpretation is based on their own sense experience. For example, when water is poured from a squat jar into a thin, taller jar, children think that there is more water in the tall jar. Similarly, if a child is shown two parallel lines of buttons with the same number in each line, when the researcher spreads out the buttons in one of the lines the child thinks there are more buttons in the longer line. The imagination runs wild in the stories children tell. Unrealistic similes abound: 'freckles look like cornflakes'. Art work contains abstract features not connected to reality. Realism and exactness are not a concern.

Concrete operational stage

The seven- to eleven-year-old child develops a new set of thinking strategies, which Piaget calls concrete operations: 'concrete' because the child can only apply them to the present context; 'operations' because they are mental actions. The junior-aged child has an enthusiasm for gathering facts and exploring what is true so he may retreat from the unbridled imagination of the previous stage, yet use the abstract. Thinking becomes more flexible through understanding, once the concept of reversibility is understood. In the conservation experiment a round ball of clay is transformed into a sausage shape. In response to the question, 'Which is larger?' a child will say, 'If you change it back, it will be the same.' The concrete-operational child can classify and order, understanding the principle of class inclusion. The limitations of thinking occur when the objects are not present, so that the question is 'abstract'. Given the problem 'Edith is fairer than Susan. Edith is darker than Lily. Who is the darkest?' the child finds difficulty since this type of abstract reasoning is unlikely before the formal operational stage. However, in depicting such characteristics with dolls he will be able to rank them. The degree of egocentrism changes in this stage. The child is able to co-ordinate two aspects of a situation simultaneously, enabling him to realize another person may have a different viewpoint. He can see the relationship of parts to a whole and begins to see the sequence of time and the significance of a point of history in understanding the world. He recognizes difference in people. This is the beginning of abstract thinking.

Formal operational stage

The formal operational stage may be reached by eleven years. The child no longer depends on objects being present. He has the capacity to think hypothetically and deductively. A child of this age can understand abstract concepts such as fairness and justice; can understand the principle of creating laws and rules to test things out as true or false; can make a hypothesis to test and solve a problem. This ability to think in the abstract allows the child to put some distance between himself and his thoughts. Subsequent research suggests that formal operational thinking develops gradually, haphazardly and is dependent on the nature of the task. It is often limited to certain areas of thinking. Moreover, the ages of eleven to fifteen years signal the possibility of formal operational thinking, rather than its achievement. Some adults never become abstract thinkers; most continue as concrete-operational thinkers in many aspects of life.

Which psychological insights are helpful to you in your contact with children?

How might psychological insights be important in pastoral care?

Piaget argued that the child thinks quite differently from the adult. Children learn actively, with the freedom to explore, touch, manipulate and experiment, rather than from passive observation. Active learning means that the child constructs knowledge for himself that he is later able to test, resulting in deeper understanding. Abstract thinking is only attained in part of adults' lives. Piaget's understanding of thought processes has considerable significance in understanding how we think religiously.

The work of Piaget has been challenged subsequently. Other researchers[19] have suggested that children are more capable than Piaget recognized and that the wording of his experimental questions inhibited children's responses. Children are active explorers of meaning and have more understanding than is revealed by what they can verbalize. Others suggest that, rather than Piaget's linear stages, development takes place in networks of sequences, which give us the basic order, rules and strategies that children develop and learn through. Piaget's cognitive developmental model may not be so central to religious thinking, which uses other non-rational kinds of knowing, such as intuitive understanding.

Parallel to Piaget's research is that of Vygotsky, whose main work was on understanding the role of language in learning.[20] Language is a natural feature of human beings, which enables communication and relationships. Vygotsky laid emphasis on social cognition, that is learning together. This insight resonates with the theological motif that humans cannot become 'an other' without 'the other' (Gen. 2.18). In the 1980s other researchers were beginning to think that social and physical contexts, together with the biological growth of the child, were equally crucial to the development of thinking. This is called situational cognition.

How important do you consider others to be in your learning? Think of examples.

What importance does a social context have for the nurture of faith?

SUMMARY POINTS FOR DISCUSSION

- Children are active learners within a few days of birth.

- Babies make sense of their world.

- The first 'image' of God is the parent.

- A child's growth is physical, emotional, intellectual, social and spiritual.

- Children's thinking is different from that of adults.

CHAPTER THREE

Insights into Spiritual and Religious Development

A toddler sensed that something was amiss in his family. He clutched his comforter, a toy monkey, and would not be parted from it. Two months ago, his sibling had been born prematurely, but the baby was no longer present. The pram was empty. His sister had died. Seeing his mother sitting tearful in a chair when usually she would be absorbed in the activities of family care, the toddler took his comforter and repeatedly gave it to his mother to hug.

> **What does this incident say to you?**
>
> **Share your evidence of signs of spirituality in children.**

In this story we have the example of a young child without language intuitively moving from his own experience to recognize an adult's feelings. His actions explicitly responded to distress in a way that was part of his experience: the toy monkey, which brought him comfort, would comfort his mother. I would suggest that this incident is an example of implicit spirituality. David Hay writes: 'Spirituality is always concerned with self-transcendence. It requires us to go beyond egocentricity to take account of our relatedness to other people, the environment and, for religion, belief in God.'[1]

This chapter explores the spiritual and religious growth of children, building on material from the previous chapter, and using anecdotes and research on spiritual and religious development. I have dealt with these aspects separately to highlight certain insights, though of course the spiritual exists alongside and builds on the everyday development of children.

SPIRITUAL AND RELIGIOUS MEANINGS

The two words 'spiritual' and 'religious' are often used inter-changeably but the origins of the words may help us distinguish them. 'Spirit' is from the Latin *spiritus*, which means 'breath', and then 'life'. Similarly, in New Testament Greek *pneuma* means 'breath' or 'wind' and then 'spirit'. Both words suggest that spirituality is, like breath, fundamental to our lives. The word 'religion', however, has its roots in the Latin word *religio*, meaning 'to bind together'. Religion is a way of giving a structure to a spirituality of beliefs and actions held by a community.

Much of Western society is dominated by secularism and adult attitudes that shun formalized religion, yet children from a young age play with ideas that are clearly spiritual and formative for religion. They wonder about the meaning of life and express their own sense of what truly matters to them. It appears that spirituality is innate in us, affirmed by the biblical insight that humans are created in 'the image and likeness of God'. Spiritual-ity is expressed for believers through religion but may also be secular. The basis for this assertion is in anecdotal stories and a growing body of research.

As humans we are distinctive in the animal kingdom in that we are 'meaning-makers', that is, we ask existential questions to help make sense of our own everyday experience and of the world in which we live. Children are particularly adept at asking ques-tions, many of which challenge adults. We are reminded of the young Jesus in the temple (Luke 2.41–52). Jerome Berryman, creator of 'Godly Play', suggests that children have four existen-tial 'limits': the knowledge that we are alone; the issue of our freedom and the lack or fear of it; concerns about the reality of death; and the need to find meaning (Who am I? What am I here for?). These questions are a reflection of a child's spiritual life and may be expressed in a religious faith.

EXPERIENCES AND STORIES THAT ILLUSTRATE 'MEANING-MAKING'

The following stories illustrate meaning-making within Jerome Berryman's 'existential' limits. The recognition of the uniqueness of each of us and of our utter aloneness is recalled by the Vic-torian writer Edmund Gosse. In his autobiography he wrote of an experience at the age of six. Edmund's father had built a rockery, supplied with water from a lead pipe which he had pierced so that when a tap was turned on there was a fountain. One day workmen left some tools by the rockery and Edmund experimented with them, making a further hole in the pipe. He forgot about the experiment until days later when his father turned on the tap and instead of the fountain a rush of water ruined the rockery. His father was furious. Edmund realized what he had done and waited for his father's wrath. His mother remarked on the visit of the plumbers two or three days before and suggested that they must have mischievously stabbed the pipe to spoil the fountain. No suspicion fell on Edmund, nor was he questioned. He wrote:

> The theory that my Father was omniscient or infallible was now dead . . . My Father as a deity . . . fell in my eyes to a human level . . . But of all the thoughts . . . the most curious was that I had found a companion and a confidant in myself. There was a secret in this world and it belonged to me and to a somebody who lived in the same body with me. There were two of us, and we could talk with one another . . . the sense of my individuality now suddenly descended upon me, and it is equally certain that it was a great solace to me to find a sympathizer in my own breast.[2]

Gosse realized that he was a unique individual, that only he could know the 'secrets' of his thoughts. He was alone.

Children have questions about the meaning of death. In a nursery class, a three-year-old boy was sitting very still, alone on one of a line of chairs in the 'home' area. The area was arranged to stimulate play relating to the topic of doctors and nurses, with white coats, nurses' uniforms, stethoscopes and bottles of 'sweetie' pills. The teacher was mystified by the boy's stillness and asked him about his play. He looked at her in amazement and said, 'I'm dead, of course!' She took the child away immediately to do something else. An experience in this boy's life had led him to connect 'hospital' and 'death'. Young children are very matter-of-fact about death; sometimes it is adults who cannot cope.

Children need to find meaning in their lives, asking such questions as 'Who am I?' and thinking about their identity. Three-year-old Abdul was excited by the birth of a baby in his family. He was asked what the baby was, to which he replied angrily, 'Black, of course'. It seemed that being 'black' was central to his identity, something to be proud of. However, his anger indicated that he had heard, or experienced, that being 'black' meant he was different from others and might not be accepted by them.

If children are given freedom to explore, they discover for themselves the world in which they live. Young children have a realism touched with a sense of mystery, awe and wonder as they make new discoveries. Teresa is nearly three. Her mother said, 'It takes ages to walk home after our mothers and toddlers group. Teresa has opened my eyes again to the world around me.' Teresa has discovered stones, feathers, ladybirds and other treasures on her walk home. Sadly, some parents have no time and so limit their children's freedom to explore. They miss the excitement of their child's sense of awe and wonder while failing to create space for the collection of these treasures.

Are we born spiritual?

What difference does spirituality make to our lives?

What early memories do you have which might be called spiritual?

Are children spiritual? Give evidence for your response.

RESEARCH ON CHILDREN'S SPIRITUALITY

Robert Coles

Research has given adults clues to the nature of children's spirituality. The Harvard professor and child psychologist Robert Coles interviewed over 500 eight- to twelve-year-olds from many different cultures and parts of the world. Some children he talked with in groups, others alone in their own homes. Some he talked to once or twice, most at least five times, and over a hundred children were interviewed 25 times over a period of time. The conversations were unstructured. Coles simply asked the children about the things and people that were most important in their lives, and about questions that puzzled them. Conversations emerged about relationships with parents and grandparents, about parental control, influence, rules and freedom. Children were concerned about wars and the suffering of other children through congenital disease and accidents, the unfairness of it all. They talked about who was ultimately responsible for events such as war and the creation of the world, which led them to talk about God and God's apparent ignoring of suffering, about ultimate destiny, heaven and hell. Coles taped the conversations. For example, twelve-year-old Eric said, 'Religion doesn't mean much to me – going to church; but I sure can stop and wonder about things.' He talked about science lessons at school, 'when we study gravity or atoms . . . that kind of stuff. Then I'll wonder how all that got going. Is there a God? Did he get it all going? Are there other people somewhere in the universe?' The conversation led to Eric's account of the death of a young male cousin he admired, who was killed by a drunken driver. Eric attempted to make sense of the accident: his cousin Ned was dead while he, Eric, was still alive, but one day he too would be no more.[3] These musings, using concepts of life and death, meaning, identity and purpose, are intensely spiritual.

Children were encouraged to draw pictures of God, Jesus, heaven and hell in an effort to portray what they could not put into words. Their words and pictures convey the religious and spiritual experiences of children in all their 'blooming buzzing confusion'.[4] It was a project, Coles stated, that 'helped me to see children as seekers, as young pilgrims well aware that life is a finite journey and as anxious to make sense of it as those of us who are farther along in the time allotted to us'.[5] He talked with children whose interest in God, the supernatural, the ultimate meaning of life and the sacred side of life was not fed by religion. Some were children of professed agnostics or atheists; others belonged to religious families but asked spiritual questions that were far from the 'orthodox' beliefs of their religious faith. In their conversations both the children and Coles became vulnerable to one another as they shared some of the intimacy of these mysteries of life. This openness and vulnerability is a characteristic of spirituality.

David Hay and Rebecca Nye

In their research on spirituality David Hay and Rebecca Nye built on the work of Alister Hardy. Hardy, a professor of zoology, proposed that what he called 'religious experience' had evolved through 'natural selection' because it had survival value for the individual. Hay used Hardy's concept but called it 'spiritual awareness'. He noted that

> there is a form of awareness, different from and transcending everyday awareness, which is potentially present in all human beings . . . The many religions of *homo sapiens* are the richly varied cultural responses of human beings to their natural spiritual awareness.'[6]

Nye held individual unstructured conversations with 38 children, boys and girls, Anglican, Roman Catholic, Muslim and of no religious affiliation. There were two groups, children of six to seven years and of ten to eleven years. Each conversation had three focuses: the child's interests and life story; a picture with the potential to generate reflective conversation;[7] and religion/spirituality if it had not emerged earlier. Nye built up a relationship of trust with each child. It was the very act of her listening to the children that enabled them all to talk and to make some sense of their experience of the spiritual in their everyday lives. Children who had grown up with the language of a secular culture found difficulties in expressing spiritual experiences. They needed a language to explore their lives and its mysteries, yet were reticent to use religious language, although some used it for its 'symbolic function'. For other children religious language had lost its potency; it was just too easy, and failed to capture 'the complexity and mystery for which they sought an expression'.[8] Their experiences sometimes could not be contained within words. Berryman commented about spirituality that 'individuals intuit that there is more meaning in such talk than the words can carry'.[9]

Children often described experiences which could be identified with adult experiences, clustered around four core spiritual qualities defined as: awareness, value, mystery, and meaningfulness or insight. Nye's conversations with children did not fit easily into any categories but two patterns appeared:

- an unusual level of *consciousness* or perceptiveness, relative to other passages of conversation spoken by the child;
- conversation expressed in a context of how the child *related* to things, other people, him/herself, and God.[10]

These she designated *relational consciousness*, characterized by relationships to self, others and a beyond, and consciousness seen

in a distinctively *reflective awareness*. 'In this "relational consciousness" seems to lie the rudimentary core of children's spirituality, out of which can arise meaningful aesthetic experiences,
religious experience, personal and traditional responses to
mystery and being, and mystical and moral insight.'[11]

Hay understood spirituality as the core of being human, representing a 'social evolution', alongside biological evolution. It is the
bedrock for the welfare of the individual and society, sustaining
the individual in times of trial, illuminating his times of joy. Since
humans are in essence social it sustains community, and politi-
cally it underlies the moral sense and striving for social justice.

Young children are spiritual. They have a sense of awe and
wonder and an innate spirituality of everyday life that challenges
the religion and spiritual atrophy of many adults. In each child is
the spark of the divine nature. Every child knows something about
God, even if they struggle to find words to explore their experience.
This innate spirituality is irrespective of learning ability or articu-
lateness.

NURTURING THE SPIRITUAL

Nurturing the spiritual lives of children is about exploring the
qualities of the relationships that make us truly human. The
spiritual experience of childhood is frequently lost as children
mature (towards the age of ten, the upper age group of the
research), first, because it is not recognized by parents as being
of worth, and second, because spirituality is not encouraged by
adults. Parents may overlook their children's sense of awe and
wonder, being too busy to simply stop and enjoy stillness or
beauty with a child. Third, spirituality may be perceived by
adults as naive and scoffed at. It is devalued in a scientific world
characterized by rationality. Spirituality is a challenge to the
rationalism, secularism and individualism of much of society –
it is counter-cultural. Hay illustrates the damaging effects of
a culture that teaches boys the self-sufficiency of macho individualism, thought necessary for survival, to the detriment of
genuine feelings of vulnerability, dependency and the need for
relationships. Fourth, religion, as a language of spirituality, has
become implausible for many adults, and children perceive and
imitate this attitude. In contrast to a culture of individualism,
spirituality is characterized by the intuitive, the creative, the
transcendent and by relationships. These comments have significant implications for pastoral care.

The pastoral care of an individual child involves the nurture of the spiritual. At home this might involve some of the suggestions in the Mothers' Union material discussed below. In children's religious and spiritual development we need to look for strengths that support a spiritual basis for faith. We need to be aware of, and use, insights from children's psychological development. Sometimes parents can be unaware of children's complex spiritual and religious development, to the detriment of their growth. Sensitivity is needed: spending time listening to and encouraging the child, watching for non-verbal signs, and reading between the lines, all enable parents to glean clues to their children's growth. This enables parents to encourage their child.

The Mothers' Union leaflet *Children and Spirituality* (see Appendix 2) suggests that spirituality gives children 'time to think about themselves, other people and the world; space to enjoy new experiences; security so that they feel able to question and explore; affirmation that their thoughts about God, life and the universe are interesting and important'. The leaflet suggests very practical ways in which the natural spirituality of all children can be nurtured by parents. These include:

- focusing and bringing to attention the five senses
- watching changes in nature
- stillness and sitting in silence together
- encouraging the collection of special objects
- having Christian symbols in the home – a cross, a dove, an angel, an ear of corn
- praying together
- creating a prayer tree in the garden.

Look at the Mothers' Union list of ways to nurture a child's spirituality (Appendix 2).

Comment on it.

Can you suggest other occasions and ways of nurturing spirituality?

Spirituality is an integral part of the school curriculum.[12] Since spirituality concerns what it means to be human, it will also be nourished in moments of reflection, in meditation, in awareness of the present moment within groups. For example, a group of junior-school children watched with bated breath as a butterfly emerged from its cocoon, letting the sunlight dry its wings before taking flight. The silence was eventually broken by one of them blurting out, 'It's resurrected'.

Children can be invited to close their eyes and listen for a few moments to attend to the here and now. A child can listen to its heartbeat or its breathing, to breathe in all that is good in the love of God and to breathe out all that spoils God's love. A further exercise designed by Dr Patrick Pietroni invited a group to experience with all their senses the physical act of eating an apple.[13] Mary Stone has devoted her energy and creativity to exploring children's spiritual awareness; her book contains many useful exercises suitable for school and church.[14]

CHILDREN AND RELIGION

Our culture is profoundly secular, yet the evidence of a religious heritage is all around us. Children encounter religion through families (though in some homes 'God' and 'Jesus' occur as swearwords) or services and hymn-singing on the television. They recognize festivals associated with public holidays; they see Christian symbols such as a 'cross' necklace or a fish brooch; they may attend ceremonies such as a christening, marriage or funeral in a church. In school, in religious education classes, clergy may be invited to explore ideas with children, taking them into church to 'enact' a christening or marriage. Children may visit a church as part of an environmental project. They experience collective worship at school. To all these words, symbols and experiences children give some sort of meaning, though their first use may be vague or inaccurate.

The children interviewed by Coles, Hay and Nye were concerned with abstract concepts such as identity, freedom, suffering, death, meaning and value; although they did not use these words, they were wrestling with the ideas. The major religious faiths have always explored these concerns. However, much religious language is symbolic, using metaphor, imagery, myth and story. The Bible uses images such as Jesus as the 'Good Shepherd' and the 'Light of the World'. It uses simile: the kingdom of God is like 'a mustard seed', 'a pearl of great price', 'yeast working in bread'. Biblical thought uses 'abstract' concepts, including God, love, forgiveness and sin. Much of this language is 'secondary language', as a writer reflects on his own (primary) experience. The Bible is an adult book; it was not written for children. It emerged from ancient cultures very different from our own. Adults may have skills, knowledge and experiences which help them to recognize and work with biblical material, but do children have these ways of thinking? What do children make of images such as the Good Shepherd and the parables of the Kingdom?

Have a conversation with a group of children you know. Ask for their help.

Find out and write down the 'big' questions that 'bother' them, that is, the questions for which they are seeking answers.

Note the language that children use.

RESEARCH ON RELIGIOUS DEVELOPMENT

Ronald Goldman

Piaget considered that the ability to think abstractly developed at about the age of twelve years; this suggests that religious concepts are beyond the comprehension of children. We need to ask how children's religious understanding develops. Has it parallels to cognitive development? Is 'understanding' more than the cognitive? Does it include emotion and attitude? How will this help us to nurture children in faith?

In the late 1960s, Ronald Goldman used Piaget's cognitive development theories within schools to discover how children's understanding of the Bible developed. He published his research findings in two books.[15] Goldman questioned 200 children about three Bible stories: Moses and the burning bush, the crossing of the Red Sea, and Jesus' temptation in the wilderness. The youngest children, aged five to seven, gave magical explanations. The seven- to eleven-year-olds employed literal reasoning with 'hands-on' ways to sort out their understanding, using 'the facts' even when these were peripheral to the meaning of the story. Only the children over twelve seemed able to think about the symbolic meanings. Goldman concluded that religious thinking was sequentially magical, literal and abstract, shaped by the same developmental processes that Piaget had identified: preoperational, concrete operational, formal/abstract operational. Goldman suggested three stages of religious thinking. These are laid out in Table 3.1.

Table 3.1 Stages of religious thinking in children

Stage 1	*Intuitive thinking*
Bible	Children use their own experience to interpret the Bible. Fantasy, magic and miracles are intermixed.
God	God is powerful and in control, depicted in children's drawings with a huge head and sitting on a cloud.
Prayer	Prayer is often a 'magic' activity.
Morality	Good things happen if you are good.
Stage 2	*Literal and concrete religious thinking*
Bible	Children enjoy Bible stories but interpret them literally. Little understanding of metaphor.
God	Jesus and God are muddled. God continues to be understood in humanistic ways.
Prayer	Prayer continues to be partly magical; and a bargaining to get things a child likes as a reward for good behaviour.
Morality	Rules are to be obeyed to earn rewards.
Stage 3	*Abstract and conceptual religious thinking*
Bible	Within the Bible poetry, symbol, metaphor can be appreciated. Some understanding of abstract concepts such as forgiveness and sacrifice.
God	Different words and concepts used for God such as love, Creator, rock.
Prayer	Prayer is seen as exploration of the child's communication with God.
Morality	Words such as rights, principles, duty, conscience are used. Understanding that sometimes rules may be broken for a greater good.

Adapted from Fraser Watts, Rebecca Nye and Sara Savage, *Psychology for Christian Ministry* (London: Routledge, 2002), p. 87.

Goldman noted that religious thinking tended to lag behind other thinking. The transition from Piaget's concrete operations (at seven to eleven years) to formal operations (abstract thinking at twelve years and over) took up to six years. Many youngsters never reached the abstract thinking required for religious thought. They simply rejected their underdeveloped religious understandings as irrational and childish compared with their thinking in other areas of life. Goldman called this '11-year-old atheism', and noted that many adults retain a childish idea of God. He questioned the wisdom of allowing a child's 'distorted' explanations to develop, since children became confused at the need to let go of a literal style of thinking and denounce what seemed a 'childlike faith'. He concluded that using the Bible and its imagery with primary school children would be destructive of their subsequent religious growth: the Bible should be left to adolescence.

Alternative perspectives on Goldman

Various aspects of Goldman's method have been questioned. First, the wording of his questions may have confused children. A seven-year-old asked about the story of Jesus' temptations, 'Why did Jesus say "Man does not live by bread alone?"', answered, 'He needed jam as well.' Within the literal thinking and experience of a seven-year-old the answer is appropriate. Second, the stage developmental model of Piaget may not be so central to religious thinking. Third, there are other non-rational kinds of knowing, such as intuitive, emotional and aesthetic understanding, which may be more appropriate to religious development than cognitive thinking. In the story of the toddler at the beginning of the chapter there is empathy as a response, a 'spiritual awareness' basic to religion. Children have more understanding than is revealed by what they can verbalize; the contrast is between implicit and explicit knowledge. This is particularly pertinent if the child is in an environment of faith such as a Christian home and a church community. Goldman's research was in day schools; within the all-age community of the church, children are able to grasp the meaning of ideas which are beyond them in a peer group. The communal understanding is significant (see Vygotsky, Chapter 7). Nye suggests that 'implicit religious understanding might mean children appreciate the frisson of a metaphor (the light of the world), or the counterpoint offered by analogy (he is the shepherd, we are the sheep) without the ability to comment explicitly on this'.[16]

Fourth, both Coles and Nye discovered in their research that the way children were invited to share their thoughts made a difference to the response. If the researcher asked for their help, children were open: they might find words to express their thinking difficult, but their free responses gave glimpses of each child's personal insights and engagement with mystery. Children are active explorers of meaning.

Fifth, Goldman was dealing with religious *thinking* but did not consider children's spontaneous questions, which can reveal the beginnings of modes of later abstract thinking. Violet Madge tells a story which is illustrative.[17] A conversation arose as six-year-olds were modelling clay.

Alan:	Who made God, then?
Gareth:	No one, he was there all the time.
Paul:	He must be old.
Sharon:	God's everywhere.
Alan:	Don't be daft, he can't be that big.
Howard:	Did God make the men of clay like we did?
Alan:	Well, if he did he must have had a lot of clay.
Mark:	Why didn't he make any children?
Deborah:	'Cos the man and the woman wasn't married then.

Ellen C. Mee

In her research Ellen C. Mee gives examples of children's questions which reflect a deep religious questioning and understanding.[18] Five- to seven-year-olds are keen to get concrete material and physical 'facts' straight in terms of their own lives. They ask: Was Jesus rich? How long did he live? Had Jesus any brothers and sisters? Are angels the souls of dead people? Was Jesus good at school? Did he read the Bible? There are questions about how things happen, especially things that seem magical: How much magic did Jesus do?

Seven- to eight-year-olds ask questions to sort fact from fantasy. In religion and science lessons children begin to appreciate there is much that we do not know and that they can share the excitement of gradually getting to know. They begin to have an interest in motive: Why did God make the world? Why did a disciple let Jesus down? They are concerned to sort out the information they have received and fill in gaps in their understanding. They are clearly trying to interpret the stories in the light of their experience. The inconsistencies in their understanding arise from comparison with their own lives and from an inability to bring together knowledge from different fields of learning.

Nine-year-olds pursue facts more deeply, asking: Is Buddha a god? Need we have churches when we can worship in our own home? They bring together science and religion: How could Jesus ascend when we have gravity? They relate philosophy and ethics: Why did God make us if we are going to die? People say God wants peace, then why do we have war? They ask questions requiring evidence: How do you know there is a God? How do we know that Jesus is the son of God? They see gaps and inconsistencies in knowledge and want an explanation.[19]

If children's questions and insights are ignored they are likely to become blasé; if they are answered in a way that offends their emerging powers of thinking, then rejection and scorn are likely consequences. Children want adults to join in with their 'wonderings'. Jesus turned back the question to the questioner (Luke 10.25–26). If we do this with a child, we may discover his mode of thinking before sharing ours with him. The message of the Bible is relevant to children if it relates to their experience. Interestingly, in church children hear the Bible reading from the Lectionary, one that is not selected with children in mind. Many of the passages chosen are difficult even for adults; however, children can cope if they are in the presence of a community of adults for whom the Bible is significant and meaningful. They can accept on this basis without necessarily understanding.

Sofia Cavalletti

The research and experience of Sofia Cavalletti help to answer some questions concerning children's religious understanding. Cavalletti worked from late 1950 until 1990 preparing young children (three- to six-year-olds) for their first communion. She discovered that children respond to religious ideas if the material used is related to their experience. She used the activity-centred methods of Maria Montessori[20] in conjunction with the story of the Good Shepherd (John 10.1–18). She told children of the love and protective presence of the Good Shepherd, who knew each of his many sheep and called each one by its own name. The Shepherd's voice is powerful and patient. The sheep turn to hear. The

Shepherd knows the needs of his sheep and guides them to good pasture. He walks ahead to show the way and to be the first to confront danger. The sheep know they are safe and protected. Cavalletti told the story using wooden figures to represent the Shepherd and sheep and a sand tray.

The children would listen to the story in silence. Then gradually they responded as they discovered for themselves the 'Good Shepherd' as a mothering, nurturing figure. They recognized that, like the sheep, they were each called by their own name. Each was precious, known and loved by God. Cavalletti offered both 'Good Shepherd' and 'Light of the World' as images for children to explore their own feelings about Jesus. The Shepherd relates to the child's need for continued mothering, while at the same time being known by name as one who is developing autonomy and individuality. Thus children found their psychological needs met in the Bible story.

Cavalletti noticed that children responded to the image of the Shepherd. She wrote:

> A deep chord within the child had been touched. The reactions . . . resemble those of a person who has found his milieu and, once having found it, does not want to leave it . . . the response the children give to the religious experience . . . seems to involve them deeply . . . lead[ing me] to believe that these arise from the depths of the child's being, as if they were natural to him.[21]

The reaction of the child was an open receiving of the story and a directness unencumbered with doubts and questions. Pier Marco (four years old) said, 'There will be one flock and one shepherd', and put even the wolf and hireling wooden figures in the fold; when his companions objected, he explained, 'But don't you understand that with the Good Shepherd everyone becomes good?'[22]

Jesus used the everyday to give clues to the nature of God's Kingdom: a tiny mustard seed growing (Mark 4.30–32), the yeast in a lump of dough (Luke 13.20–21), a pearl of great worth (Matt.13.45–46). Young children are alert to the smallest happenings, which adults have become so accustomed to that they have become banal and insignificant. Alert as they are, children spontaneously, through questions, seek for meaning as Jesus intended when telling his parables. Comments from a conversation on the parable of the leaven illustrate children's involvement:

- The leaven has God's strength because only He can make it grow.
- The leaven is the Kingdom of God.
- How big can it get?
- It can go as high as the sky because the Kingdom of God is great.
- It never stops growing.
- It's in our hearts.

Cavalletti's radical claim that the fundamental structure of the child is innately religious, and should be taken as the basis and reference point for children's humanity, is parallel to Hay and Nye's definition of children's innate spirituality as relational consciousness. This suggests that children can be nurtured and helped by using appropriate biblical material.

> **What biblical images were important to you in childhood?**
>
> **What Bible stories were important to you as a child? Why?**

Jerome Berryman

Jerome Berryman built on the work of Cavalletti and Montessori in developing 'Godly Play'. He recognized the spirituality within each child and sought to enable children to listen to their own inner spirit and encounter the sacred stories of the community of faith. Godly Play invites children to play with the Scriptures. Berryman draws on the creativity of non-verbal communication (gesture, image, symbols, awe, wonder) and verbal communication (story and metaphor). The biblical stories are carefully chosen to reflect the fourfold functions of Christian language:

- sacred story (those which formed the people of God, for example, Exodus, Sinai)
- parable (parables of the Kingdom)
- liturgical action (Advent, Christmas, Easter, baptism, Eucharist)
- contemplative silence.

Each story is told in a particular way, using the essential elements while omitting unnecessary description, thus avoiding any interpretation by the adult telling the story. In the telling the gestures and silence are as significant as the words, aided by objects from a gold box of two-dimensional figures and cloth (parable) or a basket of three-dimensional figures and objects (sacred story and liturgical action).

If possible, a room is set aside as a creative environment of sacred space. The room has shelves with the material for the stories in baskets and boxes. There is a box of sand for 'desert' stories (Abraham, the Exodus and the Exile). One side of the room, the focus, contains images of the Good Shepherd, the Holy Family, a candle (the Light of Christ), and beyond it material for Christmas and Easter. There are also resources for the children's creativity. The centre of the room is a carpeted space. Each child is invited into the room by the doorkeeper, to join the storyteller, forming a circle seated on the floor. Thus, in walking into the room the child is surrounded by symbols of the language of Christian people.

When all are ready, the storyteller walks around the room to choose the box or basket that contains materials for the day's story. This is significant since meaning comes from context, and each lesson needs the whole language system for its full meaning. The children watch where the 'story' comes from and the place to which it is returned at the end, so that they can themselves find and 'use' the story. On returning to the circle the storyteller creates a sense of wonder, by for example holding a parable box and saying, 'This box looks old. Parables are old. I wonder if there is a parable inside?' Comments are made about the box lid and 'entering' the parable. 'Entering' refers to the fact that parables bring us into a new place of understanding. They confront us with questions about our everyday view of life; they challenge, and disrupt the status quo imposed by tradition, power and social class. Sometimes this new place remains 'closed' to us; however, we can return to the parable later, when it may reveal new challenges to us. The lid is used to hide the contents, which are gradually brought out, first the felt underlay and then the figures of the story. There is wondering about the colour and shape of the pieces of felt found in the box. Each child's response is accepted. The story is then told without making eye contact with the children, since it is the story that is central to a child's encounter with God, themselves, one another and the world around them. The story is structured, with pauses, silence and gestures, so that children can absorb it and make connections with their own experience of life.

Each child is invited to make a twofold response to the story. First there are open questions, within the group, exploring meaning not facts, such as 'I wonder what part of this story you like best? I wonder what part of the story you think is most important? I wonder if you are in the story and if the story is in you?' A dialogue of equals emerges between storyteller and children, and between the children: this is a way of meditation, a contemporary experience of the ancient *lectio divina* (a meditative reading of the Scriptures). Next, the children are encouraged to make their own responses, choosing from pencils, coloured paper, paints, clay, books or the story box or basket itself. In their responses some retell the story, others interpret it, while others use the story to make sense of their own present experience. When the children return to the circle they may want to share, but this is not essential. There is space to be thankful and a feast of juice and biscuits is shared. Central to Godly Play are the following elements:

- creating sacred space
- learning a religious language
- building a sense of community
- using religious language to make one's own meaning
- sharing a feast.

The depth of response from children to Godly Play is a powerful experience. Using the parable of the mustard seed, I was thrown off balance by a child's remark: 'I wonder what happens if the bush is cut down.' There was silence until another child said, 'The roots would grow again, with runners like strawberry plants and anyway it may have produced seeds to grow new trees.' A dialogue then emerged between the children that living things don't 'end': they are recycled and used by other plants and animals. A child used the word 'eternal' and others nodded. 'Yes', one child stated, 'like the Kingdom it never ends.' On another occasion I was using the material for baptism. The script suggests putting the candle out with a snuffer and then gently raising it and moving the smoke to symbolize the flowing out of the Christ light into all our lives. The children were deeply moved and silent at this point. Godly Play is built on years of research into understanding the Scriptures and children's development, leading to a theology of childhood. It flows from a commitment to children and to nurturing their faith.

RESEARCH IN STAGES OF FAITH DEVELOPMENT

James Fowler

How does a child's faith develop? Insights into faith development emerge from the research of James Fowler. He defines faith as 'our relationship with what we would regard as our ultimate environment: the centre of our system of values, what we regard as power and how these relate to ourselves'.[23] His research, based on 400 interviews with people whose ages ranged from four to 84 years, established that all humans attempt to make some meaning of their lives. The interviews led him to discern a sequential progression of stages through which each individual will grow (see Table 3.2). The higher the stage of development, the more mature is the person's faith. Between each of the stages there is a transition, which can be traumatic and painful.

Table 3.2 Fowler's stages of faith development

Type of faith	Characteristics	Implications
Stage 1: chaotic (infants)	Formed intuitively by imitating words and actions of others	Positive relations will lead to a sense of trust in others and the world
	Pre-verbal or in early stages of verbal development	Provision of appropriate symbols on which the child can feed
	Imaginative/fantasy Responsive to feelings/moods	Belonging will contribute deep and lasting images; if children are excluded because 'they don't yet understand' they may be cut off from vital nourishment
Stage 2: mythic/literal (6–12 years)	Begins to take on the stories/ rituals of own community	Sense of belonging is important
	Belonging to a faith community is important	Narrative mode is a way of connecting feeling and thought
	Things taken literally	Story important as deeper level of experience
	Enjoys and responds to physical symbols – cross, candles	

(continued overleaf)

Table 3.2 – continued

Type of faith	Characteristics	Implications
Stage 3: synthetic (i.e. built-up) conventional (11–18 years)	Faith seen as bringing people together/belonging One faith seen as the norm and its beliefs, values and judgements as ultimate and to be adopted Other faiths not acknowledged Not everyone leaves Stage 3	Can be a time of conforming with others Need to discover own identity Reflection – being helped to give meaning to and make sense of life
Stage 4: individuative-reflective (young adult)	Faith is seen as personal to make sense of life and self Need to establish personal foundation for faith Time of tension between self/others Critical for faith development	Foundation of a clear belief of the individual Meeting others, clarifying
Stage 5: conjunctive (rare before 30)	Able to live with paradox and ambiguity More vulnerable Open to truth in others' beliefs Deepening empathy for others' journey experiences	Open to others and recognizing that one does not have all the truth Need education to intensify religious affinities Will walk alongside others
Stage 6: universalizing (later in life, a very rare stage)	A category of individuals: Gandhi, Mother Teresa, Martin Luther King Jr, Dag Hammarskjöld Faith so refined that they serve as moral or spiritual examples for communities and help others understand more clearly The self is no longer the ultimate, rather grounding in God: finding themselves by losing themselves Not perfect but have a faith which reflects a new quality of freedom with the self and with others	

Fowler's work can be a useful tool, but it needs handling with care. The criticism has been made that his research method is inadequate to test what is a general and theologically inspired hypothesis. Moreover, it is suggested that the cognitive component is too dominant and is inappropriate for faith development, which is also about the spiritual, emotional, intuitive and creative. He tends to dismiss the faith of children as merely a stage to the mature adult faith which is the Christian goal. He thus fails to recognize the deep spiritual thinking of children.

John Westerhoff

An alternative understanding of faith development is seen in the work of John H.Westerhoff.[24]

1 **Experienced Faith** The experience of the very young child whose parents mediate God through a relationship of care, love and security. The parent mediates God to the child, which helps to form an image of God in the child's mind. The experience of these early years are foundational for a child's attitude, values in life and faith development.
2 **Affiliative Faith** As a child's world expands he carries with him the powerful experience of his parents. Because he wants to please them and adopt their beliefs and values, their faith becomes his. Sometimes conflict arises when the parents' non-verbal behaviour is powerful and may be different from what they say.
3 **Searching Faith** When capable of abstracting cognitively, a child will search for himself and discover his own faith.
4 **Owned Faith** The child/young person commits to a set of beliefs and a way of life which may be very different from that of his parents.

In this model children's faith is considered to be derived from the significant adults in their lives, usually parents and to some extent the community of faith, until they make their own personal commitment to following Christ as responsible disciples. Both Fowler and Westerhoff suggest a progression of spirituality from immaturity (childhood) to maturity (adulthood); however, other research indicates an innate, rich level of maturity in children's spirituality. Coles's research and my own experience suggest that children make their own sense of faith and are active thinkers in their own right, although the influence of home and faith community is significant.

NURTURING THE RELIGIOUS LIFE OF CHILDREN

From psychological research we now recognize that infants are far more sophisticated and sensitive to their experiences and environment than was once thought. Both Winnicott and Bowlby drew attention to children's acquisition in infancy of a foundation for their sense of self. An infant's life is focused intently on a range of experiences that later will be vital ingredients of faith: intimacy, dependence, love, personhood, trust, forgiveness, power and wonder. It is only from these first-hand experiences that infants can later understand these Christian terms.

It is likely that the most fundamental experience for a child is that of feeling secure. The child then has the security to trust someone who will not fail, usually his or her mother. A relationship is formed in that trust which enables the child to grow. The quality of this experience of relationship is crucial for the child's understanding of God and precedes language. Failure of human relationships during childhood impairs growth. When language comes, the most potent words – love, trust, help, I, you – derive their power from those early experiences. Later experiences enlarge and deepen these original meanings, but can rarely erase them. Loving parental relationships are the key to nurturing the child at this stage of development.

Erikson believed the psycho-social life of the two- to five-year-old was defined by issues of power and powerlessness; autonomy and self-doubt; taking initiative and experiences of guilt and failure. It is a cauldron of intense emotions, particularly since vocabulary and conceptual skills are limited. These emotions may overwhelm the child, giving rise to a sense of a power beyond the child. Positive attitudes of parents are key in encouraging infants to experiment and resolve issues. The development of trust in significant adults is the beginning of faith.

Pre-schoolers are curious, active explorers, constantly questioning why. They are open to knowledge and relationships, including God, who is a natural fact of their lives. Cavalletti and Fowler noted the power of images at this age. Cavalletti suggests both 'Good Shepherd' and 'Light of the World' as images for children to explore their own feelings about Jesus. The Shepherd relates to the child's need for continued mothering and for being known by name as one who is developing autonomy and individuality. Children project the strong feelings that are difficult to handle, creating an external symbol of meaning from images. 'Religious images have a great power for evoking and expressing human emotions, and so often appeal to children. The feelings and meanings children invest in these images may be unconventional at this stage.'[25] For example, Edward is described at two years as having a capacity for silence and reflection, concentration and delight in play, happiness in his own company and the capacity to become totally absorbed in what he attends to – a picture, music, a puzzle.[26] There may be a spontaneous verbal response – 'how good of God' – though it is likely to be quiet, suggesting that the child is thinking aloud rather than wanting a parental response. Parents need to give encouragement, freedom and space to children simply to enjoy life, particularly discoveries in the natural world: the wind, rain, insects, flowers, conkers, the movement of their own bodies, swinging in the park, running and splashing through a puddle, to explore and engage at their own pace. Play is an important 'work' at this stage.

Pre-schoolers need structure: for example, bedtime rituals such as reading a story, particularly as they begin to be able to join in the telling. Rituals might also include reflecting on the day. Praise and thanksgiving are religious responses to which children feel naturally drawn; sharing some of the psalms of praise in creation may be helpful. Prayer may emerge as an extension of everyday life, in which children give thanks for people they love, and regret happenings for which they are sorry. Develop simple meditation with a child: listen to breathing and imagine breathing in the love of God and breathing out all that spoils God's love. 'Asking' prayers are more difficult at this age, since magic and wishful thinking predominate and may hinder an understanding of the purpose of prayer.

Children recognize an inner life of conflicts, which they explore in free play. These developments coincide with the beginning of formal education, and their widening social contacts coincide with less dependence on intuition and increased reasoning about self and others. Children of this age, despite their limited religious understanding, have religious and spiritual experiences and feelings which they recount (see Cavalletti, 1983; Coles, 1992; Hay and Nye, 1998).

Between five and seven years children are literal concrete thinkers. They begin to classify and organize their thoughts. They question and openly search, a quality to encourage in their faith development. Children want to belong and feel part of the community, participating actively in rituals such as candle lighting and processions. Stories are important, although a literalism may be evident. Use a Bible character who in some way relates to the life of the child. Ask the children to close their eyes while the story is told and imagine the scene. Then help them imagine themselves in the story. Bring them back to reality by suggesting they open their eyes gradually and return. Use imaginative exploring questions, which can later become the subjects for prayer.

Children can feel and in a sense 'know' what they may be incapable of articulating or not fully understand intellectually. The feeling side is developed through belonging to and having an experience of worship within a Christian community. Friendship is important. For older children fantasy is left behind, and replaced by a growing urge to sort fact from fiction. They bring together learning from different 'disciplines' and relate them, so that inconsistencies begin to emerge. This results in searching and questioning. When concrete thinking reaches its limits, but abstract thinking has not developed, creative drama allows a child to explore what it means to 'stand in another's shoes' and feel empathy for someone else. A local school responded to the story of a child slave by singing and entering into the experience of slavery.

Children require adults to listen and journey with them. Childhood is a significant period of religious change. Jesus said to his disciples, and says to adults today, 'unless you change and become like children' (Matt. 18.3). Openness to new meanings, the excitement of discovering an insight for oneself, the willingness to be vulnerable in the face of the mysterious and unknown and to take risks is of the essence of young children. It is these religious and spiritual characteristics in children that we adults should honour and use in our own lives. Children can awaken in adults a continuing capacity for wonder and awareness of the spiritual.

SUMMARY POINTS FOR DISCUSSION

- Children are spiritual and raise religious questions.

- We need to listen to children, to 'hear' what they are actually saying.

- Children make sense of their world, but in a different way from adults.

- Adults can learn from children, from their openness, vulnerability, spirituality, awe.

- The spiritual and religious understanding evident in children needs to be nurtured.

CHAPTER FOUR

Insights from the Scriptures

Peter was an isolate: he was bigger than the other children in his class and did not smell very fresh; nobody wanted to be his friend. The teacher was telling the story of Zacchaeus, the rejected taxman of Luke's story (Luke 19.1–10). Towards the end of the story, Peter became very excited. He was jumping up and down at the back of the room, waving his arms in the air to get his teacher's attention. 'That's me,' he shouted. He had identified with Zacchaeus the isolate, and realized that in some way he too was accepted. When Peter recognized a fellow isolate, his experience resonated with that of a tax collector in the first century of the Christian era, and so for him a gospel story became 'real'.

> **What stories from Scripture influenced you as a child?**
>
> **Can you remember why?**

In this chapter I ask how the Scriptures depict children. What insights do they give for understanding the child? An engagement with the Scriptures is essential for Christians, since they are a prime source of our understanding of God and ourselves, but our use of Scripture needs care (see Appendix 1).

INSIGHTS FROM THE HEBREW SCRIPTURES

The picture of children in the Hebrew Scriptures is multifaceted. There is no systematic thinking, yet there are a number of references to children: to the emotions of joy at their birth or sadness at infertility; to weaning, nurturing, socialization and educating;

to the care of the fatherless; to children as innocent and as sinful. These insights present us with the sense of an ambiguity and ambivalence towards children.

Incidental references to children

References to children are incidental to the great themes of Scripture such as covenant, yet the covenant was sealed with the promise of land, blessing and descendants (Gen. 12.1–3, 7; 13.14–17). Abundant children reflected God's promise to Abraham (Gen.12.1–3; 13.16; 15.5; Ps. 128.3–6; Isa. 54.1–3). Similarly, children are mentioned and included in the account of the Exodus, an event that consolidated the covenant community of God's people (Exod. 12.37). The covenant was ethical, governing the relationship between God and humans (Commandments 1–4; Deut. 5.1–15), and humans with each other (Commandments 5–10; Deut. 5.16–21). God's steadfast love was in contrast to the constant waywardness of the people. The text of Scripture is littered with relationships torn apart, yet there is a constant reminder that the people of God were aliens (Lev. 19.33) until called to become children of God's grace, and their task was to succour the alien, the widow and orphan children (Exod. 22.21–22; Deut. 24.19–22; Lev. 19.33–34). The succour was practical help for the vulnerable at the margins of society. It responded to and reflected the nature of a vulnerable God. Many children were vulnerable and orphans, ignored by all but God.

What particular significance did children have within this covenant?

Circumcision was the identifying mark of the covenant community; Jewish boys and the children of slaves and foreigners were circumcised on the eighth day (Gen. 17.12). Jensen comments, 'Children, as inheritors of the covenant, did not grow into God's promises for the community but were from birth participants in them'.[1] Children were an integral part of the community, yet paradoxically they were incomplete until they could study and practise the law. In a sense, children were marginalized.

Attitudes to birth

There was mystery surrounding conception and birth. The part played by women in reproduction was unknown – a mystery, and so women were a power often feared. Before birth there was a sense of God's presence and activity (Job 10.9–12; Jer. 1.5). Today, the importance of foetal formation is well known. Our ability to take scans during pregnancy, awareness of the movement in the womb and the mystery of growth help us to appreciate the words of the psalmist: 'You put me together in my mother's womb . . . when I was growing there in secret, you knew that I was there – you saw me before I was born' (Ps. 139.13, 15–16, GNB). The response to the birth of children was parental love, joy and pleasure (Gen. 21.6–7; 29.35; 30.12–13; 1 Sam. 2.1–10; 1 Kings 3.26; 4 Macc.15.4–5; Jer. 20.15).

> **What are the implications of Psalm 139 for how we understand the conception and foetal development of a child?**
>
> **What if the pregnancy is not wanted?**

Infertility created anguish (Gen. 15.2; 30.1–2; 1 Sam. 1.10). It was considered a divine curse and socially shameful. Laws and customs, and the so-called 'levirate marriage' (Deut. 25.5–10), safeguarded the future of the male line (Gen. 30.1–13; Deut. 25.5).[2] A barren woman could give one of her maids to her husband, and the resulting child was considered the woman's. On occasions the man took a second wife (1 Sam. 1.1–2). Sometimes 'divine intervention' led to the conception of children, who were received as answers to prayer (1 Sam. 1.19–20). Yet there was recognition of the distress of the childless woman (Isa. 54.1) and the eunuch (Isa. 56.3–5). In the twenty-first century in the developed world children are precious to many couples and infertility is a disappointment. But an increasing number of people choose singleness, and couples childlessness, for reasons that include fears about the world into which children are born or the economic and emotional cost of child-bearing and child-rearing, attitudes which might be considered selfish. This reflects a very different attitude to children from that of the Hebrew Scriptures.

Characteristics of children

Children were a sign of God's blessing (Gen. 17.6; 28.3; 49.25; Ps. 128.3–4). Sons particularly were a 'heritage' and a 'reward'. Children become a blessing to others, witnesses to their faith and 'messengers' of God. For example, several heroes and prophets were regarded as being 'called' at birth (1 Sam. 1.11, 20; Judg. 13.3–5; Isa. 44.24; 49.1; Jer. 1.4–6) and as belonging to God from the womb (Ps. 139.13–16; cf. 2 Esd. 8.7–14). The infant Moses was saved from death and grew to liberate his people (Exod. 1.22; 2.1–10; 3.9–10). Through hearing God's voice the child Samuel becomes the messenger of God to attack lax living (1 Sam. 3.1–18). David is a youth when, anointed with oil and the Spirit of the Lord, he is called to play his lyre to banish Saul's 'evil spirit' and to fight the Philistine enemy (1 Sam. 16–17). A young slave girl is the means by which Naaman is cured of leprosy (2 Kings 5.2–14). It is children who are intuitive and praise God, silencing the enemy (Ps. 8.2).

Children were seen as God's gift. Eve named her son Seth, meaning 'gift' (Gen. 4.25). The concept of gift bears the implication that, as God's, children are held in trust by parents; they are not their possessions. Hannah dedicated her child, a gift, to God (1 Sam. 1.22). Sons were a special gift (Ps. 127.3–5). The first-born male was offered as a thanksgiving to God (Exod. 22.29) and redeemed by a sacrifice (Exod. 13.1–2). The tendency today is to commodify children, seeing them as objects rather than gifts.

Humans bear God's 'image' and 'likeness' (Gen.1.26; 'likeness' is omitted in Gen.1.27 and 9.6), but nowhere in Scripture is either attribute qualified. Subsequent Christian tradition has associated 'image and likeness' with the rationality characteristic of God, yet children were considered to lack the power of reason until the development of language. Historically, this has led to a failure of theological thinking and action concerning children. The reference to 'the image of God' is likely to refer to the spiritual. Today the idea of a child created 'in the image and likeness of God' as a central premise would re-envision our understanding of their significance. It would also free us to allow our children to be themselves instead of needing them to fulfil our ambitions for them. If they are in God's image, they are not in our image. A child is not ours to mould but a new creation reflecting the abundance of the life of God. This thinking challenges the way we think of, and nurture, children today. One biblical account of

Creation includes the words 'male and female he created them' (Gen. 1.27). Humanity includes children, differentiated as male and female, and blessed. There is variety in creation, God is other than humanity, as male is other than female. Difference is to be acknowledged and celebrated.

The people of God were different from the surrounding cultures, who abandoned their unwanted offspring, particularly girls and those born deformed or handicapped. If certain birth rites were not performed (cutting the umbilical cord, washing the baby, rubbing it with salt, wrapping in cloths), it was an abomination to God (Ezek. 16.4). Today many children are considered worthless. In the developed world, abortion rates are increasing, divorce may leave children in struggling one-parent families and fathers abandon their offspring, careless of children created in the 'image of God'. In the developing world, children are exploited through child labour, recruited as child soldiers, left orphans of Aids, die of malnutrition and in war. The Scriptures remind us of the value of children.

The covenant brought humans into a relationship with God and others: 'and I will walk among you, and will be your God, and you shall be my people' (Lev. 26.12). Humanity is relational, a reflection of plurality within God (Gen. 1.26). God said, 'It is not good that the man should be alone' (Gen. 2.18). In the Hebrew Scriptures children exist within the context of family relationships. The Scriptures show that humans need one another. Today, developmental psychology parallels this theological insight. Children need others since 'the self' is formed, challenged and given meaning by other selves in a community.

Significance of the family

Jewish children were born, shaped, nourished, sustained and given identity in the family of the covenant community. The family was the central religious and social unit of the people of God, dominated by the patriarch. His power was supreme. A father might sell his daughter or son into slavery (Exod. 21.7; Neh. 5.5). Striking or cursing one's father or mother, and even stubborn disobedience, were capital crimes (Exod. 21.15, 17; Lev. 20.9; Deut. 21.18–21). Parents were to be respected. They represented God, and were trustees of a child, holding their authority from God. Adults were to 'train children in the right way' (Prov. 22.6); this involved guidance and boundaries. They were to tell children about God's faithfulness (Isa. 38.19), and teach them fear (awe) of the Lord (Prov. 1.7) and right and just living (Prov. 2.9), as found in the Torah.

The Shema, the summary of the Torah, states 'teach them', which means 'impress upon them' (Deut. 6.4–7). The instruction was 'recite them to your children and talk about them when you are at home and when you are away'. The use of 'when' suggests that there is an appropriate time to talk to children, reinforced by the words 'when your children ask you' (Deut. 6.20). The saying of the Shema was accompanied by the visual and tactile. Small boxes (phylacteries or tefillin), worn on the arms and head, contained the words of the Shema, as did the mezuzah displayed on the doorposts. The fringes (tzitzit) on the prayer shawl (tallis) were reminders of the commandments (Deut. 6.8–9; 11.13–21; Num. 15.37–41). The child's senses were actively focused on symbols of the faith, an experience which predated a child's understanding. Every seventh year the whole community of God, including children, came together to hear the public reading of the whole Torah so 'that their children, who have not known it, may hear and learn to fear the Lord' (Deut. 31.10–13).

In the home children were surrounded by daily reminders of their faith. Josephus[3] mentions three aspects of home life. The first was the food laws which distinguished Jews from others (3 Macc. 3.4). The production, buying, preparation and eating of food were daily occurrences that reinforced the relationship of food and faith. The second was the importance of the 'company' a Jew kept; persons who shared the same food customs controlled whom one might expect to marry. Third, Josephus refers to the rhythm of work and leisure. The weekly Sabbath and the annual cycle of festivals (Passover, Shavuot, Tabernacles), were celebrated and explained in the home, with children taking a leading role (Deut. 6.20–22; Exod. 12.26–27). On these occasions the family would retell the stories of God's guiding of Israel. Faith became the everyday life-blood of the child. The emphasis on the home indicates the importance of children in themselves, and of their nurture.

Each festival was celebrated with particular symbolic rites. The Passover feast (Seder) began with children asking the reason for the celebration: 'Why is this night different from all the other nights?' The questions were an occasion for teaching: '. . . you shall tell your child on that day, "It is because of what the Lord did for me when I came out of Egypt"' (Exod. 13.8). The Seder ended with a child bargaining for the return of the *afikoman* (hidden matzoh bread). In Passover, 'Four types of children (wise, wicked, simple, and those who do not know how to ask) are used to symbolize how all Israel struggles with growing in wisdom and goodness.'[4]

The developed world in the twenty-first century lays emphasis on the private nature of the family, which may exclude community support. The emphasis on individualism, personal fulfilment and an adult-orientated society challenges family relationships. Our society is one in which the family is in flux and under severe pressure. Yet we know the importance of the formative early years of a child's life. The biblical insight of the central role of the family as a nurturing environment for children is helpful. Pastoral care through and with parents needs to recapture the importance for children of stable adults in a secure family supported by the church family.

What symbols of faith might be obvious in our homes?

What special food or meals during the year symbolize our faith?

There was no education specifically for Jewish children; they learnt by listening and participating along with adults (Deut. 6.7). During the exilic period (the fourth century BCE), schools and synagogues emerged. These supplemented the teaching that took place in the home, but were not a replacement for it. Children were significant, not because of their innate qualities, but through their preoccupation with studying the Torah. Rabbi Juda Nesiah (210 CE) stated that 'the world stands only upon the breath of the schoolchildren'.[5]

Family and discipline

The 'child quieted at its mother's breast' is used as a metaphor of peace (Ps. 131.2, RSV); babies and infants praise God (Ps. 8.2); but the child is ignorant, capricious and in need of strict discipline (2 Kings 2.23–24; Wisd. 12.24–25; 15.14; Prov. 22.15; Sir. 30.1–13). Children were not idealized: they were capable of evil. These beliefs influenced nurturing styles and education. If human nature was a mixture of good and bad potentials, evil could suddenly erupt. Vigilance and restraint were required at all times.

The obedience of children was essential for the very survival of a small, yet growing, nation. A disobedient son weakened family life and brought shame on himself and his family, whereas an obedient son brought honour.[6] A boy's destiny was to study the law (Torah), participate in the public life of work, and represent the family in the outside world. Little is known of the socialization of girls. Ben Sirach (author of Ecclesiasticus) concluded that 'the birth of a daughter means loss' (Sir. 22.3)! Girls were harshly treated, having to accept a demanding role under male authority, and expected to be unobtrusive and modest. If not disciplined, a girl could become unruly and shameless, disgracing both her father and later her husband: failing to fulfil the role expected of her, she was despised by both (Sir. 22.3–5). Ben Sirach advises parents, 'Do you have daughters? . . . Be concerned for their chastity' (Sir. 7.24; 42.11). Daughters gained status only through marriage and childbirth (Gen. 21.1–7; 30.22–23).

The Hebrew Scriptures state that 'the imagination of man's heart is evil from his youth' (Gen. 8.21, NKJV) and 'behold I was brought forth in iniquity, and in sin did my mother conceive me' (Ps. 51.5, NKJV). Is this poetic licence, metaphorical language or a considered judgement by the writers that evil is present at the beginning of life? Is evil equivalent to sin? Does sin include moral judgement and intention? Judaism did not trace sin to Adam's disobedience; that understanding was developed by Paul (Rom. 5.12). Nor is sin inherited. The 'fall story' acts as a description of everyday human experience, 'self-centredness', present early in life. The rabbis debated when a child first sinned, but Judaism in general tended to affirm the innocence (vulnerability) of children, which gave them a special relationship to God.

Advocacy of harsh physical discipline and punishment concerns only sons (Prov. 19.18–20). Parental discipline, physical punishment and love are linked (Prov. 13.24; 23.13–14; Sir. 30.1), seen as reflecting God's way (Prov. 3.11–12). Discipline expected a response of obedient submission to parents who represented God. It appears to exclude understanding and can be interpreted as cultivating passivity in the child. An unruly son could disrupt, destabilize and bring shame on a family (Sir. 30.9–13), and hence obedience and duty were central (Sir. 3.2–16), key values in the context of family loyalty (Deut. 21.18–21). Discipline was valued and although today the methods suggested in the Hebrew Scriptures appear cruel, some Christians continue to take these injunctions seriously and interpret this discipline as the need to 'break the child's will'.[7] Harm is done to our children if we do not teach them and encourage the development of a moral code. Children need to be helped to recognize their own anger and jealousy, which may spill over into harmful actions. It is important to teach children forgiveness and a new beginning.

Vulnerability

Young children are vulnerable at birth, and it is likely that infant mortality was high throughout the period covered by the Scriptures. Children were caught up in the world of their parents, sometimes punished to appease the sin of a parent (Josh. 7.1–26; 2 Sam. 21). That world involved war and famine, in which children were vulnerable and suffered. In the siege of Jerusalem and the ensuing famine children were left lying in the streets begging for water (Lam. 1.16; 2.11, 21; 4.4). Children were taken as prisoners of war (Lam. 1.5–6); in desperation they were eaten by their parents (Lam. 2.20; 4.10); boys were traded for the services of a prostitute and girls for wine (Joel 3.3). Today children continue to be vulnerable as a result of adult atrocities and count for nothing. In the developing world children are recruited as soldiers, are killed in the crossfire of war, or become refugees and orphans. Hunger claims the lives of children daily in a world where food is plentiful. In the developed world children are 'sacrificed' to their parents' status and careers. Their innocence is sacrificed to the gods of individualism, materialism and capitalism.

Child sacrifice was practised in the Ancient Near East (ANE) during much of the historical period covered by the Hebrew Scriptures. It was abhorred by the people of God as a pagan rite (Lev. 18.21; 20.2–5; Deut. 12.31; 18.10) and condemned by the prophets (Jer. 7.31; 19.13; 32.35). However, two texts are particularly significant: the attempted sacrifice of Isaac and the sacrifice of the unnamed daughter of Jephthah (Judg. 11.29–40). The sacrifice of Isaac is a particularly difficult text (Gen. 22); it has to be addressed, first, because it is within the Scriptures and suggests a particular understanding of God. Second, it has been used subsequently in teaching and the disciplining of children; third it is influential in interpreting the death of Christ (see the parallels in John 3.16; Rom. 8.31–32; 1 Pet. 1.19–20).

What is the significance of this story and its implications for children? It is a multilayered story, but it is unlikely to be about child sacrifice since the practice was condemned. Did it mark the origins of the practice of redeeming the first-born by an alternative sacrifice (Exod. 13.11–16; 34.19–20)? This is unlikely; only in later Jewish texts is the story interpreted as an archetype of the sacrificial system. If we turn to the characters in the story for elucidation, Abraham is portrayed as obedient to God even at the expense of the life of his child. Theologians have interpreted Abraham as complicit and God as guilty of requiring child sacrifice, amounting to child abuse.[8] Isaac is not consulted because he is a child and culturally would be expected to obey his parents unquestioningly.

Midrashic interpretation significantly developed Isaac's active role, absolving Abraham of responsibility as a potential child-killer.[9]

> I commanded not Abraham to slay his son, but rather lay not thy hand upon the lad, to tell the nations of the world of Abraham's love, who did not withhold his only son for me, to do the will of the Creator.[10]

Von Rad suggests,

> It has to do with a road out into Godforsakenness, a road on which Abraham does not know that God is only testing him . . . But in this way Yahweh tests faith and obedience . . . in this test God confronts Abraham with the question whether he could give up God's gift of promise . . . [understood] as a pure gift.[11]

The name Isaac means 'laughter'. Would this indicate a game, or God's teasing of Abraham? The interpretation of von Rad would resonate with the concept of the child as a gift of God's grace and a concrete fulfilment of the covenant promise.

Trible explores a further interpretation. Isaac is a gift of God, yet Abraham's attachment to Isaac has become a form of idolatry. Is Abraham prepared to let go even of Isaac and worship God alone? Several of these interpretations ignore the real child Isaac; he appears a passive 'pawn' of Abraham and even of God.[12] Similarly, the death of Jephthah's daughter raises questions. It is the child who is the unwitting victim of adult actions.

In both stories the writers reflect an ambiguity in the character of God. Some pictures of God are anthropomorphic (Gen 3.8; 6.6). Elsewhere there is authority and power ('Let there be . . .'; Gen.

1.3). Gracia Ellwood[13] and David Blumenthal[14] are theologians who explore the abusive in God.

The patriarchal ideology undergirding these texts has been used subsequently to justify rigid control over women and children and to enforce submission to male authority. The texts reflect the idea that women and children are possessions available for a man's gratification; they emphasize negative attitudes to women and view children as having wills which need to be broken. The violence of authoritarian leadership was challenged by Jesus (Mark 10.43).[15] Texts need deconstructing in the light of their hierarchical and patriarchal socio-political context, together with bringing to the fore 'hidden' texts which appear counter-cultural.[16]

Read the story of the sacrifice of Isaac and retell it from the point of view of Isaac or Sarah.

Why do you think this story was a favourite to tell children?

Consider whether you would tell this story to children.

There are examples in the Hebrew Scriptures of children being healed. Ishmael and Hagar are 'near death' when God hears the boy's cries (Gen. 21.14–20). God provides water so that both mother and son might live, and promises that 'I will make a great nation of him' (Gen. 21.18). Both Elijah (1 Kings 17.8–24) and Elisha (2 Kings 4.18–37) breathed new life into boys considered dead.

In the prophetic period, God's care of the orphan was central (Isa. 1.17, 23; Jer. 7.6; 22.3; Ezek. 22.7; Ps. 68.5; Mal. 3.5). As an ethical monotheism developed in Israel the cause of the widow and the orphan became a litmus test of the nation's practice of obedient faith (Ps.146.9; Zech.7.10). However, the Hebrew Scriptures reflect a cultural context in which Jewish, like pagan, children were largely without rights, suffered and were dispensable.

CHILD AS METAPHOR

Child as saviour

The child became a sign and symbol of Israel's hope for salvation, bringing justice and a return to Eden at a period of despair, possibly after a defeat by the Assyrians. A child would come named 'Immanuel' (Isa. 7.14; 9.6–7; 11.6–8). In Isaiah's context it appears to be a royal child whose birth is a symbol of God's faithfulness. Other cultures had a parallel expectation of a golden age. In the first century BCE Virgil combined the ancient myth of a golden age with the future birth of a boy, human and divine, as saviour.[17] Children were considered to be chaste, innocent and beloved of the gods, who could act as intermediaries and messengers of the gods. In exile, the image of child as vulnerable and as victim merges with that of saviour in a story of Rabbi Juda:

> See how beloved the little children are before God. When the Sanhedrin went into captivity, the *Shechinah*, God's indwelling presence, did not go with them. The watchers of the priests went into captivity but the Shechinah did not go with them. But when the little children went into captivity, the Shechinah went with them. For it says in Lamentations: 'Her children are gone into captivity' and immediately after, 'From Zion her splendor is departed.' (Lamentations Rabbah. 1.33)[18]

Comparing these verses in Lamentations gives rise to the rabbinic concept of God's splendour attending children wherever they go.

Child as the whole people of God

'The child' is used as a metaphor for the relationship of the people to God. Israel is called 'child' and God's 'son' (Exod. 4.22–23; Hos. 11.1, cf. Deut. 1.31.). If Israel is described as a child, then it might be presumed that God is father. The image of the divine as 'father' influenced the later Judaeo-Christian civilization with its emphasis on fatherhood. But what did 'father' mean in the Hebrew Scriptures? How did the use of father as metaphor affect real children? 'Lord' was a word used of the leaders of the tribes; it conveys authority and possession of things and people. If 'father' is a synonym for 'Lord' in this sense, then it expresses a distance of relationship and a paternalism of dependence. It can refer to divine discipline, necessary to bring the 'child' of faith into God's holiness (Prov. 3.11–12; Deut. 8.5). Elsewhere, writers use the image of God as father in contexts of care, protection, encouragement and teaching (Pss. 27.10; 68.5; 89.26). References to God as father are not static; the concept evolves. For example, Jeremiah introduces the concept of friendship within that of father (Jer. 3.4, 19). As there is growth in human relationships between parent and child, so it is with God.

A contrast to the male domination of Scripture is the presence of Sophia (wisdom). She is present at the Creation and is the first created.

> The Lord created me, at the beginning of his work ... before the beginning of the earth. When there were no depths I was brought forth ... I was beside the master craftsman, delighting him day after day, ever at play in his presence, at play everywhere on his earth, delighting to be with the children of men. (Prov. 8.22–24, NRSV; Prov. 8.30–31, NJB)

The text is a difficult one; 'a beloved child' is simply one translation, but it resonates with the idea of play. Whatever the original meaning of this text, there is here a contrast to the male warrior God so often portrayed in the Hebrew Scriptures and a sensitivity to observations of children at play (cf. Isa. 11.8; Zech. 8.4–5). The imagery occurs with God as playmate in the Beguine mystics of the thirteenth century.[19]

In later writings God is reflected in both male and female images. The mother and child relationship becomes a picture of God's creativity and nurturing (Pss. 22.10; 71.6; 131.2; Isa. 46.3); a mother may forget her children but God will not (Isa. 49.15,16). Feminine attributes become metaphors for salvation following the trauma of the destruction of Jerusalem and exile in a foreign land (Isa. 66.7–13), and for divine compassion (Jer. 31.15–22). It may be that this imagery is simply the expression of an intimate relationship between God and God's people and is gender-neutral. The initiative for, and constancy of, this relationship always came from God. The fact that such imagery is present in Scripture is itself significant. The references are to birth and the nursing of children, yet they reflect a keen observation of and interest in children and God's care for them.

Look up the references depicting God's feminine aspects (Deut. 32.18; Hos. 11.1–4; Isa. 42.14; 66.12–13).

Does the use of 'child' as a metaphor for the whole people of God affect our understanding of how real children were seen?

JESUS AS A JEWISH CHILD

Jesus was formed, rooted and nurtured within a Jewish family in an occupied country. The Hebrew Scriptures shaped and re-sourced his self-understanding. He quoted the Scriptures in his teaching (Matt. 21.16) and quoted a psalm from the cross (Ps. 22.1). He challenged the Scriptures which stultified life (Mark 2.27) and sought a righteousness of the heart (Matt. 5.1—7.28). Jesus' childhood was bathed in the Scriptures and it is likely that this informed his attitudes and actions with children, as shown in the Gospels.

INSIGHTS FROM THE NEW TESTAMENT

In the Roman Empire of the first century CE there were two con-trasting, incompatible, views about children. First, children were valued for themselves and for their future contribution to society, as seen, for example, in Plutarch's letter of consolation to his wife on the death of their two-year-old daughter Timoxena.[20] Second, children were seen as weak and insignificant, and childhood as merely a preface to adulthood. The Latin word for a young child translates as 'non-speaker'. Children did not count because they lacked language and reason. Young children, particularly girls, were considered dispensable, frequently aborted or abandoned.

The references to children in the Gospels are few, yet they are significant. The central message of Jesus was the 'good news' of the Kingdom (Mark 1.15). The members of God's Kingdom were not the 'righteous', but the marginalized, such as children, those who knew their need for God. They were described as 'the poor in spirit', 'those who mourn', 'the meek', ' the pure in heart' (Matt. 5.1–11), who became a new 'family', of God, sisters and brothers, 'children of God'. Actual children were included and chosen to be models of discipleship (Mark 10.16).

Birth and childhood of Jesus

Anderson and Johnson comment,

> the truth of God is embodied in a child. It is the Child who
> carries in himself the hope for the world. The consequences of
> that event are twofold. Firstly childhood, not just our human-
> ity, is capable of bearing transcendence. Secondly we cannot
> know the fullness of God without understanding what it is to
> be a child.[21]

The birth and childhood of Jesus give insights into this. The
'foetal' Jesus is recognized in the womb (Luke 1.65, cf. Jer. 1.5).
Foetal life is sacred: Jesus made our unborn life his. The utter
weakness and vulnerability of a child are evident in the events
surrounding his birth, as a homeless refugee of dubious parent-
age, poor and caught up in political intrigue and threats to his
life. Thus, from the beginning, Jesus identifies with the children
of his day. A child is vulnerable at birth, highly dependent on
adult relationships for nurture. This is a reminder that the pastoral care of young children is within the relationship of a family.

For a child, family roots are significant, giving an identity and a
belonging. The genealogy of Jesus is through Joseph, as was
normal in a patriarchal society. The meaning of the 'virgin' birth
has been questioned. The reference is from Isaiah 7.14, where
'virgin' means 'a young woman of marriageable age', but this does
not rule out human paternity. Jesus had brothers and sisters.
Illegitimacy was a scandal for mother and child. Whatever the
symbolism of 'virgin birth', there is the possibility that Jesus
faced discrimination, as did many other children, thus identifying
with them in an 'irregular birth'.

Matthew's genealogy for Jesus (Matt. 1.1–17) includes five
women: Tamar, Rahab, Ruth, the wife of Uriah (Bathsheba) and
Mary,[22] all of whom were scandalous to the orthodox Jew. They
include an adulteress, a prostitute and a foreigner, yet each
played an important role in the tradition of the people of God.
Their inclusion suggests 'irregularity', a break with tradition;
they have no orthodox lineage. The presence of the women acts as
a clue to the Gospel, which can be interpreted as challenging and
subverting orthodox belief, particularly when set alongside Jesus'
words and actions with another marginalized group, children. In
the Gospel the children have no lineage; they are nameless, their

presence is disruptive (Matt. 19.13–15) and irregular, challenging normal life (Matt. 18.1–5). If we listen to this gospel of subversion, we too will be challenged to be advocates of children.

The infant Jesus was taken to the temple to be redeemed according to Jewish law (Luke 2.22–39; Exod. 13.11–16; 22.29). The father gave a thank-offering and was asked, 'Do you want to redeem your child?' If the answer was 'Yes', the offering was accepted with the words 'Your son is redeemed'. There was risk in the offering: 'the symbolic severing of the maternal link, the truth that the child is not hers [Mary's] but *His* . . . [God's]'.[23] This is an insight that a child is a gift, not a possession. Anna and Simeon's words parallel the joy and pain every child brings to its parents, yet this child had a destiny, to be a light 'to the Gentiles and for glory of your people Israel' (Luke 2.32). The visit concluded with the return to Nazareth, where 'the child grew and became strong, filled with wisdom; and the favour of God was upon him' (Luke 2.40). A child grows at his or her own pace. In the twenty-first century some parents attempt to rush the pace of their children's development. Luke's insights into Jesus' infancy recognize a pattern of childhood growth which resonates with today's psychological insights into child development. Children grow in body, mind and spirit.

The twelve-year-old Jesus stays in the temple at Passover, possibly inquisitive and forgetting both time and parents (Luke 2.41–52), listening to the rabbis who were honouring the festival by lecturing. Jesus listens and asks questions. In the twenty-first century this suggests an intelligent child; in the first century it was a disgrace, since a child was questioning learned adults. Finding Jesus, Mary reproaches him about the anxiety his absence caused. Jesus' response indicates a call to a wider family which transcends his own: 'Did you not know that I must be in my Father's house?' (Luke 2.49). Here is spiritual insight, the recognition of a relationship with another Father, and a greater vision. This is a typical incident with a growing child who is taking autonomy and gradually leaving parents behind. Following the incident, Luke states, 'he was obedient to them': obedience was expected in Jewish culture. Children's autonomy needs the context of wise parental guidance, which gives freedom and guidelines. The incident ends, 'Jesus increased in wisdom and in years, and in divine and human favour' (Luke 2.51–52). This is a child who has God-given gifts. The incident affirms the spirituality of children and challenges parents and the Church to listen sensitively to children in order to nurture and respond to their spirituality.

Jesus is referred to several times as 'the child' (Matt. 2.8, 9, 11, 13, 14, 20, 21), and by the phrase 'the child and his mother' (Matt. 2.11, 13, 14, 20, 21). Jesus knew what it was to be a child. Irenaeus (115–190) wrote of Jesus,

> sanctifying every age, by that period corresponding to it which belonged to Himself . . . becoming an infant for infants, thus sanctifying infants; a child for children, thus sanctifying those who are of this age, being at the same time made to them an example of piety, righteousness, and submission . . .[24]

Jesus' own childhood honoured all children. Modern scholars write of Jesus' birth as the 'humanization of God'[25] and say 'Christianity teaches that humanity was saved by the birth of a child'[26] and 'it takes the Incarnation to show us that being born has not just an anthropological, but also a theological eternal significance'.[27]

Families in the first century

Jesus spoke to children in the context of a family. He recognized a good father and parental care in his rhetorical question, 'Is there anyone among you who, if your child asks for bread, will give a stone?' (Matt. 7.9; see also Luke 11.11). He used the word 'Father' for God, although references are sparse (except in the fourth Gospel), transforming the patriarchal image from one of unquestioned authority to one of watchful loving care (Luke 15). Children were dependent on the attention of parents (Matt. 7.11; 18.25), were exposed to sickness, and suffered hunger (Matt. 14.21; 15.38) and conflicts within families (Luke 12.13–15; 15.11–32). There is a realism in Jesus' references to children which mirrors the experience of family life today.

However, there are also ambiguities in Jesus' attitude to family. Jesus affirmed the fifth commandment (Mark 7.10–13), while proclaiming a call that challenged allegiance to the family. As a boy he had answered his mother's demands of filial loyalty with those of a higher calling (Luke 2.49), but as an adult, when his family came to reprove him for shaming the family, he replied, 'Who are my mother and my brothers?' and stated, 'Whoever does the will of God is my brother and sister and mother' (Mark

3.33–35). He called on his followers to hate mother and father (Luke 14.25–26). When family responsibilities hindered the expansion of the mission, Jesus was critical (Matt. 8.18–22; Luke 9.61–62). Yet he blessed and healed children brought to him by their families. Why is there this ambiguity? Parallels with Jewish texts, such as Maccabees, indicate that love for family members is relativized under *crisis* conditions,[28] while for the evangelists the imminent crisis was the *parousia* (Christ's return at the end of time). Jesus' challenge may be a critique of a particular type of family structure. He invited his disciples into a new kin-group, which crossed culture, age, class and ethnicity, subverting commitment to family and the oppressive structures of an élite. The group required a new ethic, replacing patriarchal control and its emphasis on 'honour' and 'shame' with nurturing and life-giving care. Jesus talks of service (Mark 9.35; 10.45), love of neighbour (Mark 12.31–33) and taking the last place (Mark 10.31). His followers became sisters and brothers to each other, children of God.

Incidents with real children

Healing was a characteristic of the Kingdom (Mark 6.7–13). Jesus' healing of children marks him out as one who saw in these 'least' the presence of God. Parents are advocates for their children crying out for help: Jairus pleads for his only daughter (Mark 5.21–43; Matt. 9.18–26; Luke 8.41–56); the Syro-Phoenician woman for her daughter (Mark 7.24–30; Matt. 15.21–28); a father for his only son (Mark 9.14–29; Matt. 17.14–21; Luke 9.37–43) and the centurion for his servant (Matt. 8.5–13; Luke 7.1–10).

Jairus' child is valued and precious, an only child (Luke 8.42) and near to death (Matt. 9.18 states she has just died). Jesus honours her privacy, grasps her hand and speaks directly to her, *'Talitha cum'* (Mark 5.41). She responds to him and gets up. Her parents are asked to give her something to eat; Jesus knows the need of children for nourishment. Two healings are of children considered 'demon-possessed'. 'Possession' had social repercussions. Sufferers were isolated and feared because of their uncontrollable body movements, which were interpreted as demonic. The condition brought shame on their parents. The Syro-Phoenician woman who seeks healing for her daughter (Mark 7.25; Matt. 15.22) is oppressed not only by gender and disease but also by her race and religion. Jesus refuses, because his mission is exclusive and the woman is not Jewish. She persists, and her tenacity and faith challenge Jesus. The girl is healed. The boy healed is powerless, dehumanized by the nature of his illness, which has stolen his childhood, preventing him 'from speaking and hearing' (Mark 9.25). Jesus' command to 'come out' results in a convulsion and Jesus lifts him up. The word 'lifted up' is also used of Jairus' daughter (Mark 5.41); in its 'passive' form it is used of the resurrection (Mark 16.6). The child is liberated by Jesus. The evangelists have placed this story after the first mention of the Passion – the suffering, handing over, powerlessness, death and rising of Jesus (Luke 9.21–27). It is as if the writer is suggesting that the boy's story is parallel to the way of Jesus and of discipleship. Children caught up in illness are freed by Jesus: this is an act of liberation from all that diminishes their life (cf. Luke 4.18–19). In the context of the first century it is amazing that it is children who are healed.

The value of children to Jesus is seen in his words of condemnation against those who place stumbling-blocks in the way of faith by discouraging, misleading or despising them (Mark 9.42; Luke 17.1–2; Matt. 18.6). That children had faith would have been incomprehensible to many adults of the first century. Jesus recognizes their faith and condemns any adult who would destroy it. Children may be confident of divine protection through guardian angels (Matt. 18.10), like the shepherd who searches for the lost sheep, risking his life and making himself vulnerable (Matt. 18.10–14). An interesting example of how adults mislead children is Mark's story of 'a little girl' (Mark 6.14–29; the same word is used of Jairus' daughter) who danced, perhaps her 'party piece', to entertain her father, Herod. Not knowing what gift to ask for and desiring to please parental authority, she is manipulated by her mother to ask for the head of John the Baptist. A child is thus 'used', abused and manipulated by a parent. Today the protection and advocacy of children is paramount: to despise 'little ones' is in opposition to God.

The children cry out in the temple; the scribes demand their silence, but Jesus quotes Psalm 8.2 (Matt. 21.15–16). He rejoices that God has hidden from the wise the understanding he has revealed to babies, the unlearned (Matt. 11.25; Luke 10.21). Children are intuitive and spontaneous, in their spiritual insight and joyful praise. The irony is that it is children who have true wisdom. Children have seen acts of healing and rejoice at Jesus' God-given gifts. In adult eyes, children know nothing, but in God's eyes they know the life of the spirit.

Jesus was not an idealist about children. He noticed the behaviour of children at play in the marketplace, perhaps a memory of his own childhood (Matt. 11.16–19; Luke 7.31–35).[29] One group of children played at weddings or funerals, but the other group sulked. The details of the game are uncertain, but Jesus compares the sulking children with the perverse response of 'this generation' in failing to understand the God-given ministry of John the Baptist or of Jesus. Jesus astutely recognizes the way children can sulk and manipulate; they are not innocents but deliberately stubborn and unkind to their peers.

Imagine one of the incidents (above) from the point of view of the child or of an adult at the scene. In that 'role', what surprised or shocked you about Jesus' attitude, or about Jesus' actions?

What did you learn about children?

Significant incidents

Two incidents are central to the Gospels and children: Jesus putting a child in the disciples' midst to settle an argument about status (Mark 9.33–37; Matt. 18.1–5; Luke 9.46–48); and the children who are brought to Jesus for a blessing (Mark 10.13–16; Matt. 19.13–15; Luke 18.15–17). In both passages, children (real children and child as metaphor), their nature, discipleship, and the reception of the Kingdom interweave, challenging and subverting adult ideas of children. Children were precious as the Israel of the future; Jesus claims them of intrinsic worth in the present.

Following Jesus' first statement about his passion, the disciples fail to understand him and instead argue about their own pre-eminence (Mark 9.33–37). In a house, the home of children, Jesus asks about the argument, but the disciples are silent. He responds, 'whoever wants to be first must be last of all and servant of all' (Mark 9.35).[30] Jesus takes a child and puts it in the centre of the disciples. The child is nameless, perhaps a grubby street child or an inquisitive child of the house. This silent child by its presence becomes the teacher. Jesus flings his arms around it and hugs it to himself. Jesus speaks of welcoming children (the Greek word 'welcome' (*dechomai*) means 'receive, accept, grant

access to'; it is used of hospitality in Mark 9.37), 'Whoever welcomes one such child in my name welcomes me, and whoever
welcomes me welcomes not me but the one who sent me.'

The reaction of the disciples and those who heard of this
incident would have been amazement: in the socio-cultural
context of the first century it was revolutionary. A child was at the
centre, as a symbol of authentic discipleship and as someone to be
served (the link of 'service' and 'children' may be the Aramaic
word meaning both 'servant' and 'child'). The thought of serving a
small and grubby child was outrageous. The child also teaches
the disciples. Within the culture, teaching was in one direction,
adults to children, yet here a child implicitly 'teaches' by its silent
presence. Mark depicts Jesus, a *man*, taking a child into his arms
as an example for *male disciples* in particular and for *all* disciples.[31] Jesus risks public censure by embracing children, considered women's work. The disciple has to learn from the child how
to welcome the insignificant child. People of power often ignore
the powerless, yet Jesus, in one sense the most powerful figure in
Mark's narrative, receives and identifies with powerless children.
His embracing them implicitly passes judgement on those who
reject children. Children are symbols of God's welcome in a
culture which ignored them. Thus, they are part of God's saving
work. Furthermore, to 'welcome a child' is to welcome Jesus
himself and God who sent him (Mark 9.37). The child becomes
the representative of Jesus and the envoy of the mission of the
Kingdom.[32] The community of faith is charged to welcome children, for in every child the vulnerable God is met (Matt. 25.40).

Jesus invites disciples into a new community where the least is
the model; thus, the disciple takes up the powerlessness and vulnerability of the child. According to John Carroll, 'A child models
discipleship in a way the twelve cannot; indeed, the child is the
surprising, shocking, paradigm of God's character and ways in
the world.'[33] And, as James Francis comments, the point of the
story is not simply that Jesus chooses to recognize the children
but that he affirms their entitlement to be recognized, such is the
nature of God's unconditional love.[34]

In the blessing of children Mark again sets the incident in a
home where Jesus is explaining to the disciples his teaching on
marriage and divorce (10.10–12), but they are disturbed by the
arrival of people bringing children to Jesus. The disciples act as
'gatekeepers', preventing the access of children to Jesus. They
appear not to have learnt their lesson about welcoming the least

(Mark 9.33–37), or do they wilfully oppose God's reign? Jesus is indignant (the word used of exorcism in Mark 1.25 and 9.25) and with a double command, 'let the little children come to me' and 'do not stop them' (Mark 10.14), receives the children. Why does Jesus want to receive them? 'For it is to such as these that the kingdom of God belongs.'[35] Jesus adds, 'Truly I tell you, whoever does not receive the kingdom of God as a little child will never enter it' (Mark 10.14–15). He embraces, lays hands on and blesses each child, recognizing their physical and spiritual needs. The kingdom belongs to any and every child without qualification or exception.

The phrase 'whoever does not receive the kingdom of God as a little child' is difficult to interpret ('receive' [*dechomai* again] is almost always used for hospitality, as in Mark 9.27, 37). There are two possible meanings: the first is 'whoever does not receive the kingdom of God as one receives a child', i.e. the disciples are to receive a child as Jesus welcomes the child (Mark 9.30). This is the way of life in the Kingdom: entry is open to all (Mark 10.27). In this interpretation children are not distracted by possessions, nor do they have their hands full. They allow themselves to be picked up, to unashamedly receive from Jesus. The phrase could also mean 'whoever does not receive the kingdom of God, as a child receives the kingdom'. A child drops everything to receive a gift, snatching it and tearing it open: children are examples of how the Kingdom is to be received with rapture and joy.

Matthew has another version of the story. Jesus calls over a child and says to the disciples, 'Unless you change and become like children, you will never enter the kingdom of heaven. Whoever becomes humble like this child is the greatest in the kingdom of heaven' (Matt. 18.3–4). Children are here used as a metaphor. There are three significant words peculiar to Matthew: 'change', 'become' and 'humble'. The Greek word for 'change' (*straphete*)[36] suggests the disciples must turn in another direction, not looking for the greatest, but towards the child. 'Turning' may also 'contain the idea of leaving behind . . . the conventional value perceptions of adulthood . . . childhood, therefore, has a radical edge in that it is dependency upon God and not upon the patriarchal tradition of teachers (Matt. 11.29)'.[37] It is a radical letting go of attempts to earn God's love. It is a simple accepting and letting God work to change attitudes to achievement, merit, possessions and power over others. 'Become' implies growth. In the Kingdom all are in the process of becoming. It is more obvious in children, who know they are growing, whereas adults think 'they have arrived'. Jesus' words are a call to adults to remember and learn from children that they too are still in 'process' and dependent upon God.

'Humble' means 'lowly', 'insignificant', or as a verb 'to make oneself small, low, weak and vulnerable', 'to depress pride', 'to abase'. But being humble is not a weakness. The words humble and humility derive from *humus* (earth), suggesting a naturalness, the physical embodied world. Jesus does not attribute to children qualities such as innocence, sinlessness or simplicity. These qualities show the danger of romanticism and are additions to the tradition, particularly in art. Jesus was a realist about children. He had seen them sulking in the marketplace. We must seek elsewhere for his meaning. Humility is not a moral quality of children; most are naturally assertive of their needs, while they thrive on relationships, giving and receiving love, discovering life. Children had no status in the first century, they were 'nobodies'. James Francis notes that being childlike is about being 'humble enough to recognize dependency, that is, one's absolute need of the gift of the Kingdom'.[38] Jesus required a return to the status of powerless children. This would have startled and disturbed the disciples, as it does us today. One interpretation is the contrast between examples of greatness in the Church ('those that lord it over others'; Matt. 20.24–28) and disciples who must be self-effacing, without claims to status and privileges. Jesus makes the child the symbol and standard of the vulnerability of every Christian. Jesus reverses the traditional status of power figures. Children are not aware of their status. If children are seen as innocent or humble (as traditionally understood), they become passive recipients with no agency. Children are worthy, not because of any characteristic, but because they are created in the image of God, already full persons 'given' to us. Children are vulnerable because that is the dependent biological and psychological nature of small children. Dependency is a characteristic of all our relationships with God; it is not passive dependence but the dependence of love in a relationship. Vulnerable children are particularly in need of God's care and protection, mediated through parents and society, which calls Christians to be advocates of children. This involves ethics: attitudes and practices towards children must be consistent with the proclamation of God's reign and must challenge all who diminish and harm children.

The children in the last two Gospel stories discussed are anonymous; neither sex nor name is given, nor is the child described as someone's child (the only significance allowed them in the first century). The text is not distracted by personal identity, yet the child is central both in reality as precious to God and as a metaphor of discipleship.

Journeying and suffering

The evangelists included the incidents of 'Jesus putting a child in the midst' and 'blessing children' within the account of Jesus' final journey to Jerusalem (Mark 8.22—10.52; Luke 9.51—18.17; Matt. 17–21). Throughout this material the child is a central and implicit motif, together with motifs of suffering, the Son of Man, the Kingdom, service and discipleship.

Look at the story of Jesus' last journey to Jerusalem (Mark 8.22—10.52).

List the sections of events and teaching.

Can you see any links between the stories?

Why has the evangelist linked children and Jesus?

Mark begins the journey with the healing of a blind man (Mark 8.22–26), a metaphor of the disciples' blindness to Jesus' identity (Mark 8.18), in contrast to the children in the temple (Matt. 21.15–16). Jesus inquires what is being said of him and responds for the first time with teaching about the suffering of the Son of Man (Mark 8.27–38). Peter challenges this but learns radical kingdom values are losing life to save it (Mark 8.35), an example of Jesus' challenge to the 'honour–shame' values of his culture. It appears that Mark intentionally parallels 'the suffering Son of Man' with the sufferings and vulnerability of children. Gundry-Volf defends a parallel between the exposure of children by parents in the Graeco-Roman world and Jesus' betrayal by Judas.[39] Both were betrayals by trusted friends. There is a parallel in the acceptance by the innocent of suffering: children were the victims of adults' power and domination, and Jesus too was a victim of powerful forces, though his suffering was accepted voluntarily.

The transfiguration (Mark 9.1–13) bears the marks of the honour–shame code. The early Gospel readers were keen to establish Jesus' lineage, hence the appearance of Moses (representing the law) and Elijah (a prophet), as symbols of authenticity. The words heard reflect those at Jesus' baptism: 'this is my beloved son' (Mark 9.7, NKJV), emphasizing divine sonship and dependency on the Father, as a child on parents and God. The Transfiguration is followed by Passion sayings, on suffering and vulnerability. When they descended from the mountain, the disciples' failure to heal a boy is contrasted with Jesus' healing (9.14–29). He frees the boy to be a child again. Jesus talks again of the Passion (9.30–32): the disciples do not understand, because they have been squabbling over status. Jesus responds, putting a child in their midst (9.33–37). Marginalized children are welcomed as signs of the Kingdom. Next, John wants to marginalize and block exorcists, who use the name of Jesus but are not among the twelve disciples (9.38–41). Jesus condemns those who put a 'stumbling-block' before little ones (9.42). Teachings on marriage and divorce follow (10.1–12). Children are the link, for within families they are affected by divorce. Children are brought to Jesus for a blessing and said to belong to the Kingdom (10.13–16). A rich young man desiring the Kingdom is prevented by his wealth (10.17–27). By contrast, a child has no wealth yet receives the Kingdom. Peter states that the disciples have left everything to follow Jesus, who replies that no one has left house, families, children or fields who will not receive a hundredfold. 'But many who are first will be last, and the last will be first': the Kingdom radically reverses expectations (10.28–31). Jesus talks again of the Passion (10.32–34). When James and John ask for key positions in the Kingdom (10.35–45), Jesus responds by comparing Gentile rulers lording it over their subjects with greatness in the Kingdom, characterized by the servant (cf. Mark 9.35); even 'the Son of Man' did not come to be served but to serve (10.45). The irony is the final incident, like the first the healing of a marginalized, sightless beggar (10.46–52). Bartimaeus has the insight to proclaim Jesus as 'Son of David' and 'teacher', becoming the perceptive, seeing disciple (cf. Matt. 21.15). Both Bartimaeus and the children are the marginalized, who become metaphors of true discipleship in the new community.

Mark has crafted this section to teach about the radical nature of discipleship, for which children are implicitly and explicitly the 'model'.[40] Actual children who are dependent and children as metaphor are key to understanding discipleship and the Kingdom. Throughout this section of the Gospel, the stories about children have parallels in the statements of the suffering 'Son of Man'. The Christian community's recognition and acceptance of children become a metaphor of its receiving the vulnerable Jesus himself.

A childlike life

Jesus brought new meaning to children and to the child as a metaphor of discipleship; throughout his life he embodied what it means to live like a child of God. He reflects the simplicity and wisdom that cuts through cant and goes to the point, illustrated in the questioning in the temple (Luke 2.41–52) and his summary of the Law (Luke 10.27). His challenging of his parents' authority is typical of children (Luke 2.41–52). Jesus questions to the last breath of his life: 'My God, my God, why have you forsaken me?' (Mark 15.34). In an act of final trust in the Father, he offers himself in dependence upon God. Our pastoral care needs to realize that children too question, yet may come ultimately in faith to trust God.

Jesus lived in harmony with the created world, as children often do: his stories were about the growth of seeds and harvesting (Mark 4), the lilies of the field (Matt. 6.28), the lost sheep (Luke 15.3–7). Very young children are fascinated by the natural world; they learn from, and respect, the creatures which are around them. They love the concreteness of stories with which they can identify. Jesus' parables were stories with multiple levels of meaning; to understand them needs insight and discernment (Mark 4.24, 33). Jesus lived 'in the present', as young children do, with little concept of time. He asks his hearers not to be anxious 'about tomorrow' (Matt. 6.25; 6.34). The statement 'Today you will be with me in paradise' (Luke 23.43) is spoken with the immediacy of children.

Jesus spoke much about the necessity to forgive over and over again (Matt. 18.21–22). His words from the cross, 'Father, forgive them', are words of forgiveness (Luke 23.34). These are reminders of the willingness of children to 'forgive and forget', to move on rather than to harbour resentment. Jesus showed his emotions, being moved with pity at the sight of suffering (Mark 1.41), concerned about hunger (Mark 6.35–44), weeping at the death of a friend (John 11.35) and falling asleep at a crucial moment (Mark 4.38). Children live in their emotions. Jesus was intuitive and imagined a world where the kingdom was fully realized. It was a subversive world, where the meek inherited the earth and children were models of the Kingdom (Luke 4.17–21; Matt. 5.3–48). This intuitive playfulness of word and action is a characteristic of childhood. Jesus reversed roles (Matt. 5–7), contrasting 'authority figures' with leadership in the Kingdom, 'it shall not be so among you' (Mark 10.43). He reversed familiar ideas of those who were blessed by God (Matt. 5.3–11); the first must be last and servant of all (Mark 9.35; 10.42–43). He chose to ride into Jerusalem on a donkey, and submitted to being given a crown of thorns by the soldiers. There is a playful irony here.

As Jesus moves towards Jerusalem, the verbs used are increasingly in the passive mood, as he receives from others rather than himself taking action. He experiences at the hands of others his own vulnerability, evident in his life: 'the Son of Man has nowhere to lay his head' (Luke 9.58). The crucifixion epitomizes powerless vulnerability, a 'condition' that is the experience of many children today, caught up in violence. The vulnerability of Jesus' birth and life parallels the vulnerability of children within society, caught up in domestic and social violence not of their making, yet children have a resilience which is an expression of life-giving resurrection. In the ascension the childlike life of Jesus is taken up into the Godhead. The child for Jesus is a 'child of God' and disciples of every age are 'children of God'.

The child in the fourth Gospel

There appears little in the fourth Gospel that gives insights into children and childhood. Rebirth is essential for entry to the Kingdom, as stated in a conversation with Nicodemus through 'being born of water and Spirit', a symbol of baptism (John 3.3, 5). In the incident of the feeding of a great crowd, it is a boy who gives up his lunch, becoming the agent of liberation for powerful adults, the weak blessing the strong. It is a restoration as well as a reversal (John 6.1–21), with parallels to the Passover meal where the youngest child begins the ritual. However, the evangelist makes extensive use of the Father–Son relationship: the use of God as Father occurs 107 times, most often in the phrase 'my Father'. It gives a new model of interpersonal relationships and a new understanding of God.

The emphasis in this Gospel reveals Jesus to be the *unique* Son of the Father, as distinct from the disciples, children who are to love one another. Barton notes a 'horizontal' dimension to being a child of God which, though rather muted in John's Gospel, comes strongly to the fore in the distinctly ecclesiological concerns of the Johannine Epistles (e.g. 1 John 2.1–2, 12; 3.1–2).[41] In the fourth Gospel obedience is not forced, it is a response of love (John 3.16; 1 John 3). There is no fear in love (1 John 4.16–18). We have a relationship of loving service, as an example for the disciples in their ministry. Children are not mentioned, but ministry as service to all is, and this would include children.

The child in the Epistles

Children were present and addressed in the weekly worship (Col. 4.16), and given a place in the Christian community. They heard the Epistles read, such as the household codes which gave advice in a pattern of relationships: between 'husband and wife', 'father and child', and 'master and slave' (Eph. 5.21—6.9; Col. 3.18—4.1; 1 Pet. 2.11—3.12).[42] Family members are exhorted to behave in certain ways: 'Children, obey your parents in everything' (Col. 3.20; cf. Exod. 20.12). This appears to be like the patriarchy in Roman and Jewish cultures. Other scholars maintain the codes were intended to reverse the 'model' of male authority, through directly addressing all – wives, slaves and children, not only males. It is possible that the phrase 'children, obey your parents in the Lord' (Eph. 6.1; Col. 3.20 adding 'in all things') may give insight, though its meaning is obscure. The phrase 'the Lord' occurs seven times in Colossians (3.18, 20, 22, 23, 24 (twice) and 4.1). Dunn comments that it represents the 'motivation and orientation' of the whole Epistle.[43] In Colossians 3 there is teaching on Christ-like qualities of compassion, kindness, meekness, forgiveness and love. The child and, subsequently, the parent are addressed within the context of the Christian community and their relationship in the Lord (Col. 3.20). The supreme authority is not the earthly parent, who may be frail and fail, but the Lord who blessed children. In this interpretation there appears the beginnings of a mutuality and a recognition that children can be addressed in their own right as children and their needs recognized. Children are 'to honour' parents in addition to obeying them. The household codes reflect some of the emphases of Jesus' teaching on children, but not the most radical remarks such as

his unconditional welcome and receiving of children. In Eph-
esians and Colossians, children are viewed as members of the
community of believers, but not as models for adult believers, or
as spiritually insightful.

The Pastoral Epistles reflect dominant societal views of the
traditional patriarchal household. A cultural pattern is recogniz-
able in male descriptions of the good wife, modest in dress and
deferential to her husband (1 Tim. 2.9–12; 1 Pet. 3.1–5; Titus
2.4–5). The Epistles take the ancient family as the model for the
Church (1 Tim. 3.15). Children appear at the margins, objects of
control to maintain the honour of the family, or as 'problems' who
require proper management as a test of a parent's fitness for epis-
copal leadership in the Church (1 Tim. 3.4). It was the Pastorals
that predominated in early Christianity, losing the radical
imperative of Jesus. However, towards the end of the first century
it was important that the community should not be seen as
subverting social norms.

Hebrews portrays God as 'educating' through discipline those
whom he loves (Heb. 12.6–7; cf. Prov. 3.11–12). The human experience of suffering shapes Christians in the pattern of him who
'learned to be son' through his suffering without which a child is
considered illegitimate (not God's child). The short-lived discipline of human parents receives respect but 'he [God] disciplines
us for our good, in order that we may share his holiness' (Heb.
12.10). This, when coupled with Revelation 3.19 'I reprove and
discipline those whom I love' taken literally, has been used by
Christian parents as a sanction of physical punishment. Jesus
had a very different message: we become like God when we
become like children, so an assault against children is an assault
against God.

The child and family as metaphor

Christianity used family metaphors, in common with the surrounding culture. Paul uses the metaphor of adoption (Rom. 8.15,
23; 9.4; Gal. 4.5; Eph. 1.5) to express the Christian's new relationship to God. By adoption a Christian becomes an heir of God and
a joint heir with Christ (Rom. 8.17). Adoption has parallels in the
Johannine writings (John 1.12; 1 John 3.1–2): persons of faith
receive the identity and status of children of God by sharing
Jesus' own relation to God. This is grounded in the Synoptic
saying that those who respond to his call are his brothers and

sisters (Mark 3.35). They share his relationship to the Father (Matt. 6.9; Luke 11.2; Mark 14.36).

Paul believed 'there is no longer slave or free, there is no longer male and female; for all of you are one in Christ Jesus' (Gal. 3.28). Written in the context of baptism, this suggests an equality beyond gender. Meeks argues for a gender dissolution in baptismal actions and formulas offering a radical equality. For Sawyer, the child is an archetype of humanity and as children 'can name only God as parent, the source of their being, so believers have only one parent. There is no room for alternative human parents.'[44] Peterson notes 'baptism as a process of restoration to the virginal innocence of Adam, and an epiphany of Jesus at baptism as a form of a child or infant'.[45] Perfection is a child. I would argue that early baptismal liturgies reflect the imagery of the innocence of the infant. This is also found in the Gospel of Thomas.[46]

Both Paul (1 Cor. 4.14–15; Gal. 4.19; 1 Thess. 2.11) and John (1 John 2.1, 18, 28; 3.7, 18; 5.21) use the imagery of 'children' and 'little children' to draw attention to the pattern of guidance, nurture and pastoral care in the Church. As founders of congregations they are *in loco parentis*; however, the comparison was also used to emphasize perceived immaturity and lack of development in congregations. Paul considered the Corinthians childish (1 Cor. 3.1; 14.20) and desired them to be mature. He uses the analogy of human development, considering the child state as imperfect, to be superseded by a more perfect one, thinking common in the first century (1 Cor. 13.11). The goal of Christian discipleship is 'mature manhood, to the measure of the stature of the fullness of Christ' (Eph. 4.13, RSV); the opposite is 'children, tossed to and fro and carried about with every wind of doctrine'. The child stood for what an adult should not be: 'Do not be children in your thinking' (1 Cor. 14.20). The writer of Hebrews 5.12–14 uses the metaphor of unweaned infants who need a diet of milk to illustrate the immaturity of readers and the necessity of basic teaching. The comparison with children expresses criticism. 'Child' is used in these instances as a metaphor that releases negative messages, contradicting the thinking of Jesus and demeaning children.

However, Strange notes one positive comment (1 Pet. 2.2–3): '1 Peter speaks of the baby, not as an example of a stage of life soon (and rightly) to be left behind, but as an example of natural and insatiable appetite and this for the things of God.'[47] Jesus challenged the cultural perception of children, while the writers of the Epistles used more conventional language. Jesus recognized that children need to grow in faith, as do adults. His teaching was a nurturing of all humanity, including children (Mark 8.9; John 6.9). He recognized the spiritual insights of children (Matt. 11.25; 21.15–16), and that there were levels of maturity (and immaturity) in children, as there were in adults.

DRAWING IDEAS TOGETHER FROM THE SCRIPTURES AND HUMAN SCIENCES

The symbol of the child is universal and timeless. It taps into powerful adult memories and archetypes of childhood. 'Membership of the Kingdom' was traditionally associated with obedience to the Law, achievement and maturity; that is, with adults. However, Jesus challenged his listeners by associating the Kingdom with children. Being childlike was for Jesus the criterion of entry to the Kingdom. Ignoring children ignores the child Jesus, who lies at the centre of the Christian faith. In the Scriptures, children are given significance as 'children of God' and signs of hope for the future. Their spiritual insight, spontaneity and playfulness is needed by 'children of God' of all ages today.

If we bring together insights from the chapters on the Scriptures and on child development, we shall find clues in each to the particular characteristics of childhood that can form the basis of a theology of childhood.[48]

- uniqueness of every child
- significance of relationships
- vulnerability of children
- parents learning from the child
- mutual learning and blessing
- instruction of the child
- letting the child freely explore
- recognizing the personhood of the child
- respecting and honouring the individuality of the child
- discipline and parameters within a context of love.

These insights will guide our understanding and practice of pastoral care, to which I now turn.

SUMMARY POINTS FOR DISCUSSION

- In the Hebrew Scriptures children are understood as, first, created in the image of God, blessed, gifts held in trust and playful and, second, as vulnerable, victims, ignorant, mischievous, wilful and needing discipline.

- Nurture and education is in the family of faith.

- Jesus' concern for those at the margins, such as children, reflects a re-emergence and enlarging of the prophetic concern with 'the widow and orphan'.

- Jesus' mission was 'to bring fullness of life' (symbolized in healing children) and to challenge unjust structures (those who forbade children access to him).

- Jesus shows the child to be precious to God, a model of discipleship and a representative of Godself.

CHAPTER FIVE

Pastoral Care:
The Brass Tacks

Nine-year-old Jan's grandfather had died unexpectedly from cancer. He spent a few days in a hospice, seemed to be brighter and was due to go home when he died. Mary, the churchwarden, noticed Jan wandering aimlessly round the village churchyard and went to talk to her. She felt unable to answer Jan's questions about where her grandfather was now, and so she introduced her to the minister who happened to be in the church. The chat with the minister comforted Jan in her grief and enabled her to make some sense of the death. Later Jan discovered that Mary was doing the church cleaning that week and offered to come along and help. The following week she appeared in church but her friend Mary was not there. She left a message in the only place she could find, which was the church visitors' book. After the funeral, which was at the crematorium, Jan has come back to church to find her new friend and has now started to bring her sister. She wants to join the choir.

> **How is this incident an example of pastoral care?**
>
> **Who does pastoral care in your community?**

In this situation the minister's pastoral care was about giving a child some resources, thoughts and new ideas to empower and enable her to make sense of her experience. It is about a child looking at questions for herself: for Jan it was thinking about what death means, how we remember someone and different understandings of the afterlife. Equally important was Mary's ongoing pastoral care for Jan, the friendship, time and interest she offered to a child, sometimes while doing the ordinary things of life such as cleaning the church.

This chapter examines the nature of pastoral care, using insights from the previous chapters on the Scriptures, the human sciences and the spiritual and religious development of children. The practical questions are: What is pastoral care? Who is responsible? How is it done? What is done?

WHAT IS PASTORAL CARE?

The church has a mandate to care pastorally for children. Christians know that children matter ultimately because they matter to God. Jesus himself was a child; his life was childlike; he questioned societal attitudes to the marginalized of his society, who included children. He radically challenged those who held back children's growth and by his actions and words he was an advocate for vulnerable children.

R. A. Lambourne, a pastoral theologian, wrote of pastoral care as 'a pattern of corporate, responsible, sensitive acts motivated by a compelling vision'.[1] Our vision of growth as Christians is that we become more Christlike (Eph. 4.15; Rom. 8.29). As Jesus said, 'Be perfect, therefore, as your heavenly Father is perfect' ('perfect' means 'rounded, complete, mature'; Matt. 5.48). This is the vision for all God's children.

Is the pastoral care offered by the Church through the clergy and children's workers distinctive? How does it differ from the pastoral care offered by designated staff in our schools? I suggest that the difference lies in the understanding that undergirds the care which is offered. Both types of care are

- informed by knowledge of the nature and needs of children;
- involve interpersonal skills;
- develop positive attitudes towards children;
- work to support the home in times of celebration and crisis.

This care involves the use of the humanistic disciplines, which give insights into the ways children develop physically, emotionally, psychologically and socially in the context of the family and society. For the Christian there is a further significant factor, that of understanding what it means to be a child in the sight of God. This knowledge will come from the Scriptures and the tradition; it will involve theology and a theology of the child and will underlie all aspects of our pastoral care of children. It will challenge and subvert cultural mores and expectations. For example, the priority given to children by Jesus ('whoever does not receive the kingdom of God as a little child'; Mark 10.15) is countercultural in a society where children are not valued for themselves. The pastoral care of a bereaved child through exploring beliefs about the afterlife is similarly subversive in a society where death is considered 'not for children' and life ends at death.

WHO ARE THE PASTORAL CARERS?

Traditionally, when we think about pastoral care within the community of faith, the carer is thought of as the minister or clergy person. The minister may have trained a team of lay people to be 'eyes and ears', aware of changes for individuals (a five-year-old beginning school, a job loss) and families (moving, a new baby), needs (housebound communion), and crises (accident, hospitalization). Depending on the model of ministry in the church, the minister may be expected to respond to all pastoral care concerns. Alternatively the minister and team may work together, or specialist trained groups may be delegated. In most congregations adults will be the recipients of pastoral care. What happens to the pastoral care of children? They are considered minors and so under the care of their parents (or other carer). Thus the community of faith implicitly ignores children, and underlying this action is an unconscious acceptance of a cultural tenet – the 'privatization of the family'. However, children are an integral part of the body of Christ and their pastoral care is the concern of the church; so, for example, in the intercessions any sick child should be prayed for.

Parents

Parents have daily responsibility for a child and are those closest to and therefore most knowledgeable about the child (physical health, personality, disposition, likes and dislikes, history). In a good relationship between parent and child, it is to the parent that the child will turn for help, whether for sharing successes and failures, asking for information, or seeking help for a problem such as bullying. This is a relationship that should be affirmed. We know that Jesus grew in 'stature and wisdom' in the context of caring parents, who cared for his welfare, even though they did not always understand him (Luke 2.41–52). Although we hear nothing more of his childhood, we know that as an adult his family still sought to protect him (Mark 3.31–32). Jesus spoke of parents who knew how to provide good things for their children (Matt. 7.9–11) and of a father who, although taken advantage of by his son, still waited and looked for his prodigal son's return (Luke 15.11–32).

Parents today face a rapidly changing world. They are bombarded with messages on how to be a parent, ranging from TV programmes such as *Supernanny* to newspaper articles and government directives. This can create a pressure to succeed. Parenting models have changed over the years. Informed by all that we now know about the optimum conditions for child development, parents can feel inadequate and intimidated. In Western societies dominated by materialism, advertisements promise children that buying the goods advertised will make them happier or more successful in school, or will bring them friends. Educational toys promise 'development' out of the stage of dependency. Children pester their parents for these 'goodies'. Parents may also feel threatened by public opinion, which blames them if a child's behaviour is considered unacceptable. Parents need support.

The parent is the prime pastoral carer to the child, but this statement needs qualifying since the parent is not alone in this challenging task. The parent is able to care because she or he is loved by God. A parent who experiences the unconditional and undeserved love of God is given the strength to love a child whether it is sick, has temper tantrums or is withdrawn. The parent can see the worth of the child as a child of God. This does not mean that the task is easy, but it does mean that the parent is given strength beyond his or her own. God's care and support of the parent is mediated through people.

The pastoral care of parents may come through the encouragement of other parents, extended family, community professionals (district nurse, social worker), internet talk group,[2] clergy, the Church family or a parenting group such as those organized by the Mothers' Union (MU). Within Christian history parenting has been considered a vocation.[3] It is interesting to note that the early Church Fathers, who were celibate, recognized the vocation of parenting as a form of the religious life and the importance of education and the religious formation of children within the home. Later, Martin Luther stated,

the greatest good in married life . . . is that God grants offspring, and commands that they be brought up to worship and
serve him. In all the world this is the noblest and most precious
work, because to God there can be nothing dearer, if need be,
than the salvation of souls . . . Most certainly father and mother
are apostles, bishops, and priests to their children, for it is they
who make them acquainted with the gospel. In short, there is
no greater or nobler authority on earth than that of parents
over their children, for this authority is both spiritual and tem-
poral.[4]

Luther recognized the daily grind of child-bearing and child-
rearing in the early years, yet he says that faith looks upon those
duties as 'adorned with divine approval as with the costliest gold
and jewels'.[5]

There is an affirmation of the vocation of parenthood in all its
reality of joy and mundane tasks as it is recognized by the community of faith. Today parenthood is perceived by some as an
inconvenience, a limitation of lifestyle and career prospects. The
Christian faith has insights and understanding to bring new
meaning, in order to raise the significance of parenting as a vocation and therefore the worth of children and their nurturing.

What is Christian parenting?

How is pastoral care expressed by a parent?

Ordained clergy/minister

Pastoral care is seen as one of the charges given to a minister at
his or her ordination, the shepherd's role of 'care of the flock'.
Care is to be given to the whole congregation, including children.
However, it is rarely thought that children have separate needs
requiring pastoral care. This lack of concern for children is
reflected in the absence of any mention of children in the initial
training of ministers, except for the mechanics of how to baptize
or dedicate a baby. Sometimes training in the psychology of
human development touches on the child, but there is very little
depth of understanding of child development or of pastoral care,
teaching or preaching to children. A cleric may have experience

as a parent or prior knowledge of child development through a previous career in teaching. This prior learning can be recognized but may need building on. For example, clergy might be expected to lead all-age worship and church parades for uniformed organizations. Each of these roles needs specific skills.

The Anglican Church is becoming more proactive about its work with children. In July 2003, the Church of England document *Strategy for Children, 'Sharing the Good News with Children'* was debated by General Synod, and its aims and objectives were ratified. Work is taking place in four key areas:

1   Worship and the nurture of children
2   Children and evangelism
3   Supporting ministry among children
4   Training for ministry among children.

Other reports were produced to encourage local dioceses to take this work forward: *Children in the Midst: Theology, Principles and Curriculum Elements for Training People to Work among Children*, and *Children Included – Guidelines for Training Clergy, Readers and Lay People in a Ministry among Children*, both published in 2005. Such training is to take place after ordination or licensing. Clergy need to be aware of: child development theories; the spiritual growth of children; learning theory; resources; child protection; and issues of health and safety. The network of diocesan children's workers promotes in exciting ways the nurture, teaching and advocacy of children. It is hoped that this book will go some way to fill the gap in training by providing material on the pastoral care of children in all its aspects.

It may be that a particular minister has not the gifts or the time to concentrate on the pastoral care of children. Nevertheless, he or she is the enabler and leader of a team which will include elected church officers and congregation members. The clergy are responsible for recruiting children's workers through discerning their vocation and gifts. A church may have within its congregation members who have knowledge, skills and gifts in their paid employment (as schoolteachers, nursery group leaders, community nurses or social workers in childcare). The minister cannot necessarily expect them also to want to work with children in the church, though it is likely that they will offer to be on a rota for one Sunday a month or an occasional midweek activity and to contribute their skills regularly but not every week.

Several churches may together employ a trained children's worker.

If the minister delegates to those with skills, she or he must also continue to pastor the workers, working with them as a team. Above all, the minister is helping them to be gospel people, that is, to know the faith with heart and mind and to experience it in their own lives so that they may be models of discipleship to children. It is essential that those who work with children have sufficient time to nourish and develop their own spiritual journey.

Children's workers and Sunday school teachers

The nurture of children is too important to leave to conscripts or those who express an interest. Nor can it be expected that simply because an adult is a parent that the person has the gifts to work with groups of children. It should be considered a privilege and an honour to teach children. Work with children within the church is a significant vocation and is entered into with care. The clergy are responsible for discerning these gifts, alongside and in consultation with other church officers. This is a team task, as is attention to the appropriate training and ongoing support of those who are chosen. Encouragement may include seeking out suitable training courses, paying the course fees and travel expenses. Clergy might bring the children's work to the attention of the parochial church council (PCC) or church meeting on a regular basis, checking that there is a suitable budget to support children's work, chairing planning meetings, praying for and listening to the children's workers on regular occasions. Children's workers in our churches are representatives of the congregation and need to be supported by that congregation.

Congregation

The whole congregation has a role to play in the pastoral care of children, whether it is to babies brought for baptism (at a baptism the congregation promises to welcome and support the newly baptized) or children who regularly attend a church activity or Sunday worship. The congregation are travellers on the journey of faith alongside children; the body of Christ includes all ages. In the biblical tradition it was the whole congregation who had responsibility for handing down the faith to the next generation (Ps. 78.3–7). In the light of twenty-first-century knowledge of child development and learning theory, our understanding of the 'how' of faith transmission is different from that of previous generations, but congregation members may still be mentors[6] of faith to children.

The congregation's role in pastoral care will also include children who are not actively involved in the church, who perhaps visit with their church or community primary school, as part of an environmental project looking at the church in the community or investigating a theme of rites of passage such as baptism, marriage or funerals (topics which are on the National Curriculum for all children). The school may use the church for a Christmas carol service or an end-of-term service. Congregational members will be present on these occasions as 'welcomers' or serving refreshments, or working with the school staff to share information about the church (building and people) and its place in the community. The congregation are the community of faith, God's people, the body of Christ; they are models of faith and their attitudes, welcome and concern for children are highly significant as an expression of pastoral care to all children who visit the church.

A youngster commented, 'Whilst doing my RE project on a medieval church I thought that if all of these men had built this magnificent building with only simple tools, and risking their lives every day, they must have known something about God I don't know, and I wanted to know it too.' A helpful church guide, an ordinary member of the congregation, was there to listen and encourage this child in his spiritual journey.

Peer group

The child's peer group is significant too. It may be that a child is too frightened to talk to an adult, even a parent, or that the parent is the problem, or is too close. Piaget stated that children think in different ways from adults and it can be hard for adults to remember clearly the issues and worries that concern children. For example, a child who is told that a beloved grandfather has had a heart attack may wonder how the heart can be attacked and ask another child. Children can be very supportive to one another, offering friendship and help. A key function of pastoral care is to encourage children to form friendships with other children that are mutually enriching. An adult in the background may be useful.

CHARACTERISTIC METHODS OF PASTORAL CARE

One-to-one pastoral care

Pastoral care may be offered to a child on a one-to-one basis. Mostly, this will be the role of the parent or at the request of the parent. If the person offering the care is another adult, then the law of the land requires a Criminal Record Bureau (CRB) check. Appropriate boundaries must be set. The child may approach the parent (or another adult), or the adult may notice that the child has something to celebrate or is sad and listless. It is important to respect the child's personhood and ask if he or she would like to talk. If the child responds positively, it is important to listen acutely.

Relationships

The essence of appropriate pastoral care is the attitude of the caregiver. The relationship of carer to cared is potentially a power relationship, particularly when it is adult to child. The carer needs a humility to give and to receive. The relationship of carer and child should be one of mutual blessing and respect and honouring of each other.

Respect is a key attitude when working with children. This includes taking their concerns seriously, making attempts to stand alongside, and giving them a space in which it is safe to talk. It means recognizing when a child's issues are complex, and having the humility to suggest that someone with more experience could help.

Listening

Adults are called to listen to children creatively. Carl Rogers suggested three pillars of wisdom: empathic listening; non-judgemental acceptance; and congruence (being real and genuine). A child who is acknowledged and validated by another person is enabled to recognize that he or she is of value.

We can listen with our ears to the tone of voice, the speed of delivery, the choice of words; we can listen with our eyes to the body language of children; how they are sitting, what they are doing with their hands, feet and eyes; we can listen intuitively to what is not said, but is implied, our intuitions or hunches, how the child or situation makes us feel. Listening is an intensive activity.

As an example of listening, David, aged six, asked his mother where he came from. She took a breath and began to explain how men and women get to know one another and share interests, and get married. However, she noticed at this point that David was getting bored, so decided to find out why he wanted to know about his birth. 'Oh,' came the reply, 'my friend at school, James, comes from Kenya and I wondered where I came from.'

We need to understand the real concern of the child in order to pastor a child. The adult must not jump to conclusions but 'hear the child out'. It may be difficult for the child to find the words he or she needs. It is acceptable on these occasions to allow times of silence, while the child thinks. This can be helped by non-verbal communication from the adult: a kindly facial expression, an arm of comfort, a hand stretched out, a 'mmm'. Gentle questions may help to clarify the issue. The care of the child is conveyed as much by the total attention given by the adult as by 'hearing the child into speech'. The latter can help the problem simply by encouraging the child to voice concerns. It is easy for adults to dismiss the problems of children – fear of the dark, sadness about hurting someone else, the death of a pet or a belief that he or she is bad – but for a child these are very real issues.

Empowering

The story of Jan and her grandfather was a story of empowering her. This was done through opening up or refocusing possible ways of understanding Jan's questions about death and the afterlife. Often as adult Christians we believe that there is a right answer and that is what is necessary to give to children. It is more important to help children realize that there are no easy answers to some questions (particularly suffering and answers to prayer), rather that we are in the place of mystery. This means not that we should not question but that we should recognize our limits as humans and the provisional nature of our answers. We can give children the resources to work out the answering of a question so that it is true to their experience.

Challenging

Sometimes a conversation will involve a gentle challenge to a child's misinformation. This too is pastoral care. On one occasion I was asked by anxious parents to visit two junior-school-aged children whose grandfather had died on Holy Saturday. The children were upset because they believed that their grandfather could not be in heaven since Jesus was in the tomb and was not there to welcome him. The conversation that ensued involved facts about the historical Jesus and the continuing presence of Jesus and our sharing together how we remember people who have died, ideas about heaven and of being in God's presence.

Being present

The one-to-one pastoral care of a child may have a particular focus. For example, some ministers and church workers take an active role in the local church or community school. The regular contribution to collective worship (assembly) is one example of participation, but that can be a brief visit with little time for individuals. A minister or church member with skills and time sometimes acts as the school chaplain. However, it is helpful if the children also see this person in another capacity from leading worship and doing the 'religious thing'. If the person has a particular skill or interest that he or she can offer to the school, then the children see this adult as a 'normal' person and will 'use' them.

A friend of mine took early retirement from science teaching. Bob is an active member of his local church and is also a chess fanatic. Through offering a weekly lunchtime chess club he is able to be alongside children and listen to each child. The children know he belongs to the church from the cross he wears in his lapel and have been inquisitive about the fish sign he has on the back of his car. Here is someone who is able to offer informal pastoral care through simply being present and sharing his enthusiasm for life and chess with the children. I know of other church members who regularly go into a school to help slow learners with reading; this involves giving confidence to children and affirming their worth, which is not determined by their ability to read. The name of God may not be mentioned in these situations but God is present in the relationship. It is 'being present' that is the clue here for pastoral care.

A church worker may help the school to initiate a 'special place', a quiet area with beautiful objects and coloured drapes, cushions and beanbags. The focus of the space may be a candle or floating candles (safety rules are needed!) or a special open book or a lovely picture. This can be used as a sanctuary, a 'sacred space' for a distressed or thankful child simply to go and be. This is particularly valuable if meditation techniques are part of the curriculum and children are guided to use silence. A hovering adult may be helpful.

Pastoral care within groups

Pastoral care will also be seen within groups of children. It will involve nurture and teaching. Children need to be affirmed and nurtured, shown that they are significant and matter to God and to God's people, the community of faith, the church.

Toddlers

Many churches use their premises for mothers and toddlers clubs. These informal occasions provide a non-threatening and inexpensive social space for mothers to meet. There is pastoral care of both mother and child by the provision of space and by making it a welcoming place, with suitable toys which are clean and working to stimulate the growing minds of toddlers. A committee of parents may select speakers, including health visitors, district nurses and childcare specialists. Topics could include talking to your child, suitable books for children, the pros and cons of immunization, symptoms of childhood illnesses, discipline and spirituality. The presence of church members who are mothers but whose children are past the toddler stage acts as a resource to the younger mothers. Again, showing a keen interest in both mums and infants, remembering names and being present are acts of pastoral care.

A fortnightly Rainbow Service for mothers and pre-schoolers was held in the modern church of St Mark. The format was informal, with infants sitting on a rug in the front and mothers sitting behind, so that their children could be seen and the children knew their mothers were there. The service included lots of activity songs, a story for the children, and moments for a quiet 'thank you' prayer. Birthdays too were celebrated. Each service ended with children being brought to the front for a blessing. When their children were blessed, the parents also felt affirmed and blessed. The twenty-minute service was followed by tea, juice and biscuits, and an activity for the infants in the adjacent church rooms. When the children started school, some of them 'graduated' to attending a midweek children's activity club.

Midweek children's activities

Many churches run a weekly after-school activity. These may well begin with a fruit drink and a communal activity while the children are assembling. A mixture of quiet and noisy games and action songs follows, often selected by the children – fun for all. The session includes a story which should 'speak' to the experience and life of the child and may be secular or biblical. Some of the methods described by Berryman in Godly Play could be used. Stories can be turned into serials with 'cliff-hangers'. It is helpful if a free choice of craft work, clay, painting or drama can follow up the story so that children are expressing their personal engagement with the story. Cooking is a favourite activity, but health and safety considerations may preclude this. Word searches or puzzles can be made available for those who finish before the others. The building up of relationships of trust with children is central. Leaders act as models of discipleship. Pastoral care takes place through the acknowledgement of each child, listening and following up concerns.

If access is possible, it is helpful to take children into the church worship area at the end of the session, entering to some quiet music and low light. Once the children are seated, the lighting of a central candle suggests that this is an important moment. The children can be invited to think silently of the happenings of the day and to give thanks: children respond to silence when they are given a focus and a task. In imagination they can be asked to bring to mind someone who is ill, sad or lonely. Finally, they may be asked to think about something they are sorry about. They can be assured that God understands, forgives and helps us to make a new start. This quiet time might end by looking at something of beauty, or by saying the Lord's Prayer or the Grace together. Children value the beauty of stained-glass windows and pictures, symbols such as candles, crosses and statues, as well as actions such as kneeling, putting their hands together, closing their eyes and finding a time to be quiet and reflective. This is ministry to children at a formative time in their lives, including nurture and teaching (the latter will be addressed below).

Uniformed organizations

Uniformed organizations offer a similar programme to children's clubs, with the addition of a 'rite' of initiation, a uniform and a requirement to attend church parade. These organizations, such as Rainbows, Brownies, Guides, Cubs and Scouts, place responsibility on the local church to welcome children, and their volunteer leaders. The welcome is evident if the church parade service is interactive and accessible to all present. Children are nurtured by the concern and interest shown in them.

Holiday clubs

Holiday clubs provide a safe place during school holidays, giving children an opportunity to have fun together in a Christian context and offering a service to working parents. Events might include a sports afternoon, an outing day, a barbecue for parents and a final service. Holiday clubs entail an enormous amount of commitment in time and energy for a great number of people. In churches which have too few people with time to organize and run a club, congregation members could join up with a local authority holiday play scheme. This is another witness and commitment to children through the offering of time and skills.

Community

A small, elderly congregation in Rochdale recently ran a Fun Day for children, with games and craft activities such as kite- and sweet-making. Over a hundred children from the local community attended, many of whom were Muslims. The parents felt that they could trust the church to care for their children. The church did not want to evangelize, but simply to stretch out a hand of friendship and create networks of dialogue for both the adults and children. The need to respect each other and learn different ways of child-rearing proved of great value in enabling the congregation to serve the community.

The government department responsible for education (recently renamed the Department for Children, Schools and Families) has been concerned in recent years to offer parents greater help and provide a service to the community through local schools. This began in 1998 with the government policy of 'wrap-around childcare'. Since 2005 centres of 'extended education' have been set up to provide for children from 8 a.m. to 6 p.m. In some urban areas, church members use church premises for breakfast clubs. The funding for this extended education is something for churches to tap into. The involvement of churches affirms that they are concerned and interested in those outside their walls. By running such a club, urban churches, in particular, show that children matter. This is itself pastoral care.

ACTIONS OF PASTORAL CARE

Responding to needs

The psychologist Abraham Maslow wrote of a hierarchy of human needs, illustrated as a triangle.[7] At the base of his triangle are *physiological* needs (such as our need to be fed). Next is the need for *security*, to live in an ordered world. This is followed by the emotional need to *belong*, the need for *esteem* (self-respect and the respect of others), and finally at the apex of needs is *self-actualization*. We do well to note these for ourselves as carers and for those to whom we offer care. The *physiological* needs of the child may involve the carer in practical help for a single parent who finds it hard to 'make ends meet', finding grants or dealing with benefits offices as an advocate for a family. It must always be done alongside the family, not from a position of superiority. *Security* may be creating a safe place in which a child can be a child: for example, one who looks after a handicapped or addicted parent. Such care might involve providing an adult carer/befriender for the parent so that the child can join a group with other children and be a child. Humans are social creatures and we need to feel that we *belong* and are significant to others. For a child in a dysfunctional family or facing personal problems, the need can be met if members of the congregation have a concern for him or her. Children have many and varied gifts and if these are accepted and used the child feels and knows that belonging is reciprocal. It is only when children know that they 'matter' that they gain self-respect and are then able to respect others. Maslow suggested that the highest need was that of *self-actualization*. Within Christianity this is not seen as a narcissism but, I would suggest, relates to Fowler's 'universalizing faith', a state of letting go the ego-driven life and being open to others. Young children reflect this faith more than adults. The latter can become more conscious of what others might think, resulting in being self-absorbed. We need to nurture this openness in our children.

Some pastoral situations

- Jessie has just started secondary school. She has been a regular member of Sunday morning Junior Church but now feels too old to be with the younger children. There are no other children of her age.
- Samuel's father left home soon after he was born. He is now three and has come with his mother to the fortnightly mothers and toddlers group held in the church room. He went into the church and saw the font. He says that he wants to be christened. His mother is not sure, because she has no one to ask to be a godparent.
- Jack was excited about the prospect of having a pet. A week after its arrival his dog died. He came to Sunday school distraught.

What is the pastoral care of each of these children?

Who is responsible and how is pastoral care offered?

For Jessie pastoral care will involve listening to her feelings of still being thought a primary school pupil. It will recognize and support her in her personal changes (hormonal, teenage years) and the challenges of new school circumstances (travel to secondary school; a larger school; many other pupils that she does not know). An opportunity may arise for a conversation about growing in faith and ideas, exploring the taking of a role and joining the adult congregation, thinking about confirmation.

Samuel was taken seriously and listened to by the leaders of the mothers and toddlers group and he and his mother together were involved in the pastoral response offered to them. Samuel's mother Anna was worried by this prospect of baptism. She and her husband were immigrants to the UK, and soon after Samuel's birth his father left home. Anna had few friends and had become extremely depressed. She was ashamed to invite anyone into her home because of her poverty. Her family were in Africa, which meant that there was no one to ask to be a godparent or to invite to a celebration. The church members came to the rescue. Two couples offered to befriend Anna and Samuel with a view to being his godparents. The women's group made a celebration cake and refreshments to follow the baptismal service. Everyone was invited to stay. Through these actions Anna realized that she mattered, as did her child, and that he was as valued in the sight of God as any other child.

Jack's distress at the death of his dog was taken seriously. An adult member of the congregation who lived alone had also lost her dog recently. When she heard about Jack she identified with his loss and went to visit him. They shared photos of their dogs, and laughed and cried over the funny and difficult aspects of having a dog. Jack has learnt that adults in the congregation understand something of his feelings. Pastoral care was also expressed as a part of the following week's intercessions, when the loss of friends and pets was recognized.

These examples suggest that pastoral care is individual to the situation. It is about the recognition of uniqueness, listening, support, nurture. It may involve worship and teaching.

Quiet days

Pastoral care is also about groups. The Barnabas organization has ideas for a 'quiet day' for children: 'reflective story-telling interspersed with a balanced mix of quiet space and gentle creativity is a good outline. The emphasis should be on quietness rather than silence.'[8] Just as adults need quiet days and retreats to reflect and simply be, so do children. There is thus a recognition of the spiritual journey of the child and how this might be nurtured. Relationships are needed for us to become a self but we also need time to be alone.

SUMMARY POINTS FOR DISCUSSION

- The pastoral care of a child is given by parents, clergy, child-care workers, the faith congregation and the child's peers.

- Pastoral care is expressed through one-to-one contacts, in groups and in worship.

- Pastoral care sustains the child in times of trial and illuminates times of joy.

- Sometimes the name of 'God' is not used but God is always present in the encounter.

- Pastoral care is unconditional support, and being alongside.

CHAPTER SIX

Pastoral Care in Challenging Situations

The children were exploring the story of the rivalry between the twins Jacob and Esau when Jamie, a seven-year-old, suddenly blurted out, 'I'm a twin'. No one knew that Jamie had a twin. He continued, 'She died 'cos I was stronger and pushed her out of the way as we were being born, so she died.' There was silence in the room. Jamie's underlying sense of guilt was palpable. In one moment he had raised issues of responsibility, guilt, shame, death and loss. The occasion opened the 'floodgates' for other children to share their losses.

It started up a conversation that needed pastoral care and sensitivity for Jamie in particular but also for the other children in the group.

> **Think of difficult experiences in your childhood (getting lost, losing a favourite toy, staying in hospital, the death of a grandparent).**
>
> **Who and what helped you through the experience?**
>
> **Who were the significant adults in your life as a child? Why?**

This chapter recognizes some of the challenges in children's lives, and develops understanding so that our pastoral care may be more focused, giving support to both the child and the parents.

THE ROLE OF THE FAMILY

Some of a child's problems may arise from events outside himself but within the family, examples being marital breakdown and illness. It may be that the whole family needs support and help.

Parents know the child best and therefore we might think that they are the best people to help in identifying and resolving a child's problems. This is usually the case, but it must be remembered that parents may feel unskilled and inadequate, unable to cope, or may lack emotional engagement with their children. Parents need appropriate support and encouragement.

CHALLENGES FOR PARENTS

Parents meet together at a health clinic, a mothers and toddlers group or at the school gates, and talk about their children. They compare the development of their offspring, often proud of their children's achievement and concerned if they do not 'perform' as other children. Yet each child has its own rate and quality of growth. One child may grow fast and healthy, while another may be slower, weak or frustrated by a childhood illness or family trauma which may lengthen the 'normal' rate of growth. We live in an individualized, highly competitive society, yet a child's growth is a process, not a race to achieve adulthood. In the Hebrew Scriptures, Jacob recognized that neither his flocks with their young nor his children could be rushed; he had to go at 'the pace of children' (Gen. 33.14). Today many adults need to learn this lesson.

Childhood is a time of rapid change in physical capacities, in language, in intellectual, emotional, social and spiritual growth; it is not surprising, therefore, that there are some disturbances. Development norms help us to know what we might expect of children at different ages, yet growth is varied. Recently child experts have called this holistic growth 'a web', with interacting developments, rather than a process of growth that is even and in marked stages. However, there is a natural sequence of development: for example, children sit before they walk, jump before they hop, hop before they can skip.

Writers on Christian ministry, in a section headed 'Children's psychology', suggest that 'Children experience problems in three main areas – in behaviour (e.g. anti-social or violent behaviour), in emotion (anxiety or depression) and learning (e.g. dyslexia).'[1]

A troubled child needs adults who convey that they understand and accept the child as he is. This involves:

- conveying a real respect for each child;
- allowing time to build a trusting relationship;

- understanding how to communicate non-verbally as well as with words;
- making the environment within their control safe.

The presenting problem may not be the actual problem. For example, Martin Herbert suggests that academic underachievement and social 'friendlessness' can be understood as consequences of other psychological difficulties. Poor school performance may indicate dyslexia, a neurological condition that affects reading and writing, but is not related to IQ. Being misperceived as 'stupid' is likely to trigger negative emotional and behavioural responses such as poor self-esteem and disobedience. Friends are an important factor for learning (from peers), for emotional well-being (self-esteem, self-awareness) and for behaviour (accommodating to others' needs, making one's own needs heard in appropriate ways). Friendlessness often arises because the child has inadequate psychological skills, lacking sensitivity to others, confidence, the ability to resolve personal disputes or to work with others. Identifying these components of a general problem can help to break a negative cycle and allow work on particular issues.[2]

A clarification strategy that can help confused parents is for them to keep a journal 'recording the ABC's of the problem: the Antecedents, to learn what triggers problem episodes; the Behaviour itself; and the Consequences that this led to'.[3] A child's problem (for example, a return to bed-wetting) may be a symptom of a family problem, which draws attention from arguing parents to the child. In this case, sensitivity for all the family is needed. A child began writing all her school work in mirror-writing. She was disturbed about the squiggles because the action was involuntary. Her teacher recognized what was happening and took her aside, using a mirror to show her what she was doing. Later it transpired that the girl was missing her mother, who had died the previous year, and she was upset because she could no longer 'picture' her. The teacher inquired and discovered a favourite aunt living nearby who had photos and stories of her sister. Being able to look at these and talk to her aunt helped the child. Her writing returned to normal.

Are problems just blips? Many childhood problems are a phase and resolve themselves with time, though they cause distress and anxiety for the child and the parents during the process of identifying the causes and resolving them. Most children will develop into normal autonomous adults, but there are certain problems which need to be tackled in order to break habits that could lead to future difficulties and which, more importantly, take the fun out of life for children in the present. For example, temper tantrums are normal in toddlers, but not in an eight-year-old, who could be expected to have developed self-control and accept-able ways of expressing strong emotions.

Children are not as capable as adults of expressing their prob-lems. Parents need to become adept at recognizing distress and responding to it. This means being alert to changes in behaviour, fantasy, play and storytelling. Francis was three. His father worked away from home and barely knew his son, nor Francis his father. Nights were disturbed by Francis waking up terrified, screaming that a lion had jumped into his bedroom. He was calmed eventually by his mother, who suggested that he offer a hand to the lion and say, 'Let's be friends'. The incident may well reflect the child's insecurity in his relationship with his father, who in fantasy became a 'powerful lion'. Nye notes that children only gradually acquire the intellectual sophistication to reflect on their own mental states, but easily project their feelings on to fictional characters with whom they can identify. They may even appropriate characters from biblical stories to do this. The story at the beginning of this chapter has a resonance here.[4]

Particular problems tend to occur in specific age groups, for example:

- babies: distress from unmet needs, lack of attention and stim-ulation
- toddlers: autonomy or control; temper tantrums, eating, fears, jealousy
- pre-school: sleep, bad dreams, fear of the dark, timidity, overdependence, isolation
- junior school: bullying, aggression, uncontrolled temper, lazi-ness or over-activity.

The comments that follow illustrate examples of children's prob-lems in behaviour (anti-social behaviour), in emotion (from low self-esteem) and in learning (i.e. school performance).

ISSUES IN BEHAVIOUR

Parents want an infant to be happy and confident, so it comes as a surprise how quickly they have to say 'no' to a child. Early on, as they become physically mobile, toddlers require parameters both for their own safety and to recognize the rights and needs of others. There are two ways that 'discipline' can work: one is imposed, the other is 'self-directed'. We may discipline children by imposing rules and controlling how they behave, but this does not work when the parent is absent. Alternatively, a parent can give a child strategies to develop self-discipline, to manage his or her own behaviour. This means that when the parent is absent the child has some idea what is appropriate behaviour. Research shows that self-discipline is the only kind that is long-lasting, since it develops the child's confidence in his own powers of choice and decision. A parent acting as a role model can encourage self-discipline, because children notice and copy the feelings and reactions of the significant adults in their lives.

There are strategies to achieve self-discipline, such as negative or positive reinforcement, whereby a reward such as a sweet or small toy is given for good behaviour or taken away for bad behaviour. However, this is a short-term method and does not encourage children to think about their behaviour. 'Time out' can be used to discourage unacceptable behaviour. In this strategy children are taken to a place that is boring but safe. The child is ignored and left without toys, and needs to stay there for one minute for every year of his or her age. If the child moves, he or she is carried back without comment. 'Time out' needs to follow immediately after the incident, and must be carried out consistently. It can be exhausting for the parent, but it does eventually work. A period alone gives the infant time to calm down and think about what has happened. 'Time out' can be followed, at a later stage of the child's development, by discussion of the behaviour that has been censured. A toddler having a tantrum needs to be contained, and if possible held, so that the child knows he or she will not be abandoned and allowed to be overwhelmed by emotion. It is important to try to avoid confrontations or humiliation by respecting a child's personality and mood. The action taken needs to be within the boundaries that the child can reasonably manage. When the child becomes calm, discussion can happen. Children need to recognize that there are boundaries that they cannot cross, such as someone else being hurt, and that certain behaviour simply is not acceptable. Boundaries should be clear and consistent; children need a predictable environment in which to operate. It is important to distinguish the unacceptable behaviour from the child who is accepted: 'naughty behaviour', not 'you are naughty'.

Jane's three-year-old was being deliberately disobedient and goading her to lose her cool. Finally, Jane lost her temper and yelled at him, 'That's enough: "Time out".' She left him sitting on the stairs, then realized that in yelling at him she had not set a good example. Later on she apologized to him. The three-year-old responded, 'Time out'. This pre-schooler was beginning to learn that 'time out' meant an opportunity to rethink behaviour and to change it.

Sometimes a parent can prevent unacceptable behaviour by intervening: for example, when she notices that a child is about to hit another child, throw a toy or damage another's painting. With some infants bad behaviour and tantrums will seem to create constant battles. It is a stage that children go through in order to learn to recognize what behaviour is socially acceptable and what is not. At an early age this behaviour is connected with the forming of the self and identity, since in our relationships with others we come to learn more of who we are. It is important not to bribe or pacify a child: more attention should be given to good behaviour.

With an older child, seven or eight years old, there may be several reasons for aggressive behaviour. It may be that the child is outgrowing his or her strength, is physically tired or bored, and takes the easy option of hitting out instead of trying to solve a problem. Alternatively, the child may have too much energy and no healthy outlet. Another reason may be a diet overloaded with additives that cause hyperactivity. A child who is unhappy because of his or her parents' attitudes or behaviour, such as quarrelling, may simply be imitating this behaviour. For some children, being naughty is one way of gaining attention. A parent needs to find a space to give a child time, to listen to the reason for aggressive behaviour and to help the child find acceptable ways of acting. Parents can learn non-verbal ways of challenging their child's behaviour, such as silence, simply looking at the child, or shaking the head. These ways can be less confrontational than meeting the child 'head-on'.

Seven-year-old Mike had uncontrollable aggression and was referred to a therapist. An assessment visit with his mother helped the therapist to discover something of his background. However, the therapist was mystified until she received a clue from Mike's answer to the question, 'What is school like?' Mike said his class teacher was great because she laughed at his jokes. 'She appreciates me,' he said. It appeared Mike was not understood at home and had not experienced that unconditional love which enables a human to grow. David Richo[5] believes that children need attention (someone's undivided time), affection (unconditional love), allowance (freedom to make mistakes), appreciation (recognition of their qualities) and acceptance (of themselves as they are) to grow into healthy humans.

Parents need space to talk with others, collectively and on a 'one-to-one' basis, in order to recognize that tantrums are common in toddlers and pre-schoolers, and to learn how other parents have coped. One possibility is to establish parenting groups such as those facilitated by individuals trained through the Mothers' Union.[6] Parents need to find positive ways of affirming their children and continuing to love them despite their unacceptable behaviour.

Emotions

The story of Jamie at the beginning of the chapter illustrates excessive emotions and low self-esteem. In school he lashed out at other children and he was eventually excluded from school.[7] Jamie must have been told about the death of his twin sister at birth. His emotional energy was charged with guilt, shame and responsibility, resulting in low self-esteem and attention-seeking behaviour. The after-school church club engaged his energy and adults gave him time to talk. Children need to have an adult's listening ear.

Children may express emotional stress in a variety of ways: physical actions such as stomping around, becoming aggressive, being quiet, twisting fingers; bed-wetting; eating poorly; or returning to an earlier developmental stage. Children may experience stress when they do not have sufficient warm, consistent, loving relationships to satisfy their emotional life.

Fear is an example of emotional stress. An infant fears that his or her carer might leave; another may be fearful of thunder or strange noises, sudden movements and going to an unfamiliar place. Some children are afraid of the dark. In dealing with fears it is important to let the child talk and for parents to show they understand. The security of reassurance is needed. At night a child may be helped by an electric night-light or the bedroom door left open so that he or she can hear others in the home. The provision for imaginative play, with puppets or dressing-up clothes, helps to provide an outlet for fears. Another emotion that may cause stress is jealousy. A toddler who is jealous of a new baby can be encouraged to express feelings in an acceptable way by hitting a cushion or pillow, and in boisterous play.

Children will be helped if they are given personal space and one-to-one attention to express their feelings. They can be encouraged to be with friends and family and be part of a group. The church can be such a group.

Learning

Most children have a sense of loyalty to their birth parents, however they are treated. The divorce of parents is traumatic for children. Research suggests that breakdown in family life affects school performance and impairs the child's sense of self-worth. Children are likely to suffer emotionally during the lengthy period when the marriage is breaking up, while attempts at reconciliation, the legislative process of divorce and the establishment of a 'new family' are taking place. Children may witness the division between parents and be encouraged to take sides. Violence and domestic abuse in the presence of children increases their subsequent emotional difficulties. This adult behaviour may be considered a 'norm' by children and repeated when they become parents. Violence between parents is frightening for children, who, unlike adults, have little control over their circumstances. Children may manipulate their parents in an attempt to undermine any attempts to separate. The child may become the carer and emotional support for an unhappy parent following separation, taking on inappropriate adult responsibilities.

Divorce may involve the loss of a parent and potentially the kinship ties on one side of the family, including grandparents. The loss of a father may be permanent if custody is given to the mother, particularly if violence has been a reason for divorce. However, fathers can sometimes challenge the custody decision and obtain regular access to their biological children within supervised contact centres. Such centres provide 'absent' parents with a supported and supervised venue to meet their children. Divorce may involve moving house, resulting in the breaking of friendship groups and a change of school; the arrival of a step-parent and step-siblings; or single parenting and poverty. Losing contact with a birth parent through divorce can have a more negative impact on a child than the death of a parent (see Table 6.1). The longer-term consequences are hard to determine.

Table 6.1 Common difficulties as children deal with recently divorced parents[8]

Age	Behaviour
Pre-school	Sad, frightened, clinging, demanding. Has vivid fantasies about abandonment by or death of parent(s). Aggression towards other children.
5–8 years	Hurt, as above, more anger, often towards remaining parent (mother typically), who is blamed for situation. Absent parent is idealized.
8–12 years	Displays less hurt, hard to encourage to talk. Seeks distractions.
Teenager	Depression, opts out of family life, creates alternative 'family' of friends.

Underachievement, poor self-esteem, and serious depression may be averted if there is someone to talk to outside the immediate family. As church members we can be particularly aware of the needs of children who experience divorce and offer them a continuing support system. Help at contact centres is frequently given by Mothers' Union members.

I next turn to several challenges which have received considerable attention in the media, including the educational press.

BULLYING

In one year 31,000 children rang ChildLine for advice because they were bullied. Historically, bullying was seen as a necessary part of growing up, teaching children to stick up for themselves in the school playground. It is recognized today that children feel and suffer as much as adults, and their suffering must be taken seriously. This has led to the development of school policies on bullying, the training of particular members of staff in counselling skills, and the introduction of curricular subjects such as

Personal, Social and Health Education (PSHE) and programmes that deal with emotional events in children's lives.

Bullying is behaviour that gives one person power over another; it can take the form of calling someone names, saying or writing nasty things, teasing, threatening, taking or damaging possessions, physical attack or making someone do something he or she doesn't want to do. Children can be very cruel and will often bully other children unmercifully. Bullying happens for a variety of reasons, sometimes because a child is different in colour, religion, size or accent, is dyslexic or wears glasses.

Bullying happens in the family too, though a child when asked said, 'Oh no, my brother doesn't bully me. He's family.' The child assumed that the physical and verbal bullying from his older brother was normal sibling behaviour. A bully was someone outside the family. Some teachers bully by making a child 'feel small' in front of others. Why do adults and children bully? It may be a way of gaining attention, becoming popular, looking tough and in charge, or expressing jealousy of the person being bullied. Bullies may themselves be bullied by a family member, may need a way of making others feel afraid, or may not like themselves and take it out on someone else. The bully needs to be understood and helped to find acceptable ways of behaving.

Bullying causes children great unhappiness. They may feel scared, unsafe and frightened, or think it is their fault and that there is something wrong with them. As a result, a child loses confidence, cannot concentrate and frequently skips school. Yet a child has a right to be safe. Children are advised by ChildLine to 'tell an adult you can trust, spend time with friends – bullies hardly ever pick on people in a group, keep a record of events, try to act more confidently, check the school anti-bullying policy, remember it's not your fault'. The most important action for a parent is to listen to their child and, with the child's permission, take action alongside the school. This may involve checking the evidence. Throughout the incident, the worth of the child must be repeated to the child.

TRANSITIONS

Children find transitions difficult. These begin early in the life of a baby when, for the first time after birth, he or she is left with a relative or friend. The parent's absence is traumatic, since recognition of a parent begins early in a baby's life. However, it is now established that a baby can relate to more people than just the mother, providing that these people are constantly present in the baby's life. The transitional object (see Chapter 2) is a comfort to a young infant. A toddler attending a regular group and a pre-schooler at nursery will find the transition difficult from having the sole attention of the mother to sharing attention with other children within a strange environment. Similarly, the transition to full-time school, or leaving infant school and going to junior school, will be challenging for a child; the parent and the receiving adults need to prepare sensitively. The parent will have worries about leaving the child; therefore, appropriate body language and gestures are reassuring, as is a promise to meet the child after school. Keeping the promise proves that the parent is trustworthy. It is important that teachers help children to know and feel that they belong, are valued and respected: participation in an interesting activity can involve a child from the beginning. A designated key helper who is consistent is essential for a very young child.

HOSPITALIZATION

Going to hospital can be a disturbing experience for a child. Medical settings are unfamiliar to a child, who will see many professional people, in different coloured uniforms. There are new sights, smells and sounds, all of which can be frightening. Children need empathy and preparation for this experience so that they know what to expect and do not fantasize. They need to give their permission for treatment and not to be excluded because they are young. Children are logical, and simple explanations are best, together with honesty and reassurance. Andrew, aged seven, went into hospital for the removal of his tonsils and adenoids. While the nurse took his temperature, he asked, 'Is it true that they cut your head off to get out your tonsils?'[9]

If a child is admitted to hospital in an emergency, such preparation is not possible. Parents are likely to be worried and their behaviour may be abnormal. Taking a favourite toy and familiar nightwear gives reassurance to a child. Many hospitals allow a parent to stay with a sick child. If this is not possible, it is important that promises to visit are kept. Pastoral visits can help and support both parent and child particularly, and sometimes only, if the visiting is by a familiar person known and trusted by the child. It is helpful to take something for the child to enjoy which is a reminder of 'normal times', for example, a card made by the peer group.

Working with a child with a life-threatening illness is especially demanding. Pastoral care is about dispelling guilt (in both child and parent), honesty, open answers, listening to the child's understanding of the illness, showing love, offering security, explaining in a language the child can understand, using appropriate media such as puppets, books and creativity. Usually the child knows intuitively what is happening, but sometimes a conspiracy of silence prevails. Sensitivity is central to care, discovering from the child what he or she knows and wants to know, working in parallel with parents. A child's needs for information or not to talk should be respected.

Tricia had leukaemia. She was in hospital and knew that she was dying. When the consultant, who was a Christian, tried to talk about death in order to prepare her, Tricia told her to 'piss off'. I was sent for as the chaplain. I had met Tricia before, and I knew she loved life and enjoyed jokes, so I went armed with a Spike Milligan joke-book. We chatted and joked. Eventually, I asked her if she had seen the consultant recently. She simply said that the consultant wanted to talk about death. 'But I didn't,' she said. 'I know that I won't be here much longer. I don't need her to tell me about heaven and all that claptrap. I want to live.' She stopped talking. 'What do you enjoy about living?' I asked. There was no reply. She had fallen asleep laughing at one of the jokes in my book.

DEATH

Children are fascinated by death, such as that of a bird or hedgehog. However, when there is a death in the family, adults wrapped up in their own grief may ignore the needs of children. On some occasions a parent may refuse to allow a child to speak of a loved person because the adult is too upset. Consequently, a child is not allowed space to grieve. Children understand differently from adults, but nevertheless they do grieve. Six-year-old Jim's grandfather died. The two had been very close; his grandfather had taught Jim to fish and they fished together regularly. However, his grandmother did not want anyone to mention the death. Jim was not allowed to attend the funeral, merely told that 'Granddad has gone to be with Jesus in heaven.' He wanted to be with his grandfather, wherever he was. His parents were scared by his odd behaviour and watched him carefully, but they accepted his grandmother's request not to mention her husband's death. Jim became more and more distressed at school and eventually he was referred to a child psychiatrist. It took many months before he accepted what had happened. Opportunities to talk from the beginning would have helped Jim.

Tom was eight years old when his grandfather died, and he was angry. The family were Christians and had talked to him before and after the death. Tom was referred to a childcare bereavement specialist at a hospice. At the meetings he was very angry and repeatedly disappeared under a table. Eventually the worker decided to go under the table with him in an effort to discover why he was so angry. Tom insisted that the worker did not tell his parents what he thought. He then said he was angry with 'the f*****g angels who had taken his grandfather'. The worker was not a Christian, nor did she have any religious or spiritual beliefs. While honouring his beliefs, she helped Tom to discover for himself that what 'took' his grandfather was the f*****g cancer.

Every 30 minutes in the UK a child is bereaved of a parent: this is 53 children a day, 20,000 children every year. Many more children are bereaved of a sibling, grandparent, schoolfriend, other relative or significant adult such as a teacher. Bereaved children have various needs. First, they need respect for themselves as persons, for their presence and their distress. They need information in order to understand death and what it means to them. They need to know about the death as soon as possible; it should not be kept hidden. Treating children as ignorant is treating them with disrespect. It is important to answer the questions that children ask in a straightforward way. Children need reassurance. The death of a parent is a threat to their whole life. They need to be assured that life will go on, even though there will inevitably be changes. It is helpful for children to return to school as soon as possible, since normality and routine is helpful to them; also, they can thus escape from the anguish of their family at home. Children need to know that grief is normal, that death is accompanied by feelings of anger and sorrow expressed in a variety of ways – crying, sobbing, silence. They need to know that these expressions are OK, that adults cry in grief. Some parents, particularly fathers, do not want their children to see them cry. If it is a parent who has died, the resources of the remaining parent in supporting and parenting the child may be limited when that parent is trying to manage his or her own grief. Having familiar adults around can be a great support at this time.

Children also need space to be left alone for periods of time with their own grief. The availability of pencils and paper, paints and books can help the child to express grief. Space gives opportunities to reflect and remember the person who has died. Sometimes the use of photograph albums can help. Meeting other children who have shared similar experiences may help older children (Appendix 5 lists some useful contacts).

The effects of a parent's death on a child will vary depending on the child's developmental stage and the circumstances of the death. If the death follows a long illness and a progressive decline in the abilities of the parent, then the child will be more prepared when the death happens. Children need to be kept informed and have their questions honestly answered throughout the illness, and if possible an opportunity should be given to say goodbye. If a death is sudden, there will be no time to say goodbye, and if the last meeting involved a disagreement a child may well feel that he or she caused the death by being naughty. The child's reasoning must be listened to, and reassurances given that he or she was not the cause of death. Such reassurances must be repeated as often as necessary.

The child's relationship with the dead parent is also significant; if the relationship was very close, bereavement is going to be more difficult. A parent's death may involve practical changes for a child. It may be closely associated with disruptive events such as moving house, or school, or having to go and live with others. Blunt questions that shock adults are often asked: 'Who will take me to football now?' Table 6.2 lists some of the behaviours commonly associated with bereavement in children.

Adolescents from twelve years onwards have special needs. They oscillate between forgetting and remembering. The unremitting pace of adult grief is too intense, too much an interference with the necessary work of growing up.

Involving the child in the funeral arrangements is important. Many clergy are aware of the particular needs of children and will share ideas to involve a child if asked. The child might want to write a poem or draw a picture to go in the coffin, put a flower on the coffin, hand out service sheets or light a candle. Children above the age of six can be asked if they would like to attend the funeral. It is important, however, that they are prepared for what happens at the service and that someone sits with them. If the child does not want to attend, it might be possible for a familiar adult to light a candle and say a prayer such as the Lord's Prayer with them while the funeral is taking place, at home or somewhere quiet in school. Explanations of why the body is buried or cremated dispel myths, while help should be given so that the child is able to remember all that was important about the deceased.

Table 6.2 Behaviours and concepts connected with bereavement in children

Age	Behaviour	Concepts	Home support	School support
0–6 months	Crying, skin rashes, tummy upsets		Give consistent care, cuddles and comfort	
6 months to 2 years	Clinging, erratic sleep patterns, cranky eating, subdued mood	Separation anxiety is central. Need for security, continuity and normality of mealtimes and bedtime rituals with a familiar adult until family reorganizes a routine.	Extra cuddles, consistent care, messy toys, paints to encourage expressive play	
3 to 4 years	Clingy, tantrums, repeated questions, extra coughs and colds	Death is a vague concept that happens to flowers, insects and pets, not humans. Children tend to think of it like sleep or a journey from which someone can wake up or return. This may result in problems over going to bed.	Extra cuddles, routine explanations, reading books about loss, drawing and play help in expressing feelings. Avoid euphemisms such as 'sleep' or 'gone away'.	Important that all staff at nursery school know of a pupil's bereavement – a casual remark can hurt.

(*continued overleaf*)

Table 6.2 – continued

Age	Behaviour	Concepts	Home support	School support
5 to 8 years	Fear of dark, nightmares, return to baby talk, bed-wetting. Afraid to go to school or friends' houses.	At 7 years, accepts reality and permanence of death, that it means no longer being able to eat, sleep, laugh, cry or feel pain. Growing understanding can lead to fear.	A night-light, regular quiet time, physical affection, information, a pet, drawing, books. Child needs reassurance and comfort.	Going to school may help since it is a normal part of life. Important that the child is involved and given choices about what, how and why information is conveyed to other pupils. No right answer.
8 to 12 years	Panic, daydreaming, denial, rudeness, phobia about illness and doctors, difficulty in getting to sleep	Matter of fact about death	Give treats as well as maintaining routine, make memory book, look at photos of the dead, talk about person, physical affection for the child, visit cemetery.	Helpful if teacher communicates with child's parent. Peer group help.

How do we help children of different ages to accept death?

What difference might it mean being a Christian child?

ADOPTION

Attitudes to adoption are changing. Concern for the child's welfare is primary but it is increasingly recognized that children want to be with their genetic parents. Social services and social workers have a difficult role. At one time, if parents were considered unfit to care, their children were immediately removed and put into institutional care. Subsequently, it was recognized that children needed the emotional support of a family. As a consequence the emphasis was laid on foster homes. Unfortunately, sometimes foster homes were only able to offer short-term care and local authority social services departments came to realize that children were not helped by being placed with a series of foster carers, each with a different ethos and set of rules. Whenever possible, the aim is now to provide 'open adoption'.

In open adoption the child is involved with his or her birth family from the beginning. The Department of Health's National Adoption Standards for England state:

> The child's needs, wishes and feelings, and their welfare and safety, are the most important concerns when considering contact with birth parents, wider family members and other people who are significant to them. Children's views on contact should carry more weight, and contact arrangements should be reviewed regularly, while recognizing the issue of safety. When it is in the child's best interest for there to be ongoing links with birth parents and families, birth families will be involved in discussion about how best to achieve this.

Couples adopting children have always been encouraged to make clear to the child that he or she is adopted. It is good that adopted children are made to feel very special and chosen. In recent years all adopted children, on reaching 18, have been able to discover the details of their birth parents. For some this has been an emotional experience. It can be equally hard for the mother who gave up the child for adoption and may carry her child's birth as a secret; it can also be distressing for the parents who adopted the child. The process needs care. Social services and agencies like Barnardo's spend considerable time and energy supporting children and families in this work.

When children are adopted and continue to have contact with a birth parent, it can cause anxiety to the adopters. Natural parents may resent adopters, and be angry at what has happened. In research on contact after adoption, conducted by Dr Elsbeth Neil of the University of East Anglia, of a sample of 168 children aged under four, only 11 per cent had no contact with adult birth relatives. Eighteen per cent received letters, cards and reports, while 17 per cent saw their birth families face to face, though this did not necessarily occur regularly. Children want to know who they are. The link between children and their birth parents can never be broken, whether contact is maintained or not. The memories of birth parents and early life experiences are ones that children take with them into the new relationship with their adoptive parents. The research found that ongoing contact alleviated some of the birth parents' anguish by reassuring them that their child was all right, by making the loss of their child easier to accept, by helping them to feel more positive about the adoptive parents, and by giving them a positive role in their child's future.[10]

In most church congregations there are families who foster or adopt. There are children who have been damaged through separation from their birth parents, who live with foster or adopted families or members of their birth families such as aunts or grandparents. The likelihood is that these children will be more erratic in their behaviour and cause more concern than other children. They will be in particular need of consistent love, understanding and acceptance by the church and its congregation. Their trust and sense of security may have been severely damaged in their early, formative years, so phrases describing God as 'parent' or 'father' may be impossible for them to understand. With experiences of an unconditional love, it may be possible for them gradually to grow in trust. The foster or adopted parents too will need support and prayer.

ABUSE

Children who are abused, in whatever way, are abused spiritually in that their capacity for trust, self-esteem, giving and receiving love, security and affirmation is assaulted; delight and wonder are all too probably replaced by despair, anger and guilt. Abuse of children – emotional, psychological, social, physical and sexual – is increasing, as is internet child pornography. Definitions of abuse have been extended to include emotional abuse and neglect, covering the attitudes of some middle-class parents who are 'low in warmth and high in criticism'. This is a complex issue, which I am not competent to address. What I know from working with adults in congregations who were abused as children is that the damage is long-lasting, particularly if one parent was abusing and the other colluded through silence.

Janet Pais suggests that abuse arises from adult contempt for what is powerless and vulnerable.[11] For an adult to use a child for his or her own gratification, or to collude in such activity, is to treat a person as a thing, causing untold damage, a 'stealing of childhood'.

> Many of us, as adults, have lost touch with the child within ourselves and this has resulted in our becoming immune to the pains we once experienced. We therefore fail to see the hurts that all children experience and, in particular, the terrible pain that neglected and abused children feel.[12]

Professional help should always be sought when abuse is considered to be present. The chief fear with abuse of a child is the long-term damage which might result.

> Even abused children often seem to escape long-lasting damage if there is somebody around who doesn't turn away. A relatively brief experience of a friend or an aunt can provide children with an alternative picture of how love can work.[13]

In all the challenging situations described above there is help available. Criticism is destructive; what parents need is the positive support of a listening ear. Organizations such as Home-Start offer a friendly visitor to a family as a support and encouragement. Parenting courses are available. One-to-one counselling may help a child, provided by a GP's surgery, the school or, in the case of bereavement, by the local hospice. It is essential that the counsellor is trusted and known by the parent. Otherwise, the parent may feel inadequate in being unable to help his or her own child. However, sometimes children do not want to talk to a parent for fear of upsetting him or her or being upset themselves. A stranger is different and may empower children to find the inner resources to help themselves rather than imposing adult solutions. Listening to a child's feelings and experience is a source of healing. It is important that at least one person in our childhood affirms our true feelings and lets us know that our true self is of worth.

SUMMARY POINTS FOR DISCUSSION

- Children need the security of knowing that they are loved despite themselves.

- Parents learn gradually to let go of their child and to honour the child's autonomy.

- Childhood is a stage of rapid growth.

- Children need parameters and boundaries to guide them.

- Children need to be listened to and taken seriously.

CHAPTER SEVEN

Pastoral Care through Christian Education

Wayne was upset. He wanted to have an important role in the infants' nativity play, perhaps a king with lots of finery, but instead he was chosen to be the innkeeper. He decided that he could perhaps put in a few more words to add to the part and his own significance. On the afternoon of the play he was ready when the infant playing Joseph knocked at the door of his inn and asked for lodging. 'Welcome, come in. We have plenty of room,' Wayne said to Mary. 'But you can b****r off,' he said, turning to Joseph.[1]

Did it matter that Wayne changed the story?

How important are facts in teaching children stories from the Scriptures?

'No room in the inn' is a biblical concept (Luke 2.7) but is it central to the nativity story? Wayne's words suggest that he didn't think so. However, although he may not have realized it, his words were of supreme significance. It could be said that the heart of the story is the welcoming of the Christ child into our hearts and lives. 'No room in the inn' can be interpreted as an expression of the homelessness of Jesus, both physically and metaphorically. In his homelessness he identified with the plight of children in his day and in ours. Homelessness was about Jesus having 'nowhere to lay his head': his birth spoke of his true home as God. A theme of 'exile' and homelessness runs through the pages of Scripture, resolved in humanity's true home in God. In some ways this story illustrates that there can be a variety of interpretations of the Scriptures, the criterion being does the interpreter's truth resonate with the meaning of the congregation of faith, since our faith is both individual and corporate, leading to new vision?

This chapter takes a short detour to examine the history of Sunday school as one of the significant institutions of education for children and an influence on the Christian education of children today.[2] I then proceed to look at the aim of such education and to explore teachers, methods and learners, in order to define the contribution of Christian education to the pastoral care of our children.

THE ORIGINS OF SUNDAY SCHOOLS IN ENGLAND

To find some clues about church involvement in Christian education for the majority of children,[3] we must step back to the Industrial Revolution, which brought families in their thousands from their village homes to work in the cities. Children worked long hours in factories for six days a week, and on the Sunday they were let loose and roamed the streets in gangs. Concerned individuals responded, such as Hannah Ball, a Methodist, who began a school for children on Sundays in 1769. Perhaps better known is the work of Robert Raikes (1735–1811), a Gloucestershire printer. He was a lively evangelical Christian, with a passion for prison reform. When visiting Gloucester prison, he saw child felons there and thought that the only way to prevent working-class children falling into crime was through education.

In 1780 Raikes began what was to be the first Sunday school for working-class boys (girls were accepted later). Publicity was possible through the printing business he inherited from his father in 1757. The curriculum was simple: lessons in reading, spelling and memorizing Scripture passages and hymns, from 10 a.m. until 2 p.m., followed by an hour's break, then the boys were taken to church until 5.30 p.m. for instruction in catechism. Sometimes instruction in writing and arithmetic was added on Saturday. The Sunday school movement became a working-class institution, instilling self-discipline, industry, thrift, improvement, and creating community. In 1786 the Easter Quarter Session magistrates passed a unanimous vote of thanks for the benefits of Sunday schools in raising the morals of the young.[4] The schools were called 'ragged schools' because of the condition of the children's clothes, but no child was turned away. Gradually, the movement spread from Gloucester to other industrial cities. Raikes's idea inspired Hannah More and her sister, Martha, who were determined to add other subjects to the curriculum: sewing, cooking, hygiene and fun through playing games. In 1803 the London Sunday School Union was founded to promote the extension of schools with voluntary teachers, and the publishing of lesson guides, plans, catechisms, spellers and other aids.

It is important to note the zeal of the Sunday school movement. It was designed for children and so it created an institution separated from adults. This separation is inherited by today's Sunday schools. The use of the word 'school' is itself significant: the aim was decidedly educational. Raikes sought to educate through using the Scriptures. His method was repetition and rote learning, including considerable memorization; morality would be imbibed through this instruction. This has parallels with the intended purpose of some adults for the children in Sunday school today, although our current knowledge of how children learn is very different.

The Sunday school movement paralleled the earlier work of individuals who established dame schools and it was a factor in the creation of state primary education through highlighting the need for all children to be educated. In 1808 the Quaker Joseph Lancaster established the Royal Lancastrian Society (later the British and Foreign School Society) for the education of 'the labouring and manufacturing classes of society of every religious persuasion'. Teaching was to be nonsectarian, informed by 'general Christian principles'. Lancaster was followed in 1811 by Andrew Bell, an Anglican priest, who established the National Society for the Education of the Poor in the Principles of the Established Church. The education of children was a priority of the Church: always an education in the context of faith teaching. Gradually, day schools were replacing Sunday schools and work for children.

The first grant of public money for schools, £20,000, was in 1833, which resulted in controversy, since the money came from the rates. There were those who objected to public money being used to perpetuate religious practices and denominational differences.[5] The money was divided between the two societies. The churches (Anglican and Free, and later Roman Catholic) could not provide sufficient funds or personnel to educate the nation's children, so their voluntary provision was erratic, yet employers demanded an educated work-force, and employees wanted improvement for themselves and their children, which they saw as a product of education. Development was hindered by differences of opinion.

EDUCATION FOR ALL

The 1870 Elementary Education Act created a dual system of state education for all children: the voluntary church schools continued, helped by government funding, and were supplemented by Board schools (later called Local Authority schools), wherever voluntary provision was insufficient. Voluntary schools provided denominational religious teaching; in Board schools there was religious instruction but it came under the 'Cowper Temple' clause: 'no religious education or religious formulary which is distinctive of any particular denomination shall be taught in any school provided by a school board.' The 'dual system' of Church and Board schools has left its mark with the inclusion of religious instruction (RI) and collective worship (CW) as a 'compulsory' part of the curriculum.[6] The agreed syllabuses that emerged to teach the subject were headed RI: the methodology of teaching was didactic; the content was a series of biblical references.

Religious instruction, which until the 1960s was based on Christianity, was now given by church and state schools, where attendance was full-time and compulsory. This began the decline of the Sunday school and a willingness to leave Christian education to day schools. For many years middle-class parents would not send their children to Sunday school, believing it to be for the working class. Parallel to the development of state education, church clubs were formed for children: the Church Lads' Brigade in 1891 and Robert Baden-Powell's Boy Scouts and Girl Guides from 1907. Each of these had a religious foundation, as did the later Crusaders (in 2007 called Urban Saints). These clubs were based on having fun together in a context of Christian faith.

RI continued to be significant in state education. The 1944 Butler Education Act was written while bombs were falling around Parliament, and Hansard reports show that the religious requirements of the 1944 Act (RI and CW) were considered to be part of the moral foundation of rebuilding post-war society. The word 'collective' indicated that worship was intended to be a focal point of unity in the schools, reflecting and reinforcing a real sense of common purpose and concern, a moral stance, and offering hope and vision for the future. The 1944 Act began with the aim of education: 'the spiritual development of the child'.

The 1960s to 1980s marked a crisis of confidence in Christian education. It was a time of changes in society: greater affluence, freedom of speech, increased leisure opportunities, rising secularism, influence of Eastern faiths, pluralism, decline in church attendance and Sunday schools, intellectual challenges to belief. In education the work of Piaget led to open learning styles in primary schools, beginning with, and building on, the experience of the child. The institutional Church struggled with declining numbers, yet there was an interest in the exploring of religious ideas, encouraged by the publication of Bishop John Robinson's book *Honest to God* in 1963 and other forms of religious expression such as Transcendental Meditation and the New Age movement. Some churches began to see Christian education as a church responsibility with the development of material for the whole people of God.[7] In schools, RI became religious education (RE), with the inclusion of teaching about world faiths, while concern over the 'compulsory' character of worship was raised. The issues were the compatibility of worship and education, the difference between a church congregation and a school community, and an increasingly pluralist society. The word 'assembly' became popular, since teachers felt that it maintained their integrity, suggesting this was an educational experience that focused on what was of worth within the school. Assemblies aimed to celebrate: to build a school identity, encourage a sense of sharing, and inculcate collective moral values.

Questions about the validity of RE and CW as 'educational' continued to be raised during the passage of the 1988 Education Reform Act (ERA). The Act suggested that education had among its aims, first, to pass on culture to the next generation (instrumental and functional) and, second, to challenge 'received knowledge, attitudes, values and assumptions' in a continuous search for truth. The second aim is interesting in that underlying it is the premise that education concerns the individual's search for, and formation of, identity, yet the word 'challenge' suggests a counter-culture of subversion. This aim is very close to that of Christian education. The Gospel itself is subversive of much contemporary culture, although the aim is a continuous search for truth, which for Christians is found in the story of the life, death and resurrection of Jesus. The objectives of education in the ERA 'are to promote the spiritual, moral, cultural, mental and physical development of individual pupils and society through a) the provision of Religious Education and b) the National Curriculum'.

What do you understand by the two expressed aims of education in the ERA?

Do you think that they are close to the aims of Christian education?

Educationalists continued to express concerns about collective worship, despite fifty years of experience and experiment, and Christian teachers (such teachers have some knowledge of the purpose of worship, experience of their own church's worship and are professional educators). The former Department for Education's circular *Religious Education and Collective Worship (Circular 1/94)* offered guidance, although it was not an authoritative legal interpretation of the provisions in the 1988 and 1993 Education Acts. It stated:

> Collective worship in schools should aim to provide the opportunity for pupils to worship God, to consider spiritual and moral issues and to explore their own beliefs; to encourage participation and response, whether through active involvement in the presentation of worship or through listening to and joining in the worship offered; and to develop community spirit, promote a common ethos and shared values, and reinforce positive attitudes. (para. 50)

In further paragraphs the Circular notes,

> 'Worship' is not defined in the legislation and in the absence of any such definition it should be taken to have its natural and ordinary meaning. That is, it must in some sense reflect something special or separate from ordinary school activities and it should be concerned with reverence or veneration paid to a divine being or power. However, worship in schools will necessarily be of a different character from worship amongst a group with beliefs in common. The legislation reflects this difference in referring to 'collective worship' rather than 'corporate worship'. (para. 57)

Collective worship and assembly are distinctive activities. Although they may take place as part of the same gathering, the difference between the two should be clear. Collective worship can, nevertheless, be related to the day to day life, aspirations and concerns of the school. (para. 58)

'Taking part' in collective worship implies more than simply passive attendance. It follows that an act of collective worship should be capable of eliciting a response from pupils, even though on a particular occasion some of the pupils may not feel able actively to identify with the act of worship. (para. 59)

The debate continues. I have deliberately used full quotations since the debate over RE and CW has both challenged and affected Christian education. State schools continue to teach about Christianity. In 2004, the Qualifications and Curriculum Authority (QCA), the government agency responsible for the curriculum in state schools, issued a framework for teaching RE in state schools for all children from three to 19 years.[8] It stated that RE has a significant role in the promotion of spiritual, moral, social and cultural development. The focus is on 'ultimate questions'[9] and ethical issues. The purpose is: to enable pupils to appreciate their own and others' beliefs; to gain a clear understanding of the significance of religions and beliefs in the world today; to have a sense of self-worth and of their uniqueness as human beings; to appreciate the importance of forming and maintaining relationships; to engage in 'learning about religion' (the nature of religion, beliefs, way of life) and 'learning from religion' (reflection on, and response to, pupils' own experience in light of their learning). The teaching about Jesus, although made a priority, has not been particularly successful. Research in 2006 from the University of Exeter stated, 'Jesus appeared to children to be a rather pallid figure, the subject of respect yet also indifference. He was perceived as significant but was also the subject of misunderstanding, sometimes confusion.'[10]

I have noted social changes: the diminishing numbers attending church and Sunday school, the influence of RE and CW in both state and church schools; the challenge to didactic education and the promotion of new learning theories arising from Piagetian insights; the rise of organizations for children founded on Christian principles. The latter have increased with mid-week activities and holiday clubs. On a Sunday within some congregations there is a Junior Church or Sunday school (usually at the same time as worship, though it does not necessarily include worship), which offers Christian education, inheriting some of Raikes's fervour and principles, though there has been a move to experiential learning, beginning and ending with the child's experience. The responsibility for Christian education, for the children of the Church's families, clearly rests with parents and the congregations to which they belong. Churches also have a continuing commitment to church schools.[11] The pastoral care of children, their nurture and teaching go hand in hand.

Assess the significance of the Sunday school movement in the past and today for the pastoral care of children.

NURTURE

Pastoral care is first of all nurture in the sense of belonging to a Christian community, the celebration of its distinctive identity in worship in company with adults on the same journey (see Chapter 8).

Second, nurture is about the attitudes of those who nurture (see Chapter 5). These need to be welcoming, accepting each child as he or she is at the present moment. In nurturing we are open and walk alongside the child, recognizing the importance of each one's stage of development, his or her joys and celebrations but also mistakes, disappointment, failures and violence. Nurture remembers the significance of the early years of a child's life that shape and determine later life and attitudes.

Third, nurture is educational, including a body of knowledge, understanding the Scriptures and the tradition of the Church, but in such a way that children can find their own path and meaning for life. One metaphor for the nurture of children is the giving of a paintbox, rather than a painting, so that they possess the 'colours', the resources, to shape their future discipleship.

THE AIM OF CHRISTIAN EDUCATION

What is the aim of Christian education for children within the Church? Answers will be myriad. A central principle is that Christian education must reflect theological understanding (what it means to be human, the nature of the child, God's relationship with humanity) and have educational validity (an open search for truth and respect for the integrity, freedom and decision-making of the learner). It is about helping children to respond to the story of Jesus within the context of finding meaning in their own lives. It is being inspired by a vision of a life of human flourishing. This will be a journey with others in the community of faith, leading to a life that reflects the person and mission of Jesus, sustained by the community and worship. It is the beginning of a lifelong journey.

Children's engagement with the Christian story

Christian education involves an engagement with the biblical and historical stories of God's activity within the community of faith. These stories are the heritage of our children. They are significant for pastoral care since, first, they feed and nourish both the imagination and the intellect of children. Second, they give them the resources (language, concepts and symbols) to develop a critical faculty for living and facing this life's challenges (hurts, sin, identity, mortality, societal structures that diminish humans). Third, they initiate them into a world-view that helps them to make sense of the reality of life, which includes both good and evil. Fourth, stories form and feed children's spiritual and religious development within their search for their own identity. Nurture is one aspect, but we need to recognize children's right to choose for themselves. Fifth, stories are a stimulus to personal discovery through open 'wondering questions', such as those used in Godly Play. Stories are not channels for moralizing; as adults, by adding our interpretation, we may unwittingly obscure a child's view of God. Sixth, the stories are those of the community of God in the past (Scriptures) and today. This is the inheritance of our children and links them with the past and the experience of an ongoing community of faith today. The child is nourished by, and participates in, a continuing faith community for whom the story, particularly that of the life, death and resurrection of Jesus, gives inspiration and a vision of how life could be when lived close to God. Christian education begins with the experience of each child and leads to him or her discovering how to live in the light of faith.

Teachers

Much Christian education of the past was didactic; power was held by male clergy and used to 'control' congregations. Educated adult congregations now challenge such learning styles, but for some children the style has continued. Children do not have the same power, experience, cognitive ability or skills as adults have to question their teachers. The content of the faith has also been an issue, with the hierarchy of the Church unable to trust lay people to interpret the Scriptures for themselves. Some Christian groups believe that it is wrong to question the truths of the Bible, and so they discourage children's questions. A clerical colleague was shocked when an adolescent asked him if Jesus was gay. Within the youngster's rudimentary knowledge of Jesus' disciples as male and lack of knowledge of first-century culture, it was an appropriate question. Somehow, we are fearful of exploration, but Jesus the teacher shows us the way. He offered stories and left his listeners to make sense of them for their own lives; he turned the question back to the questioner (Luke 10.25–29); he accompanied those who were searching for meaning, clarifying their thinking (Luke 24.13–35). The teaching of Jesus set his listeners free to respond (the rich young ruler freely turned away); it is indoctrination, a fixed viewpoint that enslaves. We have also forgotten Jesus' promise that the Spirit will lead into all truth (John 16.13).

In many churches today the education for children is theologically weak and uninteresting and lacks consistency. There is insufficient reflection on the formation and nurture of children within the church. For some, working with children is considered a 'second-rate' ministry, to be left by male clergy to women. Children are considered the future church, not the present, so they are not a priority. Teachers may be ill-prepared. Sometimes teenagers are sent to work with the younger children, simply to retain their attendance, while they themselves are not spiritually 'fed'. As mentioned in Chapter 5, working with children is a vocation not given to everyone; preparation, support, training and resources are needed for those taking on this responsibility. The work of Christian education should be a focus and regularly discussed by the local church; it is too important to be left to chance, because it is at heart concerned with the formation of a Christian identity of all God's children. It reclaims the Christian culture evidenced in art, music, buildings and literature which has been clouded by our consumerist society.

There are other problems with the traditional didactic methods of Christian education. First, in such forms of learning the adult, as the authority, transmitted knowledge to the learner. The power imbalance between teacher and pupil diminishes the effectiveness of learning, whereas within a faith community child and adult should be travellers together. Second, a didactic method leads to the passivity of the learner. It is known that in this method, after three hours only 70 per cent is retained, after three days only 10 per cent and after three weeks only 5 per cent. This is a huge waste. Third, learning is concentrated on accurate content rather than skills and the imagination; it therefore loses impact. Fourth, didactic teaching tends to give the same material to all children and expects the same level of understanding and response. It ignores individual differences in learning styles and the different experiences that each child brings to learning. To be effective as Christian educators we need to be aware of the insights of educational psychology.

METHODS OF TEACHING AND LEARNING IN EDUCATION

Paulo Freire (1921–97) challenged traditional education methods in his book *Pedagogy of the Oppressed*. His emphasis was on dialogue signifying respect for one another in the pupil–teacher relationship, in contrast to what he describes as the 'banking' type of education, where the educator 'deposits' knowledge into the child. Freire used the metaphor of 'Easter' to explore how the power divide between teachers and learners could be transcended. He believed that the educator had to *die* in order to be born again and to educate alongside, both to teach and to learn from the person being taught. 'An educator is a person who has to live in the deep significance of Easter.'[12]

For Freire education was about praxis: it deepened understanding and made a difference to building community, leading to actions for justice and human flourishing. Freire believed that education was the key for those who were oppressed and had no voice. His is a pedagogy of hope. He wrote of *conscientization*,[13] that is, developing a consciousness in people that has the power to transform their thinking and attitudes. His thinking is particularly applicable to teaching children in the Church. Frequently, children's thinking is oppressed by didactic teaching and not considered significant. Their questions are thought to be inappropriate. Children can be affirmed and made aware of their significance as children of God. There is also a need to awaken adults to the needs and nurture of children by affirming the present stage of development of each child.

Learning is closely linked with development. Development is about the way a child functions. It is dependent on his or her physical progress, ability to think and observations of others. As Christians we desire that our children 'grow in grace'. We hope and pray that they will be formed in the image of Christ. Learning is provoked. It happens at a time and place when a particular problem arises for a child and needs to be tackled.[14] For the Christian parent learning is not morally neutral (no learning is neutral, though that is the claim frequently made by educationalists). Learning is a searching for truth and a belief that truth, though perhaps imperfectly and partially grasped, is found in the story of Jesus.

MODELS OF LEARNING THEORY

Transmission model

This is the theory that children learn what they are shown by adults. Locke believed that a child was a *tabula rasa*, a clean sheet, which could be imprinted by adults. Today the followers of B. F. Skinner, a behaviourist psychologist, reward appropriate behaviour through the positive reinforcement of praising good behaviour. Children recognize that doing things in a certain way brings advantages such as enjoyment and satisfaction. These reinforce their behaviour, until a point is reached when rewards are not necessary. This method of learning is the traditional, didactic approach.

Leave it to nature: a laissez-faire model

This theory emerged from Rousseau, who thought that children learnt naturally when the time was right for them. Adults help children to learn by providing a suitable environment. This method sees children as interactive in their own learning. Sigmund Freud, his daughter Anna, her student Erik Erikson, and Melanie Klein held that development in children unfolds naturally. When, for example, a child suffers a trauma, self-healing happens through experiencing the power of love, security, play and being valued found in a normal childhood.

The social constructivist/interactionist approach

Kant believed that a child's learning was an interaction between the developing child and the environment; he thus used both the previous models. Piaget believed children were active learners; however, he emphasized cognitive development and learning, making no mention of social and emotional development. Vygotsky believed social relationships were at the heart of learning. He argued that learning is a result of the social interactions between the child and those around him or her (peers, teachers, parents). Language was an important tool for the child to organize perceptions and actions through a process of reflecting and seeing in a new way. Development takes place through children's internalizing of their culture: language, art, play, dancing, music. It is the interactions between children, the significant people in their environment and their culture which promote learning.[15]

A central concept for Vygotsky is the *zone of proximal development* (ZDP), the distance between the child's present and potential level of development. Vygotsky argued that a child learns from other people who are more knowledgeable; this learning has instruction at its heart. The 'expert' (more knowledgeable one, who could be a teacher or a member of the peer group) intervenes with a challenge to new learning, beyond a child's existing development but within the ZDP, so that the child accomplishes learning he or she could not do alone.

Jerome Bruner is a US educationalist who has built on Vygotsky's work.[16] Bruner wrote of learning as a *spiral curriculum*, with increasingly sophisticated levels of understanding resulting from ideas which were revisited. This implied that young children could grasp ideas in an intuitive way and later return to the idea using more complex modes of thinking. For example, a six-year-old understood the parable of the Prodigal Son as one of paternal negligence, responding to the story with the statement, 'My Dad would not have let me go on my own.' Later, with more 'life experience' of a father who let go and gave the child space for his own decisions, the child could return to the same parable with new insight; meaning now emerges such as that of a generous father. Bruner believed that understanding the structure of a discipline (principles and concepts) was significant, rather than simply mastering the facts.

Bruner thought that adults could help a child learn anything by a method he called *scaffolding*. The adult extends and supports the child's learning, as adult and child learn together. The imagery of scaffolding suggests that the child is not asked to build all at once. It takes note of the child's existing level and how far he or she can progress with help. Instruction is necessary. The concept of scaffolding is parallel to Vygotsky's ZDP. The theories of learning of Vygotsky and Bruner share a number of key concepts:

- Social relationships are at the heart of learning
- Adults intervene to enable the child to learn more
- Instruction is at the heart of learning
- Language is an important tool
- Learning is through the child internalizing her culture
- Learning is the interaction between the child, significant people and culture
- Learning is spiral in that revisiting a concept increases levels of depth and understanding.

How useful are Vygotsky's and Bruner's insights for the Christian education of children?

EDUCATION IN THE FAITH COMMUNITY

These concepts are significant for the nurture of children in the faith through teaching, which is a facet of their pastoral care. The insights of Piaget, Vygotsky and Bruner, together with those of Freire, encourage a different type of learning which uses: active learning; the senses (objects to look at, feel and explore); the imagination (stories); different ways of learning (visual, aural, kinaesthetic); exploring together using 'scaffolding' (adult teacher and child working together); using the child's cultural heritage (art, play, dancing, music); open, exploring questions (such as the wondering questions of Godly Play). If we use these methods we discover that sense is made by the child, in relating new learning to existing learning and experience. In this way Piaget's schemas are constructed in the child. However, Piaget's concept of cognitive intelligence, which limited abstract thinking to the adolescent and adult years, has been challenged by the research of Howard Gardner and his theory of multiple intelligences. Gardner's work is marked by his desire for his own children to understand the world and to help create the conditions to change it. Gardner states, 'We must figure out how intelligence and morality can work together.'[17]

The research of Coles, Hay and Nye, Cavalletti, and Berryman indicates that children are innately and intuitively spiritual and religious, grappling with Christian concepts even if they find traditional religious language difficult. This is understandable, given the nature of religious language. Religion refers to ideas such as God, sin, Holy Spirit, love and forgiveness, which are not objects that can be seen and touched. The concepts exist as inferences, intangible but also profoundly real. Psychologists call this 'cognitive complexity'. Yet complex religious ideas, normally thought to be beyond children, can be accessed through a 'hierarchical' order of learning that begins with the experience of the child and progresses through image (objects to handle), to story, and finally attains to 'abstract' religious ideas. This happens over a period of years for a child, encouraged by the 'scaffolding' provided by adults and the 'spiral curriculum'. This may inform a way of teaching faith that does not produce literalists or a naive faith that is jettisoned in adolescence or adulthood. For example, Cavalletti used the child's experience of being loved by a parent, the image of the shepherd (a model of a shepherd) and the biblical story of the Good Shepherd to help form in children the idea of God's knowledge and care of them.

The insights of educational psychology are reflected in faith communities. Jewish culture is expressed in the Hebrew Scriptures, food laws and festivals. Children imbibe this rich culture in their daily living. Methods of learning to 'nurture and teach' children in faith are illustrated in the Jewish approach to Passover, where children learn through: being with adults; instruction; the senses; and through the culture of stories. At the annual Passover meal, a child asks, 'Why are we doing this? Why is this night special?' The environment is the Seder table laid by the parent with symbolic objects (for example, the salt water to remember the tears; the lamb shank to recall the animal sacrificed; the unleavened bread). The environment is the family of faith. As the family joke and laugh, touch, taste and eat, the Passover story is told, extending children's knowledge and nurturing them in a central story of their faith with their community.[18]

One Maundy Thursday, a Passover meal was preceded by a workshop in which adults worked together with a group of children to prepare the food, set the table, make music, hear the story and make a Haggadah book telling the story of the plagues and the deliverance from Egypt. At the meal the children asked the traditional questions and adults told the story, using all the symbols of the meal that the children had laid out on the table. We ate a meal together as we remembered the story. The passage from St John about Jesus' last meal with his friends was read, and we remembered his words and his washing of the disciples' feet (John 13.1–17). As the reader and I finished the foot-washing of two chosen adults, two of the children spontaneously came to have their feet washed too. They had learnt through the experience of the day and become part of the story.

The learner

Children are active interpreters of what they see and hear; their interpretation is different from that of adults, yet it is valid for them. On occasions a 'block' in learning may occur, when new learning contradicts previous learning. For example, a young child's understanding of God as creator is challenged when he later comes to learn about dinosaurs and evolution. How can these apparently opposing world-views be reconciled? The teacher has a role to play in helping the child experiment and find a new level of understanding. The resolution is through the process of 'play', that is, 'trying out ideas', risk, freedom to make mistakes, again and again, until there is a conclusion. The result may mean the jettisoning of the previous learning or a re-engagement between it and the new, leading to growth. This process will take time and patience and is likely to be painful. The help of parents and teachers is important, provoking through questions, giving new material, and instructing (Vygotsky's scaffolding). Children return to the Christian festivals each year, biblical stories are repeated, yet at each occasion there can be a deepening of understanding and response in the learner (Bruner's spiral curriculum).

Content: stories sacred and secular

If we engage children, they will interpret the Bible as far as they are able, bringing their abilities, limitations, feelings and experiences of life to make sense of it for themselves. In turn, the Bible may inform and challenge them. To know the Bible is not simply a question of knowing its contents; rather, it involves acting upon

it, interacting with it, asking questions of it, making interpretations of it and playing with it, imagining oneself in the story,
choosing to be formed and informed by it. It is about the forming
of an identity and about being transformed by the Spirit, a
process which is continuous throughout life for children and
adults. Gretchen Wolff Pritchard is helpful here:

> We encounter the Bible not as a source of rules and formulas,
> but as a story – and it is a story about us. We are far from home
> in a world which is full of terror, and we cannot help ourselves,
> but neither can we give up on vision and be reconciled to things
> as they are.[19]

At all ages of development children relish stories and can enter
into them imaginatively. Stories are important, although a literalism may be evident in the way young children interpret them.[20]
Here the concept of hierarchy (see above) is helpful.

> Christian education is not the communication of correct views
> about what the various works and words of Jesus might mean,
> rather it is the stocking of the imagination with the icons of
> these works and words themselves. It is most successfully
> accomplished, therefore, not by catechisms that purport to
> produce understanding, but by stories that hang the icons,
> understood or not, on the walls of the mind.[21]

The Bible must be handled sensitively. It covers a historical
period of approximately 2,500 years and a further 2,000 years
separate us from the New Testament. Children do not realize this
(incidentally, nor do many adult Christians). It may say nothing,
or a number of contradictory things, in response to issues of living
today, though it gives clues and signposts to contemporary life. It
is a book of profound adult experiences of faith, failure and inspiration, within the relationship of God and humanity. We must not
trivialize it: for example, the love of a parent for a child is a tiny
glimpse of, but cannot be equated with, the forgiving and creative
love of God. It uses different types of material, including law,
narrative and story. It is not a storybook but a record of adult
experience, though much of it uses a story form. These stories
were part of an oral tradition for years until they are written
down, so they are best told by a storyteller who draws the listeners into the experience.

When using biblical material with children we need to ask ourselves several questions. Why am I telling this story? Is the
context I am using appropriate to the context and meaning of
the original story? Are the concepts appropriate to the age of the
child I am teaching? Is there a better story to use?[22] We need to
use the parts of the Bible which resonate with the children and
help them to interpret experience and deepen understanding.
The key is the experience of the child. We need to take care to
select material whose language, style and concepts are within the
present stage of development of the child. When we consider the
meanings of some of the stories we use with children (Noah's Ark,
the sacrifice of Isaac, Moses in the bulrushes, the call of Samuel),
they are chosen because they are about other children, or animals, not because of the intrinsic meaning (e.g. Noah's ark is a
story about sin, salvation and judgement).

Parables are good stories and in the Bible their meaning is
never explained. They hold up a mirror to everyday life and challenge us to reflect and make meaning of life. This natural capacity of the story to speak to the child means it is not necessary to
explain stories. Let the parable relate to the child's experience as
it is being told. In hearing and telling stories, children will
discover layers of meaning for themselves.

Other stories will include characters from Church history such
as Gregory and Augustine (how Christianity came to Britain);
those who found faith hard (Ignatius and Benedict); those who
challenged their society with their lives (St Francis of Assisi, St
Alban, Oscar Romero); those who are prominent Christians today
(Desmond Tutu).

Much contemporary children's 'secular' literature also engages
with deep theological issues, such as identity, the conquest of evil,
meaning in life, and can sustain a child's spiritual and religious
growth. Examples include Maurice Sendak's picture book *Where
the Wild Things Are*, J. K. Rowling's Harry Potter series, Philip
Pullman's trilogy *His Dark Materials*, C. S. Lewis's *Chronicles of
Narnia* and G. P. Taylor's *Shadowmancer*. Children's literature is
about the freedom to experiment in safety, to sort out identity. In
good secular literature authors employ fantasy and magic, trans-
porting the child to 'other worlds' different from their own, where
child characters face overwhelming conflicts.[23] Children are connected intimately with 'a free-floating world of the imagination.
Their observable, active fantasy life, their fluid make-believe play
seem to give them access to a world of wisdom.'[24] Imagination is a

function of the right hemisphere of the brain, which is responsible for the non-verbal, intuitive, imaginative and visualization. Through the imagination of the writer a child is able to face the challenge of his own life.

> Children are much better than adults at projecting themselves into stories. They relish the chance to visit a 'transitional space', loosening their grip on 'real' time and on their ego, to allow inner reality and outer reality to meet and dialogue in a safe way.[25]

Story helps the child face the 'giants' in life's path, confronting his monsters such as greed and jealousy within, and bullying and isolation without. Play has the same function.

Role of the teacher

What, then, is the role of the teacher in Christian education (parent, cleric, Sunday school teacher)?[26] Socrates used the image of the 'midwife', who brings life to birth. The teacher is a participant in the birth of faith. First, teachers choose the material to be taught, reflecting the developmental stage and present experience of each child. It is helpful on Sunday if this teaching is also linked with the Christian year. Much of the content will be stories which engage the imagination. Second, the child must be provided with a safe space so that he or she is open to new ideas. We must be prepared to adventure with the child. Third, we need to help the child to make sense of the Bible. Fourth, we must respect children's questions and statements while probing and stretching their thinking. Fifth, we need to give children freedom and time to explore the Bible, putting it alongside their own experience. Sixth, we need to provide resources for creativity and the developing of the imagination – paints, pencils, wood, clay, dressing-up clothes for drama, computer technology which can help in engagement with the story.

SUMMARY POINTS FOR DISCUSSION

- Today's Sunday school inherits certain principles from Raikes.

- Christian education contributes to the pastoral care of children through giving symbols, images, stories in the formation of a Christian identity.

- Learning styles are informed by child development stages.

- Christian education can be enriched by the insights of educational psychology.

- The Christian educator works alongside the child.

CHAPTER EIGHT

Pastoral Care within Worship and Sacraments

Jane, aged eight, dashes into church ahead of her father and step-mother. Most Sundays she spends with Dad, though during the week she lives with Mum. 'Sunday school is just about to begin in the church room. Would you like to join the other children?' asks the churchwarden. The church room is entered through a door in the church. Jane declines and returns to sit with her father. She sits near the end of the pew so that she can see the service. A story is included in the sermon, which Jane enjoys. It is a eucharistic service: the prayer is said from the nave so that everyone can see and hear. As the bread and wine are distributed, we see, for the first time, the Sunday school children, who join the line to receive. The children then sit together at the front with their teachers. After the Blessing the churchwarden reads the notices and asks the children about their lesson. Today a ten-year-old reads aloud a prayer that she has written about the death of her guinea-pig. The congregation clap. After the service Jane wants to talk about her day with her father.

Think of your earliest memory of church as a child:

- **the people**
- **the building**
- **the atmosphere**
- **the content of worship.**

What might it be like to be a toddler, a three-, five-, eight- or eleven-year-old in the church?

Children are individuals. Jane was given a choice and decided to stay with her parents and the adults rather than be with the other children. She likes it that way. The children enjoy their activities and learning together; sometimes we can hear their excited voices. The children say that it is boring when they are present for the whole eucharistic service, and the congregation are not keen to have them present throughout, since they say their presence can be disruptive, but they do want the children to come to church. They bring vitality, freshness and creativity. The congregation always clap the children's contribution, whatever it is. In this way they believe they encourage the children. However, on this occasion, in response to a child's distress and heartfelt prayer, another reaction might have been more appropriate.

This chapter builds on pastoral care through Christian education. It looks at thinking and practice in the past and notes how worship and sacraments contribute to pastoral care today.

A LOOK AT THE PAST

Support for children within the Church has been patchy. Jerome Berryman states that today:

> We idealize children and yet we demonize them. We celebrate a 'year of the child' and exclude children from worship. We value them; yet spend relatively little time or money on their needs. We tout evangelism to add members, but we do not count children, already present in the Church, to be worth 'evangelizing' or even the hospitality we give to strangers.[1]

How were children received by the Church in the past? Can insights from the past help us today?

ORIGINS OF PASTORAL CARE OF CHILDREN

Jesus lived in a Jewish and Gentile culture which considered children of little significance. Babies were aborted and abandoned. Children were of no worth until they became rational adults. But children were of ultimate significance to Jesus (see Chapter 2). Jesus was innovative in giving meaning to the child's present life. Defying his disciples' attempt to prevent children being brought to him, he took them in his arms and blessed them (Mark 10.13–16). Sadly, the Epistles, which reflect the emerging

Christian community, make few references to children, who were not a priority. The infant Christian communities of the first century recognized the importance of the home for nurturing in the faith. Leaders in the early Church encouraged households in the faith formation of their young. Clement wrote in 96 CE, 'Let us instruct the young in the fear of God . . . Let our children share in the instruction which is in Christ' (1 Clement 26.6, 8).[2] The *Didache* asked parents, 'to bring them [children] up in the fear of the Lord' (*Didache* 4.9). Polycarp, Bishop of Smyrna (69–155 CE), told men to instruct their wives 'to educate the children in the fear of God'. 'Fear' relates to 'awe', a word used of worship. Children shared with adults, suggesting a mutuality and a status of worth was given to children. Polycarp at his martyrdom proclaimed, 'For eighty-six years I have been Christ's servant.' Justin Martyr, in a defence of Christianity (155 CE), remembered 'many men and women of sixty and seventy years of age, [who] became disciples of Christ from their childhood' (Justin Martyr, *First Apology* 1.15). This was a testimony to faithful parenting in the early years of a child's life. The accountability of parents to God is found in the *Apostolic Constitutions*:

> Fathers, educate your children in the Lord and bring them up in the discipline and instruction of the Lord . . . He who neglects to admonish and instruct his son hates his own child . . . by the carelessness of their parents, those who begat them will be responsible for their souls.

Similarly, Chrysostom (347–407) in *Comparison and Against the Opponents*, 132–3.B73, and Jerome (348–420), in *Epistle 107 To Laeta*, rebuked lazy parents, pointing out that their indolence risked the soul of their child. There was a concern for the pastoral care of children through teaching and sharing in worship within families and the Christian community.

ORIGINS OF THE BAPTISM OF CHILDREN

The policy of 'not counting the children' (Matt. 14.21) means that we are unsure of the relationship between baptism and children. The Acts depicts the baptism of believing adults. The only hints that infant baptism was practised are Paul's reference to the children of Christian parents being 'holy' (1 Cor. 7.14); baptism as a spiritual counterpart of circumcision (Col.

2.11–12); and household baptisms (Acts 16.15, 33; 18.8; 1 Cor. 1.16). Some scholars argue from these hints that infants were baptized from the earliest days of the Church: other scholars suggest a later date. Tertullian (160–220) questioned what appeared to be an existing practice. He wanted infant baptism postponed on the grounds that childhood was the 'age of innocence'. Children need to learn, to 'become able to know Christ', before their baptism (*On Baptism*, 18). Hippolytus (170–236) noted that children were the first to be baptized before the adults (*Apostolic Tradition*, 200 CE). Origen (185–254) described the baptism of infants as an apostolic tradition, yet asked, 'Why should children be baptized for the remission of sins?' and 'At what point had they sinned?' He declared that infants had not sinned because they had no power to decide between right and wrong. Cyprian (200–58) was concerned about the timing of baptism, insisting on the baptism of the newborn: 'Baptism confers remission of original sin so should not be delayed' (*Epistle 58, To Fidus on the Baptism of Infants*). It seems that teaching about original sin influenced the status of the child, becoming a major reason for the adoption of infant baptism. Augustine linked original sin with children and justified the practice of infant baptism. His argument was as follows: baptism cleanses from sin; even infants show sinful tendencies, though they have not themselves sinned (Rom. 9.11), therefore they must have inherited sin through conception to account for these sinful tendencies; baptism, the remedy for sin, should be administered as soon as possible after birth.

The Fathers of the Eastern (Orthodox) Church, Gregory of Nazianzus (330–89), Gregory of Nyssa (330–95) and Chrysostom, believed children did not inherit sin or personal guilt. However, baptism marked the beginning of a spiritual struggle and of growth in holiness. Children benefited from baptism, which incorporated them into the Church and provided care and discipline. Infant baptism became the normal practice at some point, probably in the fifth century.

What of the souls of children dying without baptism? Gregory of Nyssa wrote a treatise *On Infants' Early Deaths*. Infant mortality was high: it is estimated that less that half those born alive survived to a fifth birthday. Gregory saw the issue as innocent suffering versus belief in a just God, theodicy. The Church taught that infants were outside God's care if unbaptized. This was not consistent with belief in a just and merciful God. The justice of

God and children's eternal destiny mattered. These were pastoral concerns. A church historian states:

> I doubt that at any time before or after the first three decades of the fifth century were a group of celibate men so concerned with babies. Whether 'babies-in-theory', or flesh-and-blood babies, is difficult to judge: the passion with which they detail the sufferings and death of infants, their shrieks and wails upon receiving the baptismal water, might suggest the latter.[3]

Church leaders and theologians cared about children.

ORIGINS OF CHILDREN'S PARTICIPATION IN THE EUCHARIST

Little is known about the presence of children at the Eucharist. The Eucharist was the food of the baptized, so if children were baptized they received the bread and wine. Paul describes Christ as the 'Passover lamb' (1 Cor. 5.7). If the Eucharist was understood as a Passover by Jewish Christians then children might be expected to be present, as in the Jewish festival (Exod. 12.21–7). It may be that the issue was uncontroversial and that baptized children participated with their families. The first evidence of a child participating in the Eucharist is from Cyprian. He recounts an incident when a child was taken to a pagan sacrifice by her nurse, without the parents' knowledge, where she ate sacrificial food. Later, at a Christian service, she became distressed and refused 'the cup'. The deacon persisted, but, when the girl drank, she vomited. She was not able to speak, so she was of a young age (Cyprian, *On the Lapsed* 25). But it seemed normal for a child to receive the Eucharist and no comment is made about that. Cyprian also wrote of adult Christians under persecution who participated in pagan sacrifices, thus compromising their faith; this affected their children, who, Cyprian notes, were innocent yet had their spiritual nourishment polluted. In the fourth-century *Apostolic Constitutions* the order specified for receiving the Eucharist was the male officials, then female officials then children, followed by the congregation (*Apostolic Constitutions* 8.13). Augustine reasoned that if children were baptized then they should have the life of Christ in them, through participating in the Eucharist. Within the Eastern Church the child was baptized, anointed and communicated from birth. This practice has continued in the Orthodox tradition, honouring the significance of children and reflecting Jesus' acceptance of them.

ORIGINS OF CONFIRMATION OF CHILDREN

The origin of confirmation is obscure. It has been traced to Jesus laying his hands on children (Mark 10.16); or breathing on the disciples (John 20.22); the laying on of hands by the apostles following baptism (Acts 8.15; 19.6); and to the early Church (Tertullian, *On Baptism* 198 and Hippolytus, *Apostolic Tradition* 215). Early on, the meaning of confirmation came to be associated with the gift of the Holy Spirit through the laying on of hands. No distinction was made between infants and adults; babies were baptized and confirmed. Gradually it became normal practice that only the bishop could confirm. During the Middle Ages confirmation was delayed until the years of 'discretion', both because of the practical difficulty of bishops travelling to confirm all babies and because there was a sense that baptism itself conveyed the grace of the Holy Spirit and was sufficient for salvation. This led to a neglect of confirmation, which was later countered by teaching that confirmation was necessary in order to become fully Christian. Archbishop Peckham in the thirteenth century stated that no one should be admitted to Holy Communion until they had been confirmed. Various English church councils insisted that children must be confirmed by the age of two, three or seven, as a result of which seven or older became the age of confirmation. A theology developed to match these changes, teaching that baptism 'restores innocence' and gives 'new birth', while confirmation gives the strength to live the Christian life and witness. Later the Council of Trent (1566) stated that seven to 12 years was the appropriate age for confirmation, preferring the latter.

REDISCOVERY OF CHILDREN AND COMMUNION

In 1930, through the Parish Communion Movement, communion became the main Sunday service. Children could not receive communion if they were not confirmed, even though they were baptized and stood at the altar rail with their parents. This renewed thinking on the relationship of children and communion. The Ely Report of 1971 concluded that baptism was a complete sacrament of initiation, which admitted children to communion prior to confirmation. Through their baptism children were members of the body of Christ. There was, however, still no change in church practice. In 1985 *Communion before Confirmation?* (known as the Knaresborough Report) concluded, as had the Ely Report, that baptized children might receive communion before confirmation, but it raised questions about children's understanding, suggesting that they were too young to understand fully what they were doing and might be desecrating holy things. This ignored Piaget's research into child development psychology and Goldman's on children and religion.

The first world Anglican Liturgical Consultation met to address the subject of children and the Eucharist in Boston, Massachusetts, from 29 to 31 July 1985. The 'Boston Statement', which followed the consultation, called on all Anglican provinces to follow Canada, the USA and New Zealand in admitting young children to communion on the basis of their baptism. Confirmation, the Statement asserted, had a pastoral role in the renewal of faith, but was neither the completion of baptism nor necessary for admission to communion. The Church of England Synod stalled. Parish priests responded pastorally to children by giving a sweet, or 'blessed' but 'non-consecrated' bread, allowing parents to share bread with their children or by giving the child a priestly blessing. Within the Anglican Church it could be said that children were insignificant and powerless, with their spiritual needs unfed: their baptism was considered insufficient for full membership of the Church.

The General Synod's report *On the Way: Towards an Integrated Approach to Christian Initiation* (1994) noted the increase in adult, and decrease in infant, baptisms. It commented that adult candidates entered 'faith through a relationship with someone rather than an evangelistic event', had 'little sense of sin', 'found fellowship an important factor in their spiritual journey', came 'to faith within the Church rather than finding faith outside and then entering', and received 'the gospel at a non cerebral level – through human relationships and pastoral care, through mystery and emotions'. Children were not mentioned. However, there are parallels between adult motivation and children who enter a faith community. Through baptism, children are made welcome, attend church and have faith. Children, like adults, have little sense of sin. If they find a welcome in a church they stay; they are attracted by the friendship of the community, not necessarily the gospel message. Children too have a sense of the spiritual which is not cerebral, but intuitive and symbolic. However, these characteristics of children were ignored and not considered evidence of faith, though shared with adults coming to faith.

In January 1997 the House of Bishops issued guidelines on the admission of children to communion before confirmation, though some considered it a departure from 'the inherited norm'. 'Admission' could be introduced at the diocesan bishop's discretion. The bishops acknowledged there were no theological objections to baptized children receiving communion: their concerns were about 'reverence' and 'a right understanding of the sacrament', questions which might also be asked of adults. The understanding of a child is different from that of an adult but this does not mean that the former is invalid. It appeared that baptized children must understand intellectually before they received communion. Finally, in February 2006 General Synod approved the *Children and Holy Communion Regulations*, which were to apply from 15 June 2006. Permission, or not, is now to be given by the diocesan bishop, on receipt of a letter supported by the parochial church council. The bishop must be satisfied that the preparation, continuing nurture and encouragement of children are adequate. The incumbent is requested to maintain a register of children admitted to communion. A certificate of attendance may be given to a child so that he or she may attend communion in another church (for example, when on holiday).

Current baptismal liturgy found in *Common Worship: Initiation Services* (1997/8) includes a section headed 'The rediscovery of baptism'. It recognizes that in a secular society baptism is generally treated as a 'sort of birth rite'. However, it reasserts the meaning of baptism as pointing Christians to their true identity, character and calling. For much of history, baptism has reflected the metaphor of 'cleansing from sin'. Another metaphor is a new birth, on the basis of John 3.4–5. Baptism is understood as the starting-point of a journey which will constantly need to be reaffirmed and sustained through nurture and learning, but unless it is accepted as entry to communion children are not taken seriously and their nurture is often forgotten.

What from the history of the Church is helpful in thinking about the pastoral care of the child in the Church today?

It seems that in the early centuries of Christian history children were significant, though not always for reasons which we would consider appropriate today. Children belonged within their own families, and their parents were encouraged by Church leaders to see childcare as a vocation. Children were baptized, nurtured and nourished with bread and wine within the community of faith. The theologians and Church leaders in the intervening years, who were on the whole silent about children in the Church, were challenged in the twenty-first century. Recent discussion has been dominated by the debate on children and communion and, as the last chapter noted, children and Christian education.

CHILDREN IN CHURCH TODAY

How do children come to be in church on a Sunday? Many come as members of Christian families worshipping together regularly week by week. A child may be baptized as a baby, even though his or her parents are not regular worshipping members of a church. Subsequently the family may bring the child on special occasions such as festivals (Christmas and Easter) or informal services (a crib service, Christingle, Mothering Sunday). The child may join Sunday school. A child may simply walk in to see what is going on in church, like it, and stay. A grandparent may bring a child. A child may come to a family baptism, wedding or funeral. Sometimes a school friend brings a child to church. A child may come into contact with the church through attendance at a church school and attend a school carol service or end-of-term service in the church.

Children also come to church in the week. Church members, together with members of the local community, provide a range of activities for children using church premises. There are mothers and toddlers groups, nursery groups, midweek children's clubs and uniformed organizations. There are children's workshops and holiday clubs. Around 375,000 children aged between five and 16 years attend and more than 100,000 volunteers run children's activity groups sponsored by the Church of England during any one week.[4] Some of these activities include a form of worship. Twenty-five per cent of primary age children attend a church school. Other schools may visit the church as part of the National Curriculum. These children receive religious education and experience collective worship.[5] The church, through its individual members, the body of Christ, is at work with children in the community throughout the week, expressing its pastoral care.

HOW DOES THE CONGREGATION THINK ABOUT CHILDREN?

There is ambivalence towards children in many congregations; children are understood in different ways. One way is to see them as 'mini adults' and childhood as simply a preface to adulthood. Worship becomes an adult activity in which children may participate if they conform to adult patterns, demands and expectations. They must be seen and not heard. A second way is to see children as 'raw material' to be moulded and educated and finally transformed into adult Christian believers. Children are considered 'passive' receivers, with little sense of a mutual relationship between children and adults. Third, children may be seen as 'unsaved', in need of rescuing from their own sinfulness and from an evil world. Fourth, they may be seen as innocent: their simplicity and innocence must be preserved and protected. 'Christian children all must be / mild, obedient, good as he.' Fifth, in some congregations children are accepted as children, with their noise, enthusiasm and untidiness. What is the truth in these perceptions?

Children for real

If children are understood as 'mini adults', who must conform and behave like adults, their present childhood is ignored. In church they need to be themselves – children – but this does not mean that they should not learn to be aware of the needs of worshipping adults. Worship is for all, adults and children. It is helpful to introduce children to church from babyhood. Gradually, they recognize that worship is a particular and special occasion, different from anything else they experience. Mothers can have a bag of goodies to get out when an infant becomes restless, perhaps a soft toy and a handkerchief as a blanket to wrap the toy. A parent can whisper to a child, pointing out things in the church which might interest the child, the light coming in from a stained-glass window, what is happening in the service. Week by week the infant will come to look and not need talking to. Older infants may be given plain paper and coloured pencils so that they can draw during the sermon. This may help them to concentrate, and it is surprising what they hear. The Mothers' Union has produced a useful leaflet with ideas for parents to use with their children during the service: *Children in Church: A Survivor's Guide.*

If we think of children as 'raw material' to be moulded, we ignore their present faith. Children have faith, though it will be different from that of adults. If we stress their future faith, we are not valuing them today. Children search and question in order to find meaning in their lives. They are not passive but active inquirers, if as adults we are prepared to allow them to be so. They are thankful for friendship and sorrowful when they see suffering. Remembering the insights about child development, we recognize our need both to care and nurture children and to accept them as individuals who have autonomy. We need to listen to children in order to understand the sense they are making of themselves and their relationships with others, the world and God. We need to be alongside children, guiding and offering them stories and insights so that they can work on these to create their own sense of themselves, and in God's good time come to a fuller faith and mature commitment. Faith is a continuous journey for Christians young and old. Children who attend worship have made some commitment to travel along the Christian way. We need to encourage and work with them to strengthen their commitment, since their peers at school may sneer at their faith and church attendance.

If we think of children as unsaved and in need of rescue from an evil world, there is a sense in which all of us are in need of salvation, thus reflecting Paul's acknowledgement of his need, 'for I do not do the good I want, but the evil I do not want is what I do' (Rom. 7.19). Adults live in the same world as children: a world that is fractured by broken relationships and selfishness. Adults are more likely to be sinners but we all, children and adults, need forgiveness and restoration.

If we see children as 'innocent', then we are not taking them seriously. Children can indeed be sweet and thoughtful, but they can also be unthinking and spiteful to one another and to adults. We need to guide and help them to see the effects of their words and actions and, as they grow in understanding and experience, to take responsibility for their own actions and the consequences. We may think that we know the pattern of Jesus' childhood ('mild and obedient' says the hymn) and can use it as a model for children today. This picture of Jesus is inaccurate, since even as a twelve-year-old he was upsetting the elders in the temple by asking questions (Luke 2.41–47). He responded to his parents' concern about his absence with the words, 'Did you not know that I must be in my Father's house?' (Luke 2.49). Here was a thinking, questioning child. As an adult Jesus was far from mild. He was angry in the face of sickness, hypocrisy and injustice. It is unlikely that the religious leaders saw his 'brand' of Judaism as 'good'. He even disowned his own family (Mark 3.31–35).

Children who come to church vary in personality, background, understanding and maturity. They come in all their joy, enthusiasm, spontaneity, activity and consciousness of sin, in their concern about their families and the world in which they live. What do children receive within church? They look to significant adults for acceptance, care, concern and nurture. Adults are disciples on the same journey as the children, even if they are further along the road.

In baptism a baby is brought into a larger family, the community of faith, where all are invited 'to become children of God'. The words of the baptismal service are 'by one Spirit we are all baptized into one body . . . we are children of the same heavenly father; we welcome you.'[6] Infant baptism is a sacrament of inclusion. Baptized children are not recruits or trainees, they are Christians; their birthright is to be included in the life of God's people in community. In some Christian traditions, children are dedicated and the congregation and parents make promises. Within these traditions some adults believe that the child is counted as God's through the faith of the parents (1 Cor. 7.14). Other traditions hold that the child must confess to personal belief and be converted before being considered a Christian.

Jesus' harshest words were for those who put stumbling-blocks in the way of 'little ones' by discouraging, misleading or despising them (Mark 9.42; Luke 17.1–2; Matt. 18.6). The Church is called to be an advocate for children, for those who cannot always speak out for themselves. In this way adults affirm and offer pastoral care to all children.

Look at the Charters for Children (Appendix 3).

How do they differ?

Try to construct your own. Better still, ask a child to do it!

SUNDAY WORSHIP

What is worship? It has been described as a 'useless' activity in that we worship with no end product. Worship may be described as an honouring of God, through which God's people are encouraged in their belief, nurtured, nourished in faith and resourced for mission. A three-year-old, asked why she went to church, said, 'We go to church to praise God.'

Michael Taylor sees the story of Jesus as the distinctive Christian characteristic, arising from the earliest confession, 'Jesus is Lord'. He notes:

> The liturgy is . . . an act of worship or 'worth-ship'. Here we affirm the worth of the Story by telling it. Here we acknowledge that its hero is our Lord and . . . nothing surpasses it in the significance which it holds for our lives . . . it remains an encounter not merely with the projection of our own ideas but with events that are independent and not part of us . . . offering us gifts and making demands. In committing ourselves to the Liturgy we offer to live by the Story that is told . . . we believe that in telling the Story we have to do with the creative and renewing springs of life and the gracious resources we need so much.[7]

Taylor's insights are helpful in bringing together the essence of the meaning of worship and its response in our lives.

Joyce Mercer talks about worship as 'identity formation' in an:

> alternative identity . . . learned through participation in the church as a 'community of practice' that seeks to walk in the ways of Jesus and organizes its life and practices around the central symbol of the kin-dom of God, with its reordering of power and its transforming commitment to an alternative way of life.[8]

In worship we encounter God, though we need to remember that for some people their encounter is not in church: for example, it may be the sense of awe in nature; an experience of transcendence in music; meeting God in others through acts of service with the marginalized; in meditation. These examples also include children's encounters with God. Nevertheless, central to the Christian is the story of Jesus. In the accounts of the story of the historical Jesus, his birth, life, death and resurrection, we receive glimpses of the nature and activity of God. Week by week we retell his story in the eucharistic prayer.[9] Our faith in God is renewed and our commitment to serve God in our daily lives and to allow God to continue the work of making us whole. A metaphor that we can use of our growth into God is that of the mirror. Our vision of God gives us increasing self-knowledge as we are transformed into God's likeness (1 Cor. 13.13; 2 Cor. 3.10). This is true for all God's children.

Many churches today discuss worship, often because of falling numbers. Some congregations bemoan their lack of children in Sunday worship, forgetting the children who meet on church premises during the week and their church school. Members of congregations might think how they can support the children in these groups: by praying for them, taking an interest, including reports of the groups in the church magazine. In these simple ways the pastoral care of children is fostered.

Church committees debate the type of worship (eucharistic or non-eucharistic); the place of children within worship (Sunday school, receiving communion); 'all-age' worship; alternative styles of worship (coffee bar; worship within a fellowship meal); the timing of worship (Sunday is sometimes the only day of the week when all the family are together. Worship may interrupt sporting activities or a day out together. The church has to be flexible in its worship: the time, the day or the venue may need to alter).[10]

The average Sunday morning congregation is likely to include people of all ages, abilities and stages of Christian maturity. Worship in church is that of the whole community of faith. It includes people whose personalities and preferred ways of worship differ widely: silence, structure, hand-waving and story. If these differences are reflected in some measure in the act of worship, then all can be fed.

VARIATIONS IN SUNDAY WORSHIP

All-age worship[11]

The phrase 'all-age worship' is used to refer particularly to services of the word[12] attended by people who range widely in age and maturity, but who are together for the whole service. All-age services may take place once a month or just on festivals (including baptisms). A service of the word may be informal, yet it needs structure, since adults and children alike tend to prefer a familiar, predictable liturgical pattern. The pattern is fourfold:

- preparation: greeting, prayers of penitence, hymn/song, collect
- Ministry of the Word: readings from Scripture, a psalm, a sermon, a creed
- prayers: intercessions and thanksgiving, Lord's Prayer
- dismissal: hymn, blessing, the congregation sent out for mission.

It is a framework that begins with the worshipper, who then hears God's word, is challenged by the word and responds, is blessed and commissioned for mission in the world. To this framework hymns are added. A range of music and instruments (e.g. guitars and wind) uses the gifts of young and old. The words (including pictures and symbols for the non-readers) may be projected onto a screen and include actions in response. The service can be led by a group of both young and old, who have spent time together planning a theme. It uses a 'hands-on' approach, in that the Scripture readings may use a dramatic version, or be mimed. The address is interactive, using drama or mime, colour and symbols.

As an alternative for the part of the service called the 'ministry of the word' congregation members are invited to explore the meaning of the Scriptures for the day in a mixed-age group (children and adults together). There can be a choice of groups, reflecting the need of each person that day, such as: a Godly Play group; a music group; an art/clay expressive group; a Bible study/ sharing group; a meditation group; a silent reflective group. The different groups express the different ways we learn (kinaesthetic, aural, visual, cognitive). Each group is led but responsibility for the thinking and direction of the group belongs to its members. The groups meet for between twenty and thirty minutes, subsequently returning to offer to the whole congregation any insights or objects made, which can contribute to the worship. The leader then declares good news from the Gospel.[13] The pattern of worship is completed with a hymn, blessing and dismissal, followed by simple refreshments. Through working in mixed-age groups, adults and children grow to understand one another as a community of faith. They learn from one another and mutually enrich each other. Children see models of Christian identity and living but also that each adult is a flawed person in process of transformation. Children are affirmed and nurtured by being listened to, and their contribution is heard and appreciated.

Issues

The place of children within the Sunday worship for many congregations is problematic (I have already noted congregations' ambiguous understanding of the nature of children). A further reason is that adults consider children disturb their peace and concentration: babies are noisy, infants are fidgety, toddlers wander, children are bored. These issues can be addressed positively. Each child is unique and reacts differently in church. A crèche for very small ones can be helpful. An alternative service might be an option: for example, the Rainbow Service mentioned in Chapter 5.

An all-age service can become so child-orientated that it becomes 'childish' entertainment and fails to engage adults or children who are used to an adult experience. This results in the absence of some regulars from all-age services, declaring that 'they are not children' and hoping that 'normal service will be resumed as soon as possible'. However, the church belongs to children as much as to adults, and children's worship time is as important as that of adults. Key to the success of all-age services are certain principles:

- parts of the service need to be briefer, since young children cannot concentrate for long;
- there are opportunities for movement, for example, sitting, kneeling, processing;
- all the senses are used;
- different media are used – pictures, objects, drama, symbols;
- the service is shorter (50 minutes);
- the congregation participates in as much of the service as possible;
- the words of the service deal with mysteries and do not patronize.

Worship enlarges our experience, broadens our knowledge, develops our imagination and talents, and stimulates us to grow in faith at whatever age we are. It does not have to be 'dumbed down' for children: they know when this is happening and resent it. The presence of children can challenge the church to reconsider learning styles and to involve the whole person in worship. Worship is rich, involving our bodies, minds, wills and senses. It engages:

- sight – candles, the colours of stained glass, flowers
- hearing – music, voices, sounds
- taste – bread and wine
- smell – flowers, polish, incense
- touch – the handshake of welcome and of peace

This is likely to mean looking anew at church design and furnishings: it may be useful to provide free-standing chairs to give space for drama, to make banners, to introduce new music. All-age worship is not a concession to the needs of children, nor a method of increasing the congregation. It is a means of expressing the family character of the church community and enables everyone in that community to be enriched, young and old, for we are all members of each other, need each other and contribute to each other's growth in Christ. Jerome Berryman has spent a lifetime sharing worship that is accessible to all. He sees the notion of 'play' as a key to participation in liturgy: play as worship is joyful, timeless, takes risks.

The service can also become all-age learning rather than all-age worship. Worship is not in itself education, though it will be a significant educational experience. Worship forms us as Christian people, in a Christian identity.

Liturgy is 'the work of the people'. Examples of accessible worship for children can be found in the Orthodox churches, which have open spaces where the service is filled with movement, light from candles, colour from icons and scent from incense. Here children find themselves welcomed and integrated.[14] Children may not sometimes understand the thinking or language of worship, but what they experience of the total community is more important than what is said.

Adults say that children will not understand and so will get bored. Do adults always understand? Do they never become bored? Children do not get bored if they are 'engaged' and caught up in the mystery and excitement of worship. Young children have a sense of wonder, awe and mystery (as noted in the research of Coles, Nye and Hay, Cavalletti, and Berryman); this is in a greater measure than adults. Children come to church ready to be fascinated. If when they enter church they find adults in a mood of wonder and anticipation for worship (e.g. the atmosphere created by a candlelight service) children will be caught up in this experience. Children entering an ancient church building may be aware of its sheer size, or an atmosphere of reverence and prayer.

Carol's eight-year-old son was overwhelmed by the smell and censing with incense at the Gospel; a child may be drawn into a Taizé chant sung to prepare for worship or the pattern of light falling through the stained-glass windows or a central peace candle burning. The different seasons of the Christian liturgical year offer a range of emphasis and mood expressed through colour (e.g. purple for Advent and Lent) and objects (Paschal cross, candle). If children do not find this wonder and mystery and become bored, it is often because the adults around them are bored.

Worship is not necessarily made easier by more accessible and easier words. Children have a fascination with language (I remember my niece at four years chanting 'supercalifragilisticexpialidocious'). Rather the words used in liturgy need to be strong, concrete and pictorial. Non-verbal communication is important for children: symbols, pictures and mime. In worship there is a balance of word and action in which all can participate. Word is expressed in reading the Scriptures, reciting the psalms, singing hymns, hearing an address, prayers of adoration, confession, supplication and intercession. There is also action, which can include kneeling, standing, processing, clapping, singing, signing of the cross, breaking and sharing bread, pouring wine, receiving God's grace.

Look at the piece of writing by D. H. Lawrence (Appendix 4).

What are the implications of his thinking for the use of hymns and symbols with children?

The restless behaviour of children is said to disturb the service. A focus and a structured beginning to the service helps: for example, a procession of service leaders or the lighting of a candle. A good deal of restlessness is the result of boredom and inactivity. If we help children to become responsible participants, they will usually rise to the occasion. Invite them to participate in liturgical roles. Children might be on the rota as 'welcomers', participate in carrying candles at a Gospel reading procession, form a circle of candles round the Gospel, and be readers of the Scriptures. These suggestions are not tokenism but an inclusiveness of all God's children, young and old.

Family occasions are usually noisy affairs, and so it will be on occasions for the family of the church. Children, however, do appreciate the silence of a short guided meditation in the service, particularly if there is a focus such as a lit candle. If adults are expecting quiet meditation throughout the service, then perhaps the liturgy with its action is not the place.

List the arguments for and against all-age worship.

What do children contribute to your church worship?

Share good experiences your church has of being an all-age Christian community – in worship, caring for one another, witness, serving the community, or other ways.

AGE-RELATED WORSHIP WITHIN WORSHIP AND LEARNING FOR ALL

This refers to worship for all ages, within which there is time for 'age-related' worship and learning. Different age groups often want space of their own and it may be appropriate for children to meet in their own Sunday school or Junior Church while the adults worship and listen to a sermon. This does imply that children need to learn, while adults have arrived in their faith and are not growing. Children are segregated (they can feel left out), confirming the belief of some of the congregation that the classroom is the only legitimate place for children in the congregation.

There are different variations on this theme: in some churches the children do not appear at the beginning of the service, but have their own time together (Sunday school, or Junior Church) and join at, or during, the eucharistic prayer. In other churches the children are present with their families until the Gospel and are then 'dismissed' for their classes, returning for the Eucharist, blessing and dismissal. In other churches, the adults move out of the church after the Gospel and the children stay; sometimes the priest goes out with the children and another leader preaches to the adults. Some services have a 'children's address'. This is only useful if it helps the Sunday school children to participate more fully in worship, perhaps thinking about parts of the service and their purpose (the significance of the intercessions) or exploring the symbols in the church. A children's address might whet their appetite by using material that prepares or enhances their separate Sunday school session. It should be an offering to God from and for all the congregation.

In services which include age-related provision it is helpful if the community are engaged with the same truths and Scripture readings (here the Lectionary is useful), so that the part of the service that all share creates a sense of identity, enabling children to feel an integral part of the congregation. There are many resources for this pattern, such as the magazine *Roots*, Scripture Union material, CURBS (<www.curbsproject.org.uk>), books. A useful audit of the commitment of a church to children is provided by the Child Friendly Church Award scheme (Anglican Diocese of Liverpool).

> **When children are withdrawn from a service, to what extent do their activities offer substitutes for the means by which main worship conveys religious thoughts?**

The gifts of children to worship

Within the church children are invited to become part of the Christian story and to share its experience in a deeper way, to recognize the Bible as the story of those who experienced God in the past. Children may puzzle about the nature of God just as Abraham puzzled about the many gods of Ur, and seeking to know God questioned and travelled (Gen. 12.1–3). Some children feel inadequate, as Jacob did beside his outgoing brother Esau; he needed his father's approval and hid behind his mother (Gen. 27.1–45). Other children are isolated and feel unloved, as Zacchaeus did (Luke 19.1–11). Each person needs to make sense of his or her own experience. This may be assisted by insights from the Scriptures or the support of a member of the faith community, so that he or she may know and be known by God and his or her Christian identity is formed.

Children are not simply receivers from the adults in the church, they are also givers. Children give themselves, if we allow them to; they bring to worship a spontaneity and a creativity; they encourage the church to be more participatory and active in worship. They encourage questioning and searching for meaning.

We, as adults, may not know the answers. Then we must admit this and search together; we need to recognize that with some questions we are in the area of mystery.

Mercer states, 'Liturgical practices with children can function as sites to reimagine and reconfigure the social positioning of children in ways that enact God's justice for children and contribute to their thriving together with adults.'[15] Children are gifts of God to us, they are divine blessings, through them the congregation welcomes Jesus himself and the one who sent him (Mark 9.37).

Sunday school

I have referred to the significance of education in a previous chapter. Education forms an aspect of, but is not the focus of, worship. We learn implicitly and explicitly: for example, implicitly, much popular theology is coloured by the words of the hymns we sing; explicitly, we learn from the sermon, group work, Bible study and Sunday school.

In their own class recently children used the Lectionary passage which was part of John's meditation on Jesus as the Bread of Life (John 6.35–51). It described the crowd challenging Jesus' statements about himself and his activity. The crowd knew Jesus' family: he was familiar and too ordinary to substantiate his claims (John 6.41–42). An imaginative teacher discussed Jesus' identity with the eight- to nine-year-olds, who wrote speech bubbles containing comments such as 'Who does he think he is?' They had begun to do some Christology.

Too often, however, we spoon-feed children, underestimating their abilities. Children can play down their abilities to 'please' the teacher, knowing that the answer to any religious question in Sunday school is either 'Jesus' or 'God'! Children need the challenge and instruction, the 'scaffolding' provided by mature Christians. This may or may not be available in Sunday school.

Some educationalists advocate occasions of separate children's ministry. This enables children to develop their faith now, recognizing their particular developmental stage, although chronological age is not always a good indicator of faith development. However, the central reason for questioning a separate church (Sunday school or Junior Church) for children is that the distinctive activity of the people of God is worship. Worship is by the whole family of God of all ages. Worship is an activity, it requires participation. It is not possible for the community to worship together if one group, the children, is separated from the adult worshipping congregation. The 'learning about worship' of children within Sunday school is outside the activity of worship. Some Sunday schools do not include worship. Children learn to worship through participating in worship and they benefit from being alongside adults.

PASTORAL CARE THROUGH THE SACRAMENTS

Baptism

Church life begins for many with infant baptism. Jesus called the disciples, and by implication the Church today, to welcome children. The birth of a child involves challenge and change for every couple. Many parents who are not church members nevertheless turn to the Church and its rituals to celebrate the birth of a child, despite the secular alternatives available.[16] In the Anglican tradition any parent may ask for a child to be baptized. This is part of a public act of worship: a big step for some parents, if they have had little contact with the Church.[17] Whatever the reasons, the minister is called to listen, to be present for the parents and help them where they are, through responding pastorally to their request for the baptism of their child.

For some clergy a request for baptism is an opportunity to demonstrate hospitality and respond pastorally to 'non-Christian' parents. For others there are theological barriers to baptism. 'Conditions' may be placed on parents who are not members of the Church, such as church attendance or a service of thanksgiving.[18] Preparation for baptism may involve clergy, a trained lay person or a couple who are parents. An initial home visit is usual since the parents are likely to feel more comfortable in their familiar surroundings and the baby is met. This visit is usually informal, enabling visitors to admire the baby and share the experience of parenting.[19] Later, many churches invite parents to join a group of other parents at church. The meeting must set them at ease, accepting and valuing them and the understandings they bring. It can be useful to begin by inviting them to talk about the experience of being a parent, something they are familiar with. 'Leads' may emerge, enabling the discussion to move into talk about baptism: the presence of the baby may bring 'light and joy' to parents, leading to an exploration of the symbolism of light; ideas about growth may lead to discussion of nutrition and the role of water in baptism. Feelings of responsibility may lead parents to consider the promises to be made, the commitment they are making to God and their child, and the support given by the church community. Exploring the words of the sacrament links parents with parts of the previous conversations concerning their child. It is important to visit the worship area and font so that parents are familiar with the building. These are acts of pastoral care of parents and child.

The service of baptism is a public act of worship. It can be made special for the family in different ways: parents can choose a hymn; a welcome can be given at the church door, and an escort arranged to special places; if the baby is at the crawling stage, a clean blanket or rug and soft toys can be provided near the parents. For the baptism a procession of church children to the font helps, carrying a towel, water jug and candle. A card of welcome may be made and presented by church children; the baby may be carried slowly through the church to be introduced to his new brothers and sisters in Christ. These are significant pointers to parents that their child is special. Each is evidence of pastoral care since parents and baby are significant to God.

The child is 'brought' to baptism and will need help and encouragement that he 'may learn to know God . . . follow Jesus Christ in the life of faith . . . serve . . . neighbour . . . and in due course come to confirmation'.[20] The promise of the Christian community is to give 'help and encouragement'. Prayers are made for the 'help and grace of God' in guiding the child 'in the way of faith'. The Church recognizes the unique individuality of the child within his family. Parents promise to encourage their child to face life with all its ambiguities, knowing that, through the child's baptism, he or she belongs to God and is beginning a lifelong journey of faith.

Find out how your church prepares for a baptism.

What thinking underlies baptism in your church?

How can families who are not very familiar with the church be helped to feel welcome?

Some families bring a child for baptism and are not seen again until the next baby arrives. This may be due to a failure of the church to offer care and support, or a result of the pressures on family life, the unsuitable times or type of worship, or simply because a 'one-off' baptism is all the parents wanted. Whatever the reason, respect has to be shown for parents' views, while the clergy and workers have to assess whether they have shown appropriate hospitality. Some churches have found ways of following up to help the family feel nurtured and supported in their parenthood.[21]

Eucharist (Holy Communion, Mass)

For many churches (Anglican and Roman Catholic) the Eucharist is the norm for the main service of the day. In the Eucharist we are told to 'taste and see'; this order reflects the fact that our experience precedes understanding. There is an argument that the Eucharist should be the staple diet for all God's people, both adults and children, the nourishment of the Christian. Through their baptism children belong at the table, sharing. At the heart of the Eucharist is mystery. This sense needs to be enhanced through the worship. It is helpful if children are involved, for example, by creating an area for them to sit on a rug in front of the altar so that they can see and participate in the actions of the Eucharist, perhaps preparing and distributing the bread and wine.

To the four elements of the service of the word are added the four acts of the Eucharist: offering (of ourselves, symbolized by money and human work in producing bread and wine), thanksgiving (the eucharistic prayer), breaking (the bread) and sharing (receiving the bread and wine). The Eucharist takes up the reality of life: it celebrates God, active in creation, the life of Jesus, and the companionship of the Spirit, the mystery of the Trinity; it remembers human cruelty and the continuing brokenness of ourselves and our world, and in recalling the Passion narrative and the resurrection it affirms love which cannot be destroyed. In the ascension it affirms that power is with a Christ-like God. The importance of the Eucharist is in binding, strengthening, incorporating and reliving salvation. It is a remembering and a vision of a world transformed by love and service. The child's experience is receiving alongside adults.

The Eucharist may become word-bound.[22] It is frequently cerebral, visually and emotionally unengaged. Worship is often seen as an adult activity in which children are allowed to participate as long as they conform to adult patterns. However, the presence of children, both as members of the body of Christ and as a gift to the Church, needs to be valued. Eucharistic language can be a problem for them, although it may not be the difficulty but the number of words. Even in the new forms liturgy is becoming more language-based, appealing exclusively to the cognitive side of the brain. It needs to 'speak' through action and silence, to the heart as well as to the head. It can then be appropriated by children. Adults benefit if children are active participants. Worship does not need to patronize children. They have a sense of worship which needs to be taken seriously. Worship for all needs to recognize the whole person – body, mind and spirit. The content of the liturgy might include: responsive confession (*Common Worship*, p. 276); a simple response to bidding prayers (*Common Worship*, p. 284); responsive words for the affirmation of faith (*Common Worship*, pp. 144–5) and at the words of Preparation (*Common Worship*, p. 292). Some eucharistic prayers are more accessible to children since they involve responses (*Prayer A, D and F, Common Worship*, pp. 184–5). The Eucharist is a celebration of Jesus' risen life, of love that gives without limit and cannot be defeated.

Receiving communion

The giving of communion to baptized children of Christian families before confirmation is still controversial in some churches, yet this is another example of the nurture of the child. I would suggest that omitting children forgets the practice of the early Church and Jesus' unconditional receiving of children.

It is helpful for children to be guided before they receive, though we are all at the altar/communion table in the place of mystery. Preparation could include, for example, exploring the significance of family meals, remembering particular meals, recalling Jesus' last meal with his friends, his giving of himself in love, an introduction to symbols, the memory through the ages of this common act, and the idea of God's grace.

Some excellent resources are available, including: *My Communion Book* for four- to eight-year-olds, by Diana Murrie, with bright pictures and an interactive script; *Come and Join the Celebration*, by John Muir and Betty Pedley, including resource and activity sheets; and a *Communion Cube* for younger children, which unfolds to work through the aspects of the service.[23]

> **What does it mean to a baptized child to be admitted to Holy Communion?**
>
> **What does it mean to be excluded from the sacrament?**

There is plenty of material available to help children prepare for confirmation. This is a pastoral opportunity to teach children, not didactically, but by exploring with them their experience and the presence and activity of God in their lives. It is also an opportunity to stretch their understanding by asking 'What do you think of this?' or 'I wonder what Christians before us have understood by . . .' We cannot impose faith: it comes from the heart. Our understandings of the tenets of the creed vary as each of us makes sense from our experience. If I ask members of the congregation what they understand by phrases of the creed, I will receive as many answers as people asked. There will be instruction. The pastoral care of children is an attitude of excitement that helps children to recognize that faith is a journey on which they may be just beginning but which deepens and has the power to transform them throughout life. Confirmation is not an arrival station but a launch pad.

Nurture through the sacraments

Rebecca was baptized at two weeks old. Every week she was taken to the parish Eucharist. She was a great delight to the congregation, which consisted mainly of elderly folk, with no other children. As a baby she was 'shared' by the congregation until the moment came to receive the Eucharist elements, at which point her parents held her for a blessing. Though non-verbal she was a blessing and was blessed by the congregation and by God. As she grew and became mobile, she would go and sit by different members of the congregation. Gradually she became vocal. One Sunday she realized that she was 'missing out' since she did not receive the bread: it seemed she was not accepted. Rebecca asked, 'Where's mine?' Her wise mother asked the priest what to do and he suggested that she share 'Mum's bread'. Rebecca belonged by right to the community of faith. This story illustrates the growth into recognition of being an integral member of God's people.

Pastoral support of children depends on an open theology where children see God in the world through the members of the community of faith, who have no ready-made beliefs to hand on, but aim to explore and share with children the riches of their faith and equip young people for life in a pluralistic society; in brief, to nurture children in faith. In worship children join with adults to experience a vision of the Kingdom, embodied in the life, death and resurrection of Jesus of Nazareth, that is both transformative and subversive of contemporary culture. Children's identity is formed within a community enriched by Christian symbols, images and worship, and nourished by the sacraments of baptism and Eucharist.

SUMMARY POINTS FOR DISCUSSION

- Children are a blessing to the Church of today.
- Children receive and have gifts to offer the adult congregation.
- We are all children of God, whatever age we are.
- In worship children receive a vision of life in the Kingdom.
- Worship is of the whole person, body (the senses, movement), mind and spirit.

CHAPTER NINE

Gathering Together

Joseph is a four-year-old and attends a nursery school every morning. He knows about the caring work of paramedics from the experience of being taken to hospital in an ambulance. Recently, the local fire-fighters came to the nursery to show the children their vehicle and explain their work. On returning home Joseph said to his mother, 'If there is a fire in our house, I know the firemen and the ambulance men will come but will God come?' Subsequently, he asked, 'Is God a man like Jesus?'

> **Think of occasions when young children have talked about their ordinary experience and then introduced ideas about God.**

Joseph at four is wrestling with his experience – things heard in church and at home – trying to make sense of them for himself. In this book, Jan, Jamie, Wayne, Rebecca and others were each involved in a similar way. All were examples of the exercise of pastoral care.

Joseph's mother was the person who responded to his needs. She found the questions challenging, with no easy way to explain. Joseph had experienced the care of the ambulance service and the fire service. He knew that in an emergency they would be present caring for him. It is important to recognize that there are many human beings who come to our aid and care for us in a pastoral way. The carers in this case were 'professionals'; in other words, it was their paid occupation (there are volunteers in both organizations). Nevertheless, apart from paid employment, we can say that a great many ambulance staff and fire-fighters put their own lives at risk in their work and show attitudes of dedication and commitment to people; this can be called pastoral care. Some may act from a faith commitment, others not. This is not the pastoral care I am addressing in this book. I have been engaging with pastoral care given by people with Christian belief rooted in a community of faith, arising from their commitment in that community.

Joseph was putting his experience of care alongside the activity of God. He wanted to know if God would be present in an emergency. In addition he wondered if God was a man like Jesus. Joseph had picked up understandings from his family and his church attendance. People help you in situations of danger. He heard in church accounts of the activity and work of Jesus. He had made the connection that Jesus was a man like other men. In his church, God was addressed in prayers and asked for help, so God must be involved too.

The questions children ask puzzle and challenge them, as they attempt to make sense of all the varied parts of their experience. For the child this is serious 'work' and therefore it is work which we need to take seriously. How was Joseph to be taken seriously? At four years old he would not have the cognitive ability to wrestle with the idea of time (that Jesus was a man, a Jew from Galilee who lived and died two thousand years ago; that Christians believe that Jesus is 'alive today', working through men and women). He would find the idea of God difficult, since God cannot be seen and experienced like other things and people. He has experience of love, security, acceptance from his parents. These are in some sense glimpses of the love of God. His mother is helped in her pastoral care if she has some knowledge of a child's cognitive development. Knowledge of learning theories is also helpful. Knowing about Vygotsky and Bruner, learning in community, the 'spiral curriculum' and 'scaffolding' would guide her. Joseph's pastoral care is about encouraging him to continue to talk. It is about learning that the human Jesus came alongside people in times of need. It is about wondering how and why people care sacrificially for others today. Joseph can be encouraged to think of a God like Jesus and his thinking can be extended by offering other 'concrete' pictures of the activity of God, such as the Good Shepherd and light, so that as he continues to grow he will return to these questions with greater insight and faith. The community of faith may be guided to know that children ask questions like this and that they can care for children by accepting them, taking their questions seriously, loving them and nourishing children like Joseph in his faith journey. This is the congregation's pastoral care.

> **In the light of your experience and the insights you have discovered in this book, how would you respond to Joseph?**

In Chapter 5 we thought about the pastoral care offered to Jan. Jan did not have particular questions at first; rather, these arose out of the care given to her. Jan's immediate care was that of noticing her grief, of being alongside in her grief, listening and offering friendship. It was only after there had been this encounter that questions began to flood out. It was than that the cleric was able to care in giving Jan information and resources to think, helping her to clarify her experience of her grandfather's death. This conversation may have surprised her. Children may not realize that adults do not know all the answers but help with questions and travel beside you. Following this encounter Jan chose to return to find the churchwarden, and it was Mary's hospitality that led to her wanting to join the choir, coming to church and later bringing her sister.

Jamie's needs were for a response to his declaration of what was worrying him. He told us about his twin and her death at birth, for which he felt responsible. His blurted-out 'confession' was in the context of a group of children sitting round me listening to a story of the twins Jacob and Esau. He experienced pastoral care through his peer group. They sat in silence, maybe challenged, perhaps shocked, by Jamie's words but their silence was only broken by accounts of their experiences of loss and death. Indirectly the group supported Jamie by their silence and also by their stories, which showed an empathy of experience. Jamie was not alone. My pastoral care was offering a safe space for the children to talk. Occasionally I shared with them, responding and gently challenging their comments about responsibility, helping them to see that there are different ways of looking at an event, that we should not judge, and that sometimes things happened, such as the death of Jamie's twin, that we do not understand. I was later able to talk to Jamie on his own, and later still with him and his mother. In all this process Jamie recognized that he was valued by the group, that he mattered as a person. This helped him. Knowledge of Maslow and child development theory helped inform my understanding of what was happening in this situation.

Wayne didn't ask for pastoral care, perhaps he did not realize he needed it. His remarks in trying to upstage Joseph in the nativity play may have been born of anger, jealousy, malice or the self-assertion of a four-year-old. The result of Wayne's activities was a frustrated Joseph, a Mary who didn't know what to do, and a potential fight between Wayne and other members of the cast. Immediate action was needed for the play to continue. The audience smiled. Tension was released. Probably Mary and Joseph ignored the interruption and continued on their way. Wayne needed care as a person, since he needed to realize that he was important for himself and that his self-assertion could prevent others being themselves.

Rebecca was baptized when she was two weeks old, and from that day she grew up in a Christian faith community. At three years old she realized that something did not make sense. She was not treated like everyone else. This community which had loved and nurtured her were denying her the bread which was a central part of their worship shared by everyone. Her question, 'Where's mine?' can be seen as the self-focus of a young child. At a deeper level it is about a child's sense of exclusion from the church family that was an integral part of her young life and of which she thought that she was a member. The care of mother and vicar helped her know that she did belong. At some time in the future, through this knowledge of belonging, she may in God's time come to her own commitment to the Christian journey.

Pastoral care was defined as 'a pattern of corporate, responsible, sensitive acts motivated by a compelling vision'. I have suggested that pastoral care exists in a cultural context; for us, that of the developed world of the twenty-first century. Our society is dominated by an individualistic, materialistic and secular attitude to life. Society is ambivalent in its attitudes to children, seeing them both as little angels and little devils. This challenges Christian insights of a God seen in Jesus (incarnation), who is relational (the Trinity, creation of a community of friends, the church), vulnerable (birth and cross) and sacrificial (gives himself for others in love), who invites others to join a life inspired by love (church). Jesus saw children realistically as affected by a society flawed by human selfishness and sin, yet as little ones made in the image of God, who were vulnerable. In hugging and blessing children he declared their worth to God, he advocated for them, and saw in them a pattern of life for all his followers. I have stated that the gospel of Jesus is subversive of our contemporary culture, and this will be expressed in pastoral care.

In our examples of pastoral care I have indicated that our society is adult-dominated and not caring of children. For example, it is not sensitive to the fact that children grieve as adults do (story of Jan); parents are careless in what they say in the hearing of children (only adults could have told Jamie about his birth); that the church adopts societal values that maturity is to do with age, rather than a deep sense of belonging (Rebecca's story). Those who cared for these children did so by challenging societal attitudes.

Pastoral care of children uses as a resource the insights of child development theories and accounts of spiritual and religious development. It recognizes individual rates of growth, the infant as an individual from birth, the uniqueness of each child, a child's need for security and love, all of which are as important as physical sustenance. Pastoral care reflects the need of a child for space and time, for learning by exploration and activity within the guidance of a family and community. Learning is by questioning (Joseph's story), by scaffolding with others who have greater knowledge, by returning to a story as in the spiral curriculum. Learning theories give insight into pastoral care.

Pastoral care is rooted in theology, that is, in understandings of the child as made in the image of God, growing in an environment which is deeply flawed by self-seeking and becoming part of this; of 'original blessings' and 'original sin', creation and redemption; of a child's vulnerability; of growing through and in relationships with others. These abiding truths about human beings exist within the Christian belief in God as Trinity (relational); God as creator and redeemer; a Christlike God (incarnation); the transforming power of God's Spirit; God's justice and mercy for creation. These truths emerge from biblical understandings. There is recognition of the Bible as a resource which contains diverse material, in parts contradictory, which is interpreted in many different ways. The Bible is a guide, its truths to be worked at within a community to which it belongs. The word of God is a person: 'the word became flesh and lived among us'. Commitment to the truths and guiding principles to be discovered in Scripture and expressed in worship through word and sacrament are the distinctive characteristics of Christian pastoral care.

With children pastoral care will be a walking alongside, honouring and respecting a growing and maturing individual who because of age and immaturity is vulnerable. It will be the work of individuals (parents, clergy, childcare workers, Sunday school teachers, peer group). It will be listening, empowering, travelling, sharing insights, story-telling, teaching, challenging, guiding in joy and sorrow. It will respond to a child's life experiences of making sense, questioning, illness, bullying, shame, guilt and death. It will be encouraging the formation of an identity within and alongside others in a community of faith travelling together. It will be in moments of encounter with mystery and joy in word and sacrament, of being transformed by the Spirit of God. Pastoral care will be expressed at times in challenging societal attitudes inimical to children and being advocates for them. The Church is called by its Lord to be an advocate for all voiceless children, not in a paternalistic mode but by standing alongside them. In debates about genetics, abortion and divorce, education, special schools, the ethical issues of today that affect children, the community of faith needs to be involved, offering informed and sensitive comment. The community of faith thus has a message to society.

Pastoral care will be a work of grace in which all share as children of the same father. The Church is called to be a sign and a call to all Christians that all people are called to be 'children of God'; this is our true identity. 'We cannot know the fullness of God without understanding what it is to be a child.'[1] In the power of the Spirit we are called to offer pastoral care to children.

> In unexperienc'd Infancy
> Many a sweet Mistake doth ly;
> Mistake tho false, intending tru;
> A *Seeming* somewhat more than *View*;
>> That doth instruct the Mind
>> In Things that ly behind,
> And many Secrets to us show
> Which afterwards we com to know.
>
> Thus did I by the Water's brink
> Another World beneath me think;
> And while the lofty spacious Skies
> Reversed there abus'd mine Eys,
>> I fancy'd other Feet
>> Came mine to touch and meet
> As by som Puddle I did play
> Another World within it lay.
>
> Thomas Traherne, 'Shadows in the Water'[2]

SUMMARY POINTS FOR DISCUSSION

- Theology brings together insights from psychology, sociology, history and the Scriptures and tradition of the community of faith in a creative dialogue.

- Each of us is called a child of God.

- Adults are called to accept children as they are.

- Our nurture of children is a travelling alongside, listening, accepting, sometimes provoking new insights.

- In serving the child we meet Christ.

Guides for Engaging with Scripture

The context of the Hebrew Scriptures is a historical period of over two thousand years. Within the Scriptures are history, narrative, poetry, hymns and story. Biblical scholars maintain that the earliest traditions were the oral story-telling sagas of nomadic groups, the patriarchs. Later, with the creation of a community following the Exodus and settlement in Canaan, law codes were evolved and written. Court histories and worship material were written in the period of the monarchy. Documents were lost and forgotten: rediscovery led to a renewal of faith following apostasy (Josiah's discovery in 622 BCE of a text thought to be Deuteronomy is described in 2 Kings 22.8–20). It is thought that an educated, intellectual, male, priestly caste in the Babylonian and Persian Exile (587–333 BCE) edited these documents, reflecting the élite of the community rather than the poor. The texts must be considered ideologically biased, since they ignore trends in society and deny a voice to the subliterate, the vast majority. Not only is there extensive exclusion from the texts of women and children but also instances of their 'abuse'.

The beliefs and practices of the exilic community reflect the cultural milieu of the Ancient Near East (ANE). The Scriptures are the nation's reflection on its 'history', in a search for identity and mission. There is a sifting of material: interpretation and judgements are made. The transmission of material and the editing and writing of texts was a complex process, of which little is known. Did the writing reflect the period when the incident happened, in a quite different culture, or the time when it was edited (which could have been a different culture again)? Did the writing reflect the writer's ideas that might bear little relation to the incident in the author's lifetime or the time in which he was writing?

The Scriptures are not 'self-interpreting'. Through the centuries the Scriptures have been interpreted in many and varying ways, through allegory and metaphor, literally and symbolically in liturgy and art. The test of authority is the discerning of the meaning of the text in the life of the believer and the community of faith, but the interpreter can be deluded. It is the nature of the risk of faith, tested in experience, which brings forth 'good' fruit (John 15.5; 16.1; Gal. 5.22). The interpretation of Scriptures will be judged in answer to questions concerning their potential to give and affirm life in all its fullness, to challenge unjust structures that limit life, and to imitate the principles shown in the life and Passion of Jesus of Nazareth. The Scriptures are to lead readers into all truth, even if that truth disturbs and is difficult.

THE GOSPELS

The Gospels are also complicated documents. To understand their meaning a process is involved: we need to discover, first, what Jesus said and did; second, what Jesus meant by his words and actions; third, what meaning was made by his hearers; fourth, the processes of the writing of the incidents; fifth, the collecting, editing and reinterpreting of the gospel for a different situation beyond Palestine in the Roman Empire; sixth, the meaning made by the recipients of the written gospel. We need to search for meaning in a particular story, and understand it in the context of the whole gospel. On occasions a plethora of interpretations may add to the richness of the material: at other times the exegete is left with making an informed guess. However, Jesus' words and actions regarding family and children are at such variance with a Judaism for which the family was central, not children *per se*, that it is likely that these pericopes represent the thinking of Jesus himself.

INSIGHTS FROM THEOLOGY

Historically theologians have acknowledged the presence of children, though this has not been systematic: for example, Augustine and Chrysostom (nature of the child, child-rearing), Gregory (the soul of the child), Luther (significance of the home, influence of fathers, catechisms, hymns for children), Calvin, Schleiermacher (moral and spiritual formation). In recent years Karl Barth, Karl Rahner, Jürgen Moltmann and Hans Urs von Balthasar have all made contributions.[1] In 1979 (the Year of the

Child), Hans-Ruedi Weber wrote a useful book of biblical exegesis of the gospel material within the context of the culture of the first century.[2]

Systematic references to children and childhood in theological scholarship are limited. Liberation theologies have highlighted Western theology as white and male, and advocated a preferential option for the poor and marginalized, yet they have failed to attend to children. Feminist theology, a liberation theology, has contributed little substantial material, though this is changing. Neither of two reference works, Lisa Isherwood and Dorothea McEwan (eds), *A–Z of Feminist Theology* (Sheffield: Sheffield Academic Press, 1996) and Letty Russell and J. Shannon Clarkson (eds), *Dictionary of Feminist Theologies* (Louisville, KY: Westminster John Knox Press, 1996), has an entry for 'children'. In Practical (Pastoral) theology, much of which is feminist, there is a burgeoning area of insight, particularly in the twenty-first century. This includes work by Pamela Courture, Bonnie Miller-McLemore, David H. Jensen, Joyce Ann Mercer and Kristin Herzog.[3]

Children occur but are not referred to in their own right: references to 'the child' tend to be indirect rather than direct, including theological engagement with marriage, the family, abuse, the ethics of genetic technology, global stewardship, nurture, faith development and the cultural metaphor of the child. There are articles on human rights, ethics, liturgy, metaphor, working mothers and child abuse.

Recently there have been several major projects on families, but even there 'children' were not the focus: the Chicago School of Divinity's Religion, Culture and Family Project, headed by Don Browning, from which emerged the work of Herbert Anderson and Susan B. W. Johnson; and a volume of historical theology contributing to the development of a theology of childhood edited by Marcia J. Bunge.[4] '*The Child in Law, Religion and Society*' (2003–2006) from the Centre for the Interdisciplinary Study of Religion (CISR) at Emory University is 'using insights and methods from law, theology and the humanities'. The Child Theology Movement is also significant. Several journals have devoted issues to children: 'Little children suffer', *Concilium*, 1996/2; 'The child', *Interpretation*, Vol. 55, No. 2 (April 2001); articles on a theology of childhood by Mitchell, DeVries and Bunge.[5]

Within the discipline of Church history there have been various contributions, including papers read at meetings of the Ecclesiastical History Society in 1993 and 1994, edited by Diane

Wood, covering historical periods from the early Church to recent times. William Strange worked on children in the early Church, introducing original resources to illustrate his material, whereas Peter O. M. Bakke extensively quotes documents of the Fathers.[6]

The spiritual life of children has been the focus of recent literature from Robert Coles, a Harvard child psychiatrist; David Hay and Rebecca Nye (a small in-depth structured piece of research in the UK); and the volumes of Karen-Marie Yust, Aostre N. Johnson, Sandy Eisenberg Sasso and Eugene C. Roehlkepartain, on nurturing spirituality, and Eugene C. Roehlkepartain, Pamela Ebstyne King, Linda Wagener and Peter L. Bensen on spiritual development.[7] The work of Clive and Jane Erricker has been significant in conferences, research and the *Journal of Spirituality*.

UK groups in Christian education have produced reports on children, but because work with children is considered the work of women, little significant theology has emerged from these reports.[8] Sofia Cavalletti influenced Jerome W. Berryman, and his Godly Play has had a significant influence in challenging approaches to children and Scriptures (see Chapter 4).[9] James Fowler and John Westerhoff have offered understandings of faith development (see Chapter 3); however, these are limited, relying heavily on psychological models of development, and have few distinctive insights about children.[10]

The General Synod of the Church of England has been patchy in its response to children. A Doctrine Commission report, *Being Human* (2003) used the adult as 'normality'. It seems that the child is not considered a person. In liturgy, recommended new ways of looking at baptism propose a single rite for both adults and children, yet the report is light on thinking about children (1995). Material has been published on child protection; these documents are significant but fail to engage with the meaning of being a child. It was in reaction to child abuse, rather than a preferential option for children, that the House of Anglican Bishops made clear the Church's advocacy of children, 'to be alongside the marginalized and the powerless – hence being alongside, listening to and theologizing about children, and acting with and for them as advocate in a prophetic ministry' (November 1998).[11] Following consultations and working parties, the Church of England has issued reports on the significance and theology of children in aspects of the Church's work and the training of its clergy (2005).[12] The Children's Society of the Church of England launched a website to consider 'a good childhood' in 2006.

Nurturing the Spiritual

Practical things to do:

- Focus on the five senses and find ways of bringing them to your attention.
- Take time to sit for even 30 seconds and enjoy complete silence and stillness.
- Help your child to notice the shape of clouds, the phases of the moon, or how a tree changes through the seasons.
- Listen to and appreciate your child's enthusiasm about animals, plants, rocks.
- Help your child to listen to others, as well as to experience being listened to. Ask your children about their day, and tell them about yours.
- Talk about thoughts and feelings.
- Encourage your child to collect 'treasures' like feathers or leaves.
- Make a prayer tree or net in your house or garden. Tie on a ribbon for each prayer.
- Go for an 'eyes-shut' walk, with one of you guiding and describing what you see.
- Imagine what life would have been like at the time of Jesus or one of the saints. What would you say to them, or ask them?
- Choose a special place where you keep a children's Bible, a cross or a religious picture. This could be a place where your child can go to be quiet or to say a prayer.
- As part of the bedtime routine, bless your child with the sign of the cross or sing a special song.
- Let your child watch or listen when you pray silently or out loud.

- When you go to church, give your children time to explore and make sure they can see what is happening.

(Derived from the Mothers' Union leaflet, *Children and Spirituality*. It is obtainable from Mothers' Union, Mary Sumner House, 24 Tufton Street, London SW1P 3RB.)

Two Charters for Children

CHARTER FOR CHILDREN

- The Church will welcome you.
- The Church will accept you and value you.
- The Church will work to meet your needs.
- The Church will be Christlike in its approach to you.
- The Church will nurture you in faith and worship.
- The Church will provide you with appropriate teaching.
- The Church will offer you relevant worship.
- The Church will encourage you to serve others.
- The Church will endeavour to provide you with a sense of community.
- The Church will support you in sharing the Good News of Christ in word and deed.

(Written by the Children's Committee, Diocese of Blackburn, 1997.)

A CHARTER FOR CHILDREN IN THE CHURCH

1 Children are equal partners with adults in the life of the church.
2 The full diet of Christian worship is for children as well as for adults.
3 Learning is for the whole church, adults and children.
4 Fellowship is for all – each belonging meaningfully to the rest.
5 Service is for children to give, as well as adults.
6 The call to evangelism comes to all God's people of whatever age.

7 The Holy Spirit speaks powerfully through children as well as adults.
8 The discovery and development of gifts in children and adults is a key function of the church.
9 As a church community we must learn to do only those things in separate age groups which we cannot in all conscience do together.
10 The concept of 'the priesthood of all believers' includes children.

(From the United Reformed Church)

APPENDIX 4

Hymns in a Man's Life

Nothing is more difficult than to determine what a child takes in, and does not take in, of its environment and its teaching. This fact is brought home to me by the hymns which I learnt as a child, and never forget. They mean to me almost more than the finest poetry, and they have for me a more permanent value, somehow or other. It is almost shameful to confess that the poems which have meant most to me, like Wordsworth's 'Ode to Immortality' and Keats' Odes, and pieces of *Macbeth* or *As You Like It* or *Midsummer Night's Dream*, and Goethe's lyrics, such as 'Über allen Gipfeln ist Ruh', and Verlaine's 'Ayant poussé la porte [étroite] qui chancelle' – all these lovely poems which after all give the ultimate shape to one's life; all these lovely poems, woven deep into a man's consciousness, are still not woven so deep in me as the rather banal Nonconformist hymns that penetrated through and through my childhood.

> Each gentle dove
> And sighing bough
> That makes the eve
> So fair to me
> Has something far
> Diviner now
> To draw me back
> To Galilee. –
> O Galilee, sweet Galilee
> Where Jesus loved so much to be,
> O Galilee, sweet Galilee
> Come sing thy songs again to me!

To me the word Galilee has a wonderful sound. The Lake of Galilee! I don't want to know where it is. I never want to go to Palestine: Galilee is one of those lovely glamorous worlds, not places, that exist in the golden haze of a child's half-formed imagination. And in my man's imagination it is just the same. It has been left untouched. With regard to the hymns which had such a profound influence on my childish consciousness, there has been no crystallising out, no dwindling into actuality, no hardening into the commonplace. They are the same to my man's experience as they were to me nearly forty years ago. . . .

The sheer delight of a child's apperception is based on *wonder*: and deny it as we may, knowledge and wonder counteract one another. So that as knowledge increases, wonder decreases. We say again: Familiarity breeds contempt. So that as we grow older, and become more familiar with phenomena, we become more contemptuous of them. – But that is only partly true. It has taken some races of men thousands of years to become contemptuous of the moon, and to the Hindu the cow is still wondrous. It is not familiarity that breeds contempt, it is the assumption of knowledge. Anybody who looks at the moon and says, 'I know all about that poor orb,' is , of course, bored by the moon.

Now the great and fatal fruit of our civilisation, which is a civilisation based on knowledge, and hostile to experience, is boredom. All our wonderful education and learning is producing a grand sum-total of boredom. Modern people are inwardly thoroughly bored. Do as they may, they are bored.

They are bored because they experience nothing. And they experience nothing because the wonder has gone out of them. And when the wonder has gone out of a man, he is dead. He is henceforth only an insect.

When all come to all, the most precious element in life is wonder. . . .

Somebody says that mystery is nothing, because mystery is something you don't know, and what you don't know is nothing to you. But there are two ways of knowing. . . .

Even the real scientist works in the sense of wonder. The pity is, when he comes out of his laboratory he puts aside his wonder along with his apparatus, and tries to make it all perfectly didactic. Science in its true condition of wonder is as religious as any religion. But didactic science is as dead and boring as dogmatic religion. Both are wonderless and productive of boredom, endless boredom.

Now we come back to hymns. They live and glisten in the depths of the man's consciousness in undimmed wonder, . . . [s]o that the miracle of the loaves and fishes is just as good to me now as when I was a child. I don't care whether it is historically a fact or not. What does it matter? It is part of the genuine wonder. The same with all the religious teaching I had as a child, *apart* from the didacticism and sentimentalism. I am eternally grateful for the wonder with which it filled my childhood.

> Sun of my soul, thou Saviour dear
> It is not night if Thou be near –

That was the last hymn at the Board School. It did not mean to me any christian dogma or any salvation. Just the words 'Sun of my soul, thou Saviour dear,' penetrated me with wonder and the mystery of twilight.

The ghastly sentimentalism that came like a leprosy over religion had not yet got hold of our colliery village. I remember when I was in Class II in the Sunday School, when I was about seven, a woman teacher trying to harrow us about the crucifixion. And she kept saying: 'And aren't you sorry for Jesus? Aren't you sorry?' And most of the children wept. I believe I shed a crocodile tear or two, but very vivid is my memory of saying to myself 'I don't really care a bit'. And I could never go back to it. I never cared about the crucifixion, one way or another. Yet the wonder of it penetrated very deep in me.

(D. H. Lawrence, first published in the *Evening News*,
13 October 1928. Abridged from *The Cambridge Edition of the
Works of D. H. Lawrence: Late Essays and Articles*,
Cambridge University Press, 2004.)

Support Agencies

BEREAVEMENT

Child Bereavement Network
c/o National Children's Bureau (NCB)
8 Wakley Street
London EC1V 7QE
Tel.: 020 7843 6309
Website: www.childhoodbereavementnetwork.org.uk

The Child Bereavement Trust
Aston House
West Wycombe
Bucks HP14 3AG
Tel.: 01494 446648
Website: www.childbereavement.org.uk
Useful publications and information service.

The Compassionate Friends
53 North Street
Bristol BS3 1EN
Helpline: 08451 232304
Website: www.tcf.org.uk
A national self-help organization which assists families in the positive
resolution of grief following the death of a child.

Cruse Bereavement Care
Cruse House
126 Sheen Road
Richmond
Surrey TW9 1UR
Helpline: 0870 167 1677
Helpline for young people: 0808 808 1677

Website: www.crusebereavementcare.org.uk
Cruse Bereavement Care's Youth Involvement Project includes the
website <www.rd4u.org.uk> designed by young people for young people
who have been bereaved.

Macmillan Cancer Relief
89 Albert Embankment
London SE1 1UQ
Macmillan CancerLine: 0808 808 2020 (9 a.m. to 10 p.m., Monday to
Friday)
Website: www.macmillan.org.uk

National Children's Bureau
Website: www.ncb.org.uk
Resource for those working with bereaved children and young people,
their families and other caregivers.

www.riprap.org.uk
Advice, stories and support for young people aged between 12 and 16
who are coping with a parent who has terminal cancer.

Winston's Wish
Website: www.winstonswish.org.uk
Practical support for children and young people who have been
bereaved.

BULLYING

Advisory Centre for Education (ACE)
Website: www.ace-ed.org.uk
Publishes a series of booklets aimed at parents and those working with
them, including school governors and local education authority officers.

www.bbc.co.uk/schools/bullying

ChildLine
45 Folgate Street
London E1 6GL
Helpline: 0800 1111 (24 hours, for children needing free confidential
help on a range of issues including bullying)
Website: www.childline.org.uk

FOR PARENT AND FAMILY SUPPORT

Childwatch
19 Spring Bank
Hull, East Yorkshire
HU3 1AF
Tel.: 01482 325 552 (9 a.m. to 5 p.m., Monday to Friday)
Assists children and adults who have been abused.

www.christianmums.com

Church of England
Website: www.cofe.anglican.org/info/education/children
This part of the Church's website deals with its work with children in
parish churches, including worship, liturgy, ministry and child protection.

Families Need Fathers
134 Curtain Road
London EC2A 3AR
Tel.: 08707 607111
Helpline: 08707 607496
Website: www.fnf.org.uk
Provides support to divorced and separated parents, irrespective of
gender or marital status, on shared issues arising from family break-
down, especially on maintaining the child's relationships with both
parents.

Fathers Direct
Herald House
Lamb's Passage
Bunhill Row
London EC1Y 8TQ
Tel.: 0845 634 1328
Website: www.fathersdirect.com
The National Information Centre on Fatherhood, partly government-
sponsored, providing new policy updates, publications and guides to
support fathers and their families.

Home-Start
2 Salisbury Road
Leicester LE1 7QR
Freephone: 0800 3068 6368
Website: www.home-start.org.uk
Email: info@home-start.org.uk
This organization is made up of a network of trained parent volunteers

who support other parents who are struggling to cope for all sorts of reasons, including post-natal illness, disability, bereavement or social isolation. Email to find your local group.

Kidscape
2 Grosvenor Gardens
London SW1W 0DH
Helpline: 08451 205204
Website: www.kidscape.org.uk
Campaigns on all aspects of children's safety, and includes information about bullying and child abuse.

Mothers' Union Parenting Training Programme
Mary Sumner House
24 Tufton Street
London SW1P 3RB
Tel.: 020 7222 5533
Website: www.themothersunion.org/parenting.aspx
This Christian organization welcomes male or female, single or married members. Its Parenting Training Programme explores ways of supporting marriage in the UK and around the world.

National Society for the Prevention of Cruelty to Children (NSPCC)
Weston House
42 Curtain Road
London EC2A 3NH
Child Protection Helpline: 0808 800 5000
Website: www.nspcc.org.uk

Parenting UK (formerly Parenting Education and Support Forum)
Unit 431, Highgate Studios
53–79 Highgate Road
London NW5 1TL
Tel.: 020 7284 8370
Website: www.parentinguk.org
National umbrella organization for people who work with parents.

Parentline Plus
520 Highgate Studios
53–79 Highgate Road
London NW5 1TL
Helpline: 0808 800 2222
Website: www.parentlineplus.org.uk
Offers support to anyone parenting a child.

Notes

1 Our Children: Context and Perceptions

1. Philippe Ariès, *Centuries of Childhood,* tr. Robert Baldick (London: Cape, 1962).
2. Medieval historians, such as Shulamith Shahar in *Childhood in the Middle Ages* (London: Routledge, 1990), have challenged this thesis. Hugh Cunningham considered that one problem with Ariès was that the English translation used the word 'idea', which failed to convey the meaning of the French *sentiment,* a sense of 'feeling and affection about childhood'. Ariès distinguished between a *sentiment* about childhood and the nature of childhood.
3. Hugh Cunningham, *Children and Childhood in Western Society since 1500* (London: Longman, 1995).
4. Individuals such as Robert Raikes, Hannah More, Lord Shaftesbury and Thomas Barnardo had become appalled by the scale of the brutalization and exploitation of children. Shaftesbury reckoned there were 30,000 children abandoned in London alone. When caught in acts of lawlessness, they were punished alongside adults, imprisoned and deported.
5. Lloyd de Mause, *The History of Childhood: The Untold Story of Child Abuse* (London: Bellew, 1991; first published 1974); Edward Shorter, *The Making of the Modern Family* (London: Collins, 1976); and Lawrence Stone, *The Family, Sex and Marriage in England 1500–1800* (London: Weidenfeld and Nicolson, 1977).
6. Neil Postman, *The Disappearance of Childhood* (London: W. H. Allen, 1983); John Sommerville, *The Rise and Fall of Childhood* (London: Sage, 1982); and Harry Hendrick, *Children, Childhood and English Society, 1880–1990* (Cambridge: Cambridge University Press, 1997).
7. An example of a social construct in developed societies is how 'being human' is understood (construed) as being a certain age, educated, fluent in language, and independent. It therefore excludes, downgrades and stigmatizes those who do not fulfil these criteria, children. Within the developed world there is a range in the age of criminal responsibility.
8. Lucy Ward, "'Databases could be danger to young,' says study', *Guardian,* 21 November 2006, p. 4. (The study was carried out by the Foundation for Information Policy Research.)
9. <www.everychildmatters.gov.uk/strategy/childrenscommissioner> (accessed 21/04/06).
10. <extended.schools@dfes.gsi.gov.uk> (accessed 26/7/06).
11. United Nations document, *Study on Violence against Children;* <www.violencestudy.org/r25>.

12. The sinful condition of humanity is only found in Genesis 3. Today theologians recognize that Adam is not a proper name but means 'human'. The story is a myth to account for evil, which is found in humanity's rebellion against God.

13. Augustine, *Confessions*, tr. R. S. Pine-Coffin (Harmondsworth: Penguin Classics, 1961), Book.1, sect.7.

14. For example, James Dobson's books (all published by Living Books in Wheaton, IL), *Dare to Discipline* (1996), *The Strong-Willed Child* (2004), *Bringing up Boys* (2002), *Parenting Isn't for Cowards* (1994); J. Richard Fugate, *What the Bible Says about . . . Child Training*, 2nd edn (Apache Junction, AZ: Foundation for Biblical Research, 1996).

15. Jean-Jacques Rousseau, *Émile*, tr. Barbara Foxley (London: Dent, Everyman's Library, 1911).

16. P. Monroe, *Fundamental Teachings of Rousseau*, p. 561.

17. *Rousseau on Education*, tr. R. L. Archer (London: Arnold, 1912), pp. 49–50.

18. Cunningham, *Children and Childhood*, p. 73.

19. Quoted in Cunningham, *Children and Childhood*, p. 74.

20. Blake Morrison, *As If* (London: Granta Books, 1997), p. 48.

21. Marina Warner, *Managing Monsters: Six Myths of Our Time* (London: Vintage, 1994), p. 44.

22. Viviana A. Zelizer, *Pricing the Priceless Child: The Changing Social Value of Children* (New York: Basic Books, 1985).

23. Jon Davies, 'Welcome to the Pied Piper', in Adrian Thatcher (ed.), *Celebrating Christian Marriage* (Edinburgh: T&T Clark, 2002), pp. 240–9.

24. David Popenoe, *Disturbing the Nest: Family Change and Decline in Modern Societies* (New York: Walter de Gruyter, 1988), p. 330.

25 Hans-Ruedi Weber, *Jesus and the Children* (Geneva: World Council of Churches, 1979), p. 6.

26. Thomas Wiedemann, *Adults and Children in the Roman Empire* (New Haven: Yale University Press; London: Routledge, 1989), p. 18.

27. Wiedemann, *Adults and Children,* pp. 21–2.

28. Thomas Aquinas, *Summa Theologiae* (Cambridge: Blackfriars, 1964), II–II.q.10.a.12.

29. Herbert Anderson and Susan B. W. Johnson, *Regarding Children: A New Respect for Childhood and Families* (Louisville, KY: Westminster John Knox Press, 1994), p. 10.

30. Virgil, *Eclogues*, IV, 4–20.

31. Henry Scott Holland, *Facts of the Faith (Being a Collection of Sermons not Hitherto Published in Book Form)*, ed. Christopher Cheshire (London: Longmans, Green and Co, 1919), pp. 110–11.

32. Bonnie J. Miller-McLemore, *Let the Children Come: Reimagining Childhood from a Christian Perspective* (San Francisco: Jossey-Bass, 2003), pp. 1–2.

2 Insights from Child Development

1. African children in rural villages can estimate volume and capacity because from an early age a daily activity is measuring cups of rice into baskets. The experience and the ability are not present in urban European children.

2. *British Nursing News*, 25 September 2005.

3. Penelope Leach, *Children First* (New York: Vintage Books, 1995), pp. 43–8.

4. Leach, *Children First*, p. 36.

5. Herbert Anderson and Susan B. W. Johnson, *Regarding Children: A New Respect for Childhood and Families* (Louisville, KY: Westminster John Knox Press, 1994), p. 45.

6. John Bowlby (1907–90) is influential for his theory of attachment (how babies become attached to the mother figure), separation (what happens when babies are separated from the mother figure) and loss (what happens when babies experience loss, having been separated from people they feel close to). Subsequent research has identified different types of attachment such as anxious/avoidant, secure/insecure and anxious/resistant.

7. Donald Winnicott (1896–1971), in his book *The Child, the Family and the Outside World* (Harmondsworth: Penguin, 1964).

8. Erik Erikson, 'Identity and the life cycle: selected papers', *Psychological Issues*, vol. 1 (1959). Here I have limited the stages to those covered by my theme of childhood.

9. This trust may be extended to other people. There can be several carers, apart from the mother or father; it is the quality of time that determines whether or not the child becomes attached to another carer, such as a neighbour or grandparent. In parts of rural Africa the child belongs to the whole adult community, choosing as its 'parent' the adult from whom love and security is received. This is helpful if the biological parent is ill, tired, did not want the infant or is cruel: the child can find support elsewhere.

10. Sometimes a child may have an imaginary friend who is a source of assurance. This 'friend' is very real to the child and parents need to take its 'presence' seriously.

11. Such knowledge has increased as women with insight as mothers have entered the field of psychology, technology such as the video recorder has been used in psychological 'tests', and developments in computer technology have enabled parallels to be drawn between computers and the workings of the human brain.

12. In the 1960s child study research focused on psychology and education. It was assumed that children were socialized into a *set* of values and behaviours that were universal and fixed, and they were thus transformed from asocial beings into social adults. A society that sees children as different, inferior and in need of socialization has consequences for children. Adults create hierarchical boundaries between themselves and children on the basis of supposed differences, and maintain children in structurally powerless positions. Subtle mechanisms allow adults to dominate children (e.g. control over their bodies, voices, time and behaviour). Children are on the receiving end of family values. They are presumed to 'belong to' or be the 'possessions of' their parents. The concept of family is seen in functionalist and essentialist terms, and is often equated with parental agency. Children are marginalized. Gradually, social scientists in the 1990s acknowledged childhood as part of society and culture rather than a precursor to it. The cross-cultural variation in childhood identified children as already social actors, not passive and incomplete beings in the process of becoming socialized adults.

13. Virginia Axline, *Dibs: In Search of Self* (Harmondsworth: Penguin, 1964), p. 16.

14. Tina Bruce and Carolyn Meggitt, *Child Care and Education*, 4th edn (London: Hodder Education, 2006), p. 466.

15. S. Woodruff, *Meditations with Mechtild of Magdeburg* (Santa Fe, NM: Bear and Co, 1982), pp. 47, 54.

16. Alison M. Gopnik, Andrew N. Meltzoff and Patricia K. Kuhl, *The Scientist in the Crib: Minds, Brains and How Children Learn* (New York: William Morrow, 1999), p. 208.

17. Jean Piaget (1896–1980) was influential in the UK from the 1960s to the 1990s, dominating approaches to the understanding of cognitive development in primary education. He described childhood stages as preverbal, precognitive, inexperienced and immature and less valuable than adult stages. This is negative and undervalues children, concentrating on what they cannot do. It is more helpful to observe what children can do and how their thinking develops.

18. Peter K. Smith and Helen Cowie, *Understanding Children's Development* (Oxford: Blackwell, 1988), p. 327.

19. Writers such as Gopnik, Meltzoff and Kuhl, in *Scientist in the Crib.*

20. Child development theories arise out of research, but it is crucial to ask who is doing the research. There is no such thing as objective research; the subjectivity of the researcher always enters the thinking and the hypothesis. For example, Piaget grew up in Western Europe. He was an only child and his child developmental theory emphasizes the child as an individual. Lev Vygotsky (born the same year as Piaget) was a Russian, from a large family and was dominated by Marxist ideas. It is hardly surprising, therefore, that his theory of learning emphasizes social relationships.

3 Insights into Spiritual and Religious Development

1. David Hay with Rebecca Nye, *The Spirit of the Child: A Child's Voice in Education* (London: Fount, 1998), p. 172.

2. Edmund Gosse, *Father and Son*, ed. J. Hepburn (London: Oxford University Press, 1974), p. 23.

3. Robert Coles, *The Spiritual Life of Children* (London: HarperCollins, 1992), pp. 286–9.

4. Coles, *Spiritual Life of Children,* p. 39, quoting William James.

5. Coles, *Spiritual Life of Children,* p. xvi.

6. Hay and Nye, *Spirit of the Child,* p. 10.

7. The pictures were: a girl gazing into a fire; a boy looking out at the night sky; a girl looking tearfully at her dead pet gerbil in its cage; a boy standing alone in a playground, ignored and perhaps unhappy; a boy on a wet pavement, with some dropped food at his feet, looking upwards with his hands spread out.

8. Hay and Nye, *Spirit of the Child,* p. 106.

9. Jerome Berryman, 'Children and mature spirituality'; <www.godlyplay.org>.

10. Hay and Nye, *Spirit of the Child*, p. 113.

11. Hay and Nye, *Spirit of the Child*, p. 114.

12. A list of how spiritual development (and religious development) is promoted can be found in Qualifications and Curriculum Authority (QCA), *Religious Education (the Non-statutory National Framework)*, p. 14; <www.qca.org.uk>.

13. Hay and Nye, *Spirit of the Child*, p. 170.

14. Mary K. Stone, *Don't Just Do Something, Sit There* (Norwich: Religious and Moral Education Press, 1995); Marian Carter and Cathy Bowness, 'Bread not stones: nurturing spirituality', in Adrian Thatcher (ed.), *Spirituality in the Curriculum* (London: Cassell, 1999).

15. Ronald Goldman, *Religious Thinking from Childhood to Adolescence* (New York: Seabury Press, 1968), *Readiness for Religion* (New York: Seabury Press, 1970).

16. Rebecca Nye, in Fraser Watts, Rebecca Nye and Sara Savage, *Psychology for Christian Ministry* (London: Routledge, 2002), p. 86.

17. Violet Madge, 'The Bible in the classroom', in Robert C. Walton (ed.), *A Source Book of the Bible for Teachers* (London: SCM Press, 1970), p. 36.

18. Ellen C. Mee, 'Children growing up: the role of religion', in Robert C. Walton (ed.), *A Source Book of the Bible for Teachers* (London: SCM Press, 1970), p. 17.

19. Mee, 'Children growing up', p. 27.

20. Maria Montessori (1870–1952) developed an educational environment where the child was at the centre. Sofia Cavalletti, *The Religious Potential of the Child* (Ramsey, NJ: Paulist Press, 1983).

21. Cavalletti, *Religious Potential of the Child*, p. 42.

22. Cavalletti, *Religious Potential of the Child*, p. 69.
23. James Fowler, *Stages of Faith: The Psychology of Human Development and the Quest for Meaning* (Victoria, Australia: Collins Dove, 1987).
24. John H. Westerhoff, *Will Our Children Have Faith?* (New York: Seabury Press, 1976).
25. Watts, Nye and Savage, *Psychology for Christian Ministry*, p. 90.
26. Pat Milner and Birgit Carolin, *Time to Listen to Children: Personal and Professional Communication* (London: Routledge, 1999), p. 83.

4 Insights from the Scriptures

1. David H. Jensen, *Graced Vulnerability: A Theology of Childhood* (Cleveland: The Pilgrim Press, 2005), p. 2.
2. If a married man died childless, his brother was required to marry the widow so that a son might be born to continue the brother's name (Deut. 25.6–10). The first son of this union was to succeed to the name of the dead brother.
3. Flavius Josephus (37–100 CE) was a Palestinian Jew whose historical works are the primary source for Palestine in the New Testament period. His works include *The Jewish War*, *Jewish Antiquities* and his autobiography.
4. Michael Shire, 'Learning to be righteous: a Jewish theology of childhood', in Karen-Marie Yust, Aostre N. Johnson, Sandy Eisenberg Sasso and Eugene C. Roehlkepartain (eds), *Nurturing Child and Adolescent Spirituality: Perspectives from the World's Religious Traditions* (Lanham, MD: Rowman and Littlefield, 2006), p. 51.
5. Hans-Ruedi Weber, *Jesus and the Children* (Geneva: World Council of Churches, 1979), pp. 42, 75.
6. The honour–shame code appears to have been a cultural value in the culture of the Ancient Near East. The two concepts are evident in Proverbs.
7. For example, James Dobson, *Dare to Discipline* (Wheaton, IL: Living Books, 1996), *The Strong-Willed Child* (2004), *Bringing up Boys* (2002), *Parenting Isn't for Cowards* (1994); Richard J. Fugate, *What the Bible Says about . . . Child Training*, 2nd edn (Apache Junction, AZ: Foundation for Biblical Research, 1996).
8. Terence E. Fretheim, 'God, Abraham, and the abuse of Isaac', *Word and World*, vol. 15, no. 1 (Winter 1995), p. 49.
9. Geza Vermes, *Scripture and Tradition in Judaism* (Leiden: Brill, 1973), pp. 193–227.
10. *Tanhuma Haksdum*, cited in S. Valler, 'The story of Jephthah's daughter in the Midrash', in A. Brenner (ed.), *Judges: A Feminist Companion to the Bible*, Second Series (Sheffield: Sheffield Academic Press, 1999), pp. 48–66.
11. Gerhard von Rad, *Genesis – A Commentary* (London: SCM Press, 1981), p. 244.
12. Phyllis Trible, 'Genesis 22: the sacrifice of Sarah', in Alice Bach (ed.), *Women in the Hebrew Bible: A Reader* (London: Routledge, 1999), pp. 271–90.
13. Gracia F. Ellwood, *Batter, My Heart* (Wallingford, PA: Pendle Hill Pamphlets, 1988). She writes that God is depicted as an abusive husband who wounds, heals and wounds again (Deut. 32.39; Isa. 42.24–25; 51.17–23). God is a humiliator of oppressed women (Jer. 13.25–26; Isa. 3.16–17). God sexually abuses Israel and then takes her back in love (Hos. 2.12, 21–22; Ezek. 16.6–8, 36–42). God curses the people (Lev. 26.27–28; Deut. 28.63, 67).
14. David R. Blumenthal, in *Facing the Abusing God: A Theology of Protest* (Louisville, KY: Westminster John Knox Press, 1993), claims that it is not possible to deny 'that Scripture does portray God as an abusing person; that God, as agent in our sacred texts, does indeed act abusively; that God as described in the Bible, acts like an abusing male, husband, father and lord' (p. 242).

15. Jesus argued, 'but it is not so among you; but whoever wishes to become great among you must be your servant' (Mark 10.43). Jesus' background was the structural violence of the first century CE, arising from a fractured society. Jesus created a new community of faithful followers (Matt. 16.18–20). The Greek word εκκλησια (*ekklesia*) translates the Hebrew *qahal*, meaning an 'assembly called together', in the Hebrew Scriptures 'the community of the chosen people'. Here is an egalitarianism which challenges stories of authoritarian action.

16. Scholars such as the feminist biblical scholar Elizabeth Fiorenza have distinguished strategies to deal with texts. She suggests a hermeneutic of suspicion, one of remembrance and one of proclamation. Elizabeth Schüssler Fiorenza, *Bread Not Stone: The Challenge of Feminist Biblical Interpretation* (Edinburgh: T&T Clark, 1990).

17. Virgil, *Eclogues*, IV, 4–20.

18. Shire, 'Learning to be righteous', p. 45.

19. 'I, God, am your playmate! I will lead the child in you in wonderful ways for I have chosen you. Beloved child, come swiftly to Me, for I am truly in you ... God says: "I am your playmate! Your childhood was a companion of my Holy Spirit." ' S. Woodruff, *Meditations with Mechtild of Magdeburg* (Santa Fe, NM: Bear and Co, 1982), pp. 47, 54.

20. 'She made it possible for me to call her by your name. Our affection for children so young has, furthermore, a poignancy all its own: the delight it gives is quite pure and free from all reproach. She had herself ... a surprisingly natural gift of mildness and good temper, and her way of responding to friendship and of bestowing favours gave us pleasure while it afforded us an insight into her kindness.' Plutarch, 'Consolation to His Wife', *Moralia*, 7.575–605, quoted in William A. Strange, *Children in the Early Church* (Carlisle: Paternoster Press, 1996), p. 8.

21. Herbert Anderson and Susan B. W. Johnson, *Regarding Children: A New Respect for Childhood and Families* (Louisville, KY: Westminster John Knox Press, 1994), p. 20.

22. Tamar (Gen. 38) and the wife of Uriah, Bathsheba (2 Sam. 11), are called adulteresses, yet Tamar is pronounced more righteous than Judah (Gen. 38.26). Rahab (Josh. 2), a prostitute, saved by her good action, is declared justified (Jas. 2.25; cf. Heb. 11.31). Ruth is a Moabite. In Amos, Jeremiah, Ezekiel and Zephaniah there are oracles against the Moabites. In Deuteronomy 23.2–3, a Moabite and an Ammonite were forbidden to enter the congregation until the tenth generation.

23. Robin Maas, 'Christ as the logos of childhood: reflections on the meaning and mission of the child', *Theology Today*, vol. 56, no. 4 (2000), p. 461.

24. Irenaeus, *Against Heresies*, Book 2, chapter XXII, sect. 4; <www.ccel.org/fathers/ANF-01/iren2/-1K>

25. J. Moltmann, 'Child and childhood as metaphors of hope', *Theology Today*, vol. 56, no. 4 (2000), p. 592.

26. Stephen G. Post, *More Lasting Unions: Christianity, the Family and Society* (Grand Rapids, MI: Eerdmans, 2000), p. 104.

27. Hans von Balthasar, 'Jesus as child and his praise of the child', *Communio*, vol. 22 (Winter 1995), p. 633.

28. Post, *More Lasting Unions*, pp. 57–9.

29. The context of the story is the question asked by John the Baptist, 'Are you the one or do we look for another?' In reply, Jesus speaks of the signs of good news: healings, exorcisms and prisoners released. When his listeners dispute these signs, Jesus responds by observing children at play (Luke 7.18–19).

30. The use of 'the first' to indicate social and political status occurs in ancient literature. Josephus described leading men and ruling priests of his day as the 'first men' (*Antiquities*, 11.5.3).

31. J. M. Gundry-Volf, 'The least and the greatest: children in the New Testament', in Marcia J. Bunge (ed.), *The Child in Christian Thought* (Grand Rapids, MI: Eerdmans, 2001), p. 44. She contrasts this with Hellenistic texts, Plutarch and Diodorus, who wrote of *women* taking children in their arms as exemplary for other *women*.

32. In the Jewish custom of *shaliach*, or law of agency, a man's representative is to be treated as the man himself. For example, see Matthew 21.33–41.

33. John Carroll, 'Children in the Bible', *Interpretation*, vol. 55, no. 2 (2001), p. 129.

34. James Francis, 'Children and childhood in the New Testament', in Stephen C. Barton (ed.), *The Family in Theological Perspective* (Edinburgh: T&T Clark, 1996), pp. 74–5. Luke changes Mark's words to 'this child' rather than 'children as such', allowing the interpretation 'which of them is ready to receive this child', that is, Jesus himself. Jesus is childlike.

35. The pronoun translated 'of such' is a correlation demonstrative pronoun, with the meaning that the kingdom belongs to children as well as to those like them. This insight was provided by John Pridmore.

36. The word *straphete* has the same root as the verb for conversion, yet in almost all the 22 occurrences it means to 'physically turn around towards' rather than religious conversion. Moreover, the saying is addressed to disciples who are already believers.

37. Francis, 'Children and childhood in the New Testament', p. 77.

38. Francis, 'Children and childhood in the New Testament', p. 77.

39. Gundry-Volf, 'The least and the greatest', p. 45.

40. This makes sense for Mark's readership, living after the destruction of Jerusalem, a vulnerable minority in an alien world, experiencing persecution and powerless. Jesus is depicted as the vulnerable 'Son of Man', who preached a kingdom which put the vulnerable child in the midst. The disciples, who had become leaders of the Church, are depicted as slow of faith, doubting and 'blind' to the gospel. This knowledge would bring comfort and reassurance to persecuted readers of the gospel who were themselves 'little ones'.

41. Stephen Barton, 'Jesus – friend of little children?' in Jeff Astley and David Day (eds), *The Contours of Christian Education* (Great Wakering, Essex: McCrimmons, 1992), p. 39.

42. Scholars consider the source of the texts is the Graeco-Roman culture deriving from Aristotelian politics, with parallels in the Jewish tradition. A household's good ordering is a Christian responsibility, a witness to society (cf. 1 Tim. 3.2–5, 12; 1 Cor. 11.2–16).

43. J. D. G. Dunn, 'The household rules in the New Testament', in Stephen C. Barton (ed.), *The Family in Theological Perspective* (Edinburgh: T&T Clark, 1996), p. 53.

44. Deborah F. Sawyer, *God, Gender and the Bible* (London: Routledge, 2002), p.136.

45. E. Peterson, 'Einige Bemerkungen zum Hamburger Papyrus', in *Frühkirke, Judentum und Gnosis* (Rome: Herder, 1959), pp. 194–6, quoted in Sawyer, *God, Gender and the Bible*, p. 137.

46. 'Jesus saw the children who were being suckled and said to the disciples, "These children who are being suckled are like those who enter the kingdom." The disciples said to Jesus, "Shall we then, being children, enter the kingdom?" Jesus answered, "When you make the two one, and when you make the inner as the outer and the outer as the inner and the above as the below, and when you make the male and female into a single one, so that the male will not be male and the female will not be female . . . then you will enter the kingdom." ' Bentley Layton (tr. and intro.), *The Gnostic Scriptures* (London: SCM Press, 1987), p. 384, sec. 20–24. Elsewhere the male dominates. 'Simon Peter said to them: Let Mary go out from among us, because women are not worthy of the Life. Jesus said: See, I

shall lead her, so that I will make her male, that she too may become a living spirit, resembling you males.' *Ibid.,* logion 114.

47. Strange, *Children in the Early Church*, p. 69.
48. Historically, theology has been reluctant to engage with any theology of the child (see Appendix 1).

5 Pastoral Care: The Brass Tacks

1. R. A. Lambourne, *Contact*, no. 35 (1971).
2. <Parentingnewsletter-reply@bbc.co.uk>
3. Parenting as a vocation was central to some of the early Church Fathers such as Chrysostom; to Luther, who wrote catechisms for the home; to Schleiermacher. It is beginning to be 'rediscovered' in the twenty-first century by Adrian Thatcher and some of the feminist pastoral theologians.
4. Martin Luther, *Babylonian Captivity of the Church,* in *Luther's Works*, Book 45, ed. Jaroslav Pelikan and Helmut Lehmann (St Louis: Concordia, 1955–1986), p. 46.
5. Luther, *Works,* Book 45, p. 39.
6. Mentors are those who stand alongside children and guide by their example and response to children's questions. Such mentors can be parents, family members and members of the congregation.
7. Abraham Maslow (1908–1970) proposed the hierarchy of needs in his 1943 paper 'A theory of human motivation'. He contended that as humans meet 'basic needs' they seek to satisfy successively 'higher needs' that occupy a set hierarchy.
8. <www.barnabasinchurches.org.uk>

6 Pastoral Care in Challenging Situations

1. Fraser Watts, Rebecca Nye and Sara Savage, *Psychology for Christian Ministry* (London: Routledge, 2002), p. 80.
2. Martin Herbert, *Working with Children and Their Families* (London: Routledge and British Psychological Society, 1988).
3. Watts, Nye and Savage, *Psychology for Christian Ministry,* p. 81.
4. Watts, Nye and Savage, *Psychology for Christian Ministry*, p. 82.
5. David Richo is an American psychotherapist, teacher and writer. He combines Jungian, transpersonal and mythic perspectives in his work; <www.davericho.com/Bio.htm>.
6. At present there are 50 different schemes in England, e.g. Triple P (Positive Parenting Programme).
7. Exclusions from school have increased in recent years, particularly in primary schools. This may be because children have become more complex or because problem behaviour is less acceptable and teachers under pressure are not willing to listen and deal with issues.
8. Table taken from Watts, Nye and Savage, *Psychology for Christian Ministry*, p. 82.
9. Pat Milner and Birgit Carolin, *Time to Listen to Children: Personal and Professional Communication* (London: Routledge, 1999), p. 128.
10. <www.adoption.org.uk> (see also Appendix 5).
11. Janet Pais, *Suffer the Children: A Theology of Liberation by a Victim of Child Abuse* (Mahwah, NJ: Paulist Press, 1991).
12. Milner and Carolin, *Time to Listen,* p. 112.
13. Alison M. Gopnik, Andrew N. Meltzoff and Patricia K. Kuhl, *The Scientist in the*

Crib: Minds, Brains and How Children Learn (New York: William Morrow, 1999), p. 49.

7 Pastoral Care Through Christian Education

1. I acknowledge here my adaptation of a story in Gervase Phinn's *A Wayne in a Manger* (Harmondsworth: Penguin, 2006).
2. The term 'Christian education' is used in this chapter to refer to the teaching of Christianity within the committed faith perspective of the Church.
3. The upper classes always had the leisure and finance for the education of their young through private tutors or monastic schools; the majority of the population had only the experience they gained from life.
4. This expressed a different point of view from the Sabbatarians, who objected to schools on Sunday, while other Christians objected to the teaching of children *per se*.
5. This was a period when there was intense rivalry among the Churches.
6. So-called 'conscience clauses' were included, which gave the right of withdrawal from collective worship for teachers and for pupils at the request of parents.
7. *Partners in Learning* (Redhill: National Christian Education Council); *Alive in God's World* (London: Church House Publishing, 1968).
8. This is a 'non-statutory national framework'. Each local authority has a Standing Advisory Council for Religious Education (SACRE), composed of educationalists and representatives of churches, which is responsible for the construction of a local syllabus. QCA hoped that its framework would inform these groups and be used as a basis.
9. Ultimate questions are defined as questions such as 'Is God real?', 'Why are we alive?', 'What is meant by good and evil?', 'Why do people suffer?' These are powerful questions about beliefs and values.
10. School of Education, University of Exeter, *Teaching about Jesus in Religious Education: Improving Children's Learning*, 2006.
11. Some church schools in the North-West have an overwhelming proportion of Muslim children, and recently a Muslim was appointed as head of a church school. I strongly believe that Christians should also be involved on the governing boards of state schools, being concerned with the whole curriculum of the schools and the education of our children, as well as the provision for religious education and collective worship.
12. Paul Taylor, *The Texts of Paulo Freire* (Buckingham: Open University Press, 1993), p. 53.
13. Freire's concept of conscientization is much debated. Does it create a value-neutral learning environment for the learner or is it preconditioned to a set of political or religious views?
14. For example, a teenage non-reader received a letter from her boyfriend, who was abroad in the army. She did not want the letter to be read by anyone other than herself. At last she saw the point of being able to read, and a gifted teacher was able to help her.
15. Lev Vygotsky (1896–1934) was unknown in the West until his work was translated into English in the 1960s and 1970s.
16. Bruner considered that cognitive development is the distinct way a child represents the world. First, there is the *enactive mode*, when the child represents the world through activity, found in motor responses. Learning grows out of action and perception (e.g. by using building blocks the child learns that over a particular height the blocks topple). Between two and six years the child represents the

world through images or spatial schemas, the *iconic mode* (a child begins to use language to stand for objects). By seven years, reaching the *symbolic mode*, the child is freed from the immediate environment and able to symbolize (in language, writing and drawing). The child begins to be able to go beyond the information given and represent the world symbolically. This is at the heart of children's capacity to think abstractly and to make knowledge their own.

17. <www.infed.org/thinkers/gardner.htm>

18. We need to reinherit the culture of the Western world, which is rooted in Christianity and evidenced in art, music, morality, images, metaphors and symbols.

19. Gretchen Wolff Pritchard, *Offering the Gospel to Children* (Cambridge, MA: Cowley, 1992), p. 5.

20. One methodology is to use the story of a Bible character who in some way relates to children's lives. Ask them to close their eyes while the story is being told and imagine the scene. Then help them imagine themselves in the story. Bring them back to reality by suggesting they open their eyes gradually and return. Use open and exploring imaginative questions. Ask some open questions about how they felt in the story and where they were in it. The answers can become the subjects for prayer.

21. Robert Farrar Capon, *The Parables of Grace* (Grand Rapids, MI: Eerdmans, 1988).

22. I acknowledge the insights here of John M. Sutcliffe, *Learning and Teaching Together* (London: Chester House Publications, 1980), pp. 65–70.

23. Bruno Bettelheim, *The Uses of Enchantment: The Meaning and Importance of Fairy Tales* (Harmondsworth: Penguin, 1978) [first published Thames and Hudson, 1976].

24. Marina Warner, *Managing Monsters: Six Myths of Our Time: The Reith Lectures, 1994* (London: Vintage, 1994), p. 37.

25. Fraser Watts, Rebecca Nye and Sara Savage, *Psychology for Christian Ministry* (London: Routledge, 2002), p. 93.

26. In past generations the home taught the faith; later the school did so through Religious Education lessons and assembly. Neither is now the case. For example, the school teaches about the major world faiths, of which Christianity is only one. The result is that many children without home or church backing have a mishmash of beliefs, as seen in research done by the Exeter School of Education (see note 10 above).

8 Pastoral Care within Worship and Sacraments

1. Jerome W. Berryman, *The Complete Guide to Godly Play*, Vol. 1 (Denver: Living the Good News, 2002), p. 112.

2. <www.ccel.org/fathers2ANF-05/anf05-51.htm>

3. Elizabeth A. Clark, 'From Origenism to Pelagianism: elusive issues in an ancient debate', *Princeton Seminary Bulletin* (1991), p. 283.

4. Church statistics for 2003/4 found at <www.cofe.anglican.org/info/cofegazette/comms2003> .

5. One in four primary schools and one in 16 secondary schools in England are Church of England (C. of E.) schools. Nearly one million pupils are educated in more than 4,700 such schools.

6. Central Board of Finance of the Church of England, *Common Worship, Initiation Services* (London: Church House Publishing, 1998), p. 69.

7. Michael H. Taylor, *Variations on a Theme* (London: Galliard, Stainer and Bell, 1973), p. 23.

8. Joyce Ann Mercer, *Welcoming Children: A Practical Theology of Childhood* (St Louis: Chalice Press, 2005), p. 162.

9. In the Eastern Church the congregation is taught to 'read' the Christian story into all that is going on. When the bread and wine is prepared before the service begins, they think of Jesus' birth and the hidden years of his childhood and youth. When the Gospel is carried in to be read (known as the Little Entrance), the thought is of Jesus emerging from obscurity into his public ministry. At the Great Entrance, when the bread and wine are processed through the congregation, Christ is on his way to his suffering and death. As the gifts are laid on the table, he is buried in the tomb; at the consecration of bread and wine thoughts turn to resurrection; and when the chalice is brought to the congregation for communion, the risen Christ appears to his disciples. The blessing at the end of the service is that of our ascended Lord. Thus, every week the story is told. I am grateful to Michael Taylor for this insight.

10. One possibility is to invite all the members of the congregation to share their skills in an 'all-age Saturday workshop' in preparation for a festival (Christmas, Easter or Harvest). Working in groups, they can create banners or an altar frontal, compose and perform dance, drama, music, prayers and liturgy. It is valuable if children can be involved in making bread and wine for the Eucharist. Working with adults in self-chosen groups affirms children as an integral part of the community of faith. Other churches have a regular midweek family evening, which includes games, creativity and worship.

11. 'All-age-worship' is thought by some to be a preferable title to 'Family worship', which might be seen to exclude single people, childless couples and others.

12. One intention is that a service of the word is a bridge to eucharistic worship. The 'bridge' might be made by using the structure of a service like Morning Prayer (as above), or by using particular prayers from the eucharistic service. All-age worship can ease newcomers into worship by its informality. The use of visual aids, drama, art and dance adds a new dimension to worship. It can encourage adult members of the congregation to use their skills and gifts together with children, in contributing to the planning of a service. Worship can then relate more closely to everyday experience expressed in praise, confession and commitment. It becomes an act of nourishment for children and adults. All-age worship is costly in time and preparation but through it the community of faith become committed to one another in a central Christian activity: worship.

13. This declaration is not a summary of the discussion but a short reflection to encourage everyone in their discipleship.

14. See St Gregory's Church, San Francisco (<www.saintgregorys.org>), and Portsmouth Cathedral (<www.portsmouthcathedral.org.uk>).

15. Mercer, *Welcoming Children,* p. 226.

16. For example, local council register offices, a commercial 'Baby Naming Society' and the British Humanist Association.

17. The reasons for requesting baptism are multiple, including the desire to please a mother-in-law, to ensure future attendance at a successful church primary school, and an intuitive need for help 'from beyond themselves' in their task of parenthood. It may be that the parents have moved geographically from their place of origin and want to make a statement about themselves as a new family.

18. Sometimes clergy suggest the service of Thanksgiving, but on the whole this is not what parents want. They often feel cheated if the water and the godparents are omitted, as they are in this service. A Thanksgiving service is intended for parents to express thanks at the safe arrival of their child; baptism has the child as its focus.

19. Sensitivity is needed here, in case the parents have guilty feelings about the

baby. It may be unwanted, the parents may not be married, or the mother may be on her own.

20. Central Board of Finance of the Church of England, *Common Worship: Services and Prayer for the Church of England* (London: Church House Publishing, 2000), p. 358.

21. Examples are: a church diary of baptisms, which are read out on the nearest Sunday to the anniversary of the baptism of the child; a card sent to the child for the first five years on the anniversary of the baptism; a birthday card sent each year. Parents may be invited personally to more 'informal' worship occasions, such as the Christmas Crib service, Christingle, Mothering Sunday or Harvest Festival. There may be parent and toddler groups. The Mothers' Union runs parenting groups to support parents in their new roles.

22. This is a problem in the Reformed tradition. In many evangelical churches, the Eucharist is marginalized. In the Baptist tradition it may be tacked on to the end of a service. In the past this was done so that unbaptized believers could leave at that point.

23. Diane Murrie, *My Communion Book – a Child's Guide to Holy Communion* (London: National Society and Church House Publishing, 2002) and the *Communion Cube* from the same source; John Muir and Betty Pedley, *Come and Join the Celebration* (London: Church House Publishing, 2001).

9 Gathering Together

1. Herbert Anderson and Susan B. W. Johnson, *Regarding Children: A New Respect for Childhood and Families* (Louisville, KY: Westminster John Knox Press, 1994), p. 20.

2. Denise Inge (ed.), *Thomas Traherne: Poetry and Prose* (London: SPCK, 2002), pp. 51–2.

Appendix 1: Guides for Engaging with Scripture

1. Karl Rahner, tr. D. Bourke, *Theological Investigations. Vol. VIII: Further Theology of the Spiritual Life* (London: Darton, Longman & Todd, 1971), pp. 33–50; Hans Urs von Balthasar, *Unless You Become Like This Child* (San Francisco: Ignatius Press, 1991).

2. Hans-Ruedi Weber, *Jesus and the Children* (Geneva: World Council of Churches, 1979).

3. Pamela D. Courture, *Seeing Children, Seeing God: A Practical Theology of Children and Poverty* (Nashville: Abingdon Press, 2000); J. Bradley Wigger, *The Power of God at Home: Nurturing Our Children in Love and Grace* (San Francisco: Jossey-Bass, 2003); Bonnie J. Miller-McLemore, *Let the Children Come: Reimagining Childhood from a Christian Perspective* (San Francisco: Jossey-Bass, 2003); David H. Jensen, *Graced Vulnerability: A Theology of Childhood* (Cleveland: The Pilgrim Press, 2005); Joyce Ann Mercer, *Welcoming Children: A Practical Theology of Childhood* (St Louis: Chalice Press, 2005); Kristin Herzog, *Our Global Future: Theological and Social Challenges* (Cleveland: The Pilgrim Press, 2005).

4. Marcia J. Bunge (ed.), *The Child in Christian Thought* (Grand Rapids, IL: Eerdmans, 2001).

5. Nathan Mitchell, 'The once and future child: towards a theology of childhood', *Living Light*, vol. 12 (1975), pp. 423–37; Dawn DeVries, 'Toward a theology of childhood', *Interpretation*, vol. 55 (2001), pp. 168–70; Marcia Bunge, 'A more vibrant theology of children', *Christian Reflection*, vol. 8 (Summer 2003), pp. 11–19.

6. Diane Wood (ed.), *Studies in Church History. 31: The Church and Childhood*

(Oxford: Blackwell, 1994); William Strange, *Children in the Early Church* (Carlisle: Paternoster Press, 1996); Peter O. M. Bakke, *When Children Became People: The Birth of Childhood in Early Christianity* (Minneapolis: Augsburg Fortress, 2005).

7. Robert Coles, *The Spiritual Life of Children* (London: HarperCollins, 1992); David Hay with Rebecca Nye, *The Spirit of the Child: A Child's Voice in Education* (London: Fount, 1998); Karen-Marie Yust, Aostre N. Johnson, Sandy Eisenberg Sasso and Eugene C. Roehlkepartain (eds), *Nurturing Child and Adolescent Spirituality: Perspectives from the World's Religious Traditions* (Lanham, MD: Rowman and Littlefield, 2006); Eugene C. Roehlkepartain, Pamela Ebstyne King, Linda Wagener and Peter L. Bensen (eds), *The Handbook of Spiritual Development in Childhood and Adolescence* (Thousand Oaks, CA: Sage Publications, 2006).

8. Church reports: British Council of Churches, *The Child in the Church* (London: British Council of Churches, 1976), *Understanding Christian Nurture* (London: British Council of Churches, 1981); General Synod Board of Education, *Children in the Way – New Directions for the Church's Children* (London: National Society/Church House Publishing, 1988), *How Faith Grows, Faith Development and Christian Education* (London: National Society/Church House Publishing, 1991), *All God's Children (Children's Evangelism in Crisis)* (London: National Society/Church House Publishing, 1991); Council of Churches for Britain and Ireland, *Unfinished Business* (London: Council of Churches for Britain and Ireland,1995). Extracts and comments on documents are found in John Sutcliffe (ed.), *Tuesday's Child: A Reader for Christian Education* (Birmingham: Christian Education Publications, 2001).

9. Sofia Cavalletti, *The Religious Potential of the Child* (Ramsey, NJ: Paulist Press, 1983); Jerome W. Berryman, *Godly Play: An Imaginative Approach to Religious Education* (Minneapolis: Augsburg Fortress, 1991).

10. James Fowler, *Stages of Faith: The Psychology of Human Development and the Quest for Meaning* (Victoria, Australia: Collins Dove, 1987); John H. Westerhoff, *Will Our Children Have Faith?* (New York: Seabury Press, 1976).

11. The House of Anglican Bishops issued a *Statement on Child Abuse* in July 1995, superseded in November 1998 by a *Policy on Child Protection*, which begins, 'Christians are called to recognize the unique status of children. There is a special need to respect them in their vulnerability. Jesus warned that those who exploited or abused children deserved profound condemnation. Within the kingdom of God children matter in their own right and are to be taken seriously.' The policy includes words on the nurture of children, which is to be physical and emotional as well as spiritual, within 'pastoral, counselling, educational, worship and recreational situations'. The Church 'is called to challenge the status quo of power and the abuse of children, the attitude of indifference, and to be alongside the marginalized and the powerless – hence being alongside, listening to and theologizing about children, and acting with and for them as advocate in a prophetic ministry'.

12. General Synod of the Church of England, Doctrine Commission, *Being Human – A Christian Understanding of Personhood Illustrated with Reference to Power, Money, Sex and Time* (London: Church House Publishing, 2003); *On the Way: Towards an Integrated Approach to Christian Initiation*, GS Misc. 444 (London: Church House Publishing, 1995); Archbishops' Council, *Policy on Child Protection* (London: Church House Publishing, 1999); General Synod of the Church of England, *Children in the Midst: Theology, Principles and Curriculum Elements for Training People to Work among Children*, GS Misc. 871 (London: Church House Publishing, 2005), *Children Included – Guidelines for Training Clergy, Readers and Lay People in a Ministry among Children* (GS Misc. 804 (London: Church House Publishing, 2005).

Select Bibliography

Anderson, Herbert, and Johnson, Susan B. W., *Regarding Children: A New Respect for Childhood and Families* (Louisville, KY: Westminster John Knox Press, 1994).

Ariès, Philippe, *Centuries of Childhood,* tr. Robert Baldick (London: Cape, 1962).

Berryman, Jerome W., *The Complete Guide to Godly Play*, Vol. 1 (Denver, CO: Living the Good News, 2002).

Bowlby, John, *Attachment and Loss: Vol.1, Attachment* (London: Hogarth Press, 1969).

Bruce, Tina, and Meggitt, Carolyn, *Child Care and Education*, 4th edn (London: Hodder Arnold, 2006).

Bunge, Marcia J., *The Child in Christian Thought* (Grand Rapids, IL: Eerdmans, 2001).

Cavalletti, Sofia, *The Religious Potential of the Child* (Ramsey, NJ: Paulist Press, 1983).

Coles, Robert, *The Spiritual Life of Children* (London: HarperCollins, 1992).

Copsey, Kathryn, *From the Ground Up* (Oxford: Bible Reading Fellowship, 2005).

Cunningham, Hugh, *Children and Childhood in Western Society since 1500* (London: Longman, 1995).

Fowler, James, *Stages of Faith: The Psychology of Human Development and the Quest for Meaning* (Victoria, Australia: Collins Dove, 1987).

General Synod Board of Education, *How Faith Grows: Faith Development and Christian Education* (London: National Society/Church House Publishing, 1991).

General Synod of the Church of England, *Children in the Midst: Theology, Principles and Curriculum Elements for Training People to Work among Children*, GS Misc. 871 (London: Church House Publishing, 2005).

General Synod of the Church of England, *Sharing the Good News with Children: The Church of England's Children's Strategy*, GS 1515 (London: Church House Publishing, 2003).

General Synod of the Church of England, *Children Included – Guidelines for Training Clergy, Readers and Lay People in a Ministry among Children,* GS Misc. 804 (London: Church House Publishing, 2005).

Gerhardt, Sue, *Why Love Matters – How Affection Shapes a Baby's Brain* (Hove: Brunner-Routledge: 2004).

Hay, David, with Nye, Rebecca, *The Spirit of the Child: A Child's Voice in Education* (London: Fount, 1998).

Jensen, David H., *Graced Vulnerability* (Cleveland, OH: The Pilgrim Press, 2005).

Leach, Penelope, *Children First* (New York: Vintage Books, 1995).

Mercer, Joyce Ann, *Welcoming Children: A Practical Theology of Childhood* (St Louis, MO: Chalice Press, 2005).

Miller-McLemore, Bonnie J., *Let the Children Come: Reimagining Childhood from a Christian Perspective* (San Francisco, CA: Jossey-Bass, 2003).

Milner, Pat, and Carolin, Birgit (eds), *Time to Listen to Children: Personal and Professional Communication* (London: Routledge, 1999).

Rizzuto, Ana-Maria, *The Birth of the Living God* (Chicago, IL: Chicago University Press, 1979).

Rousseau, Jean-Jacques, *Émile*, tr. Barbara Foxley (London: Dent, Everyman's Library, 1911).

Smith, Peter K., and Cowie, Helen, *Understanding Children's Development* (Oxford: Blackwell Publishers, 1988).

Vygotsky, Lev S., *Mind in Society: The Development of Higher Psychological Processes* (Cambridge, MA: Harvard University Press, 1978).

Watts, Fraser, Nye, Rebecca, and Savage, Sara, *Psychology for Christian Ministry* (London: Routledge, 2002).

Weber, Hans-Ruedi, *Jesus and the Children* (Geneva: World Council of Churches, 1979).

Wiedemann, Thomas, *Adults and Children in the Roman Empire* (New Haven, CT: Yale University Press; London: Routledge, 1989).

Winnicott, Donald, *The Child, the Family and the Outside World* (Harmondsworth: Penguin, 1964).

Yust, Karen-Marie, Johnson, Aostre N., Sasso, Sandy Eisenberg, and Roehlkepartain, Eugene C. (eds), *Nurturing Child and Adolescent Spirituality: Perspectives from the World's Religious Traditions* (Lanham, MD: Rowman and Littlefield, 2006).

Index